*Back Row, L to R:*
*Calvin Grinnell or Running Elk,*
*Bernie Fox or Yellow Dog,*
*Dr. Gerard Baker or Yellow Wolf*

*Front Row, L to R:*
*Carol Newman or Sweet Grass,*
*Wanda Sheppard or Plenty Sage*

*All are relatives of Sacagawea.*
*— Photo by Bernie Fox*

The *Sacagawea* Project Board of tribal elders was established to gather and review information and provide oversight, and a university researcher was located to find information gathered by outside historians. Over a six year period, the group worked with funding provided by the MHA Tribal Council. Other interested tribal members joined the effort. All involved in the development of this book did research and brought findings. This book is the result of all of their efforts.

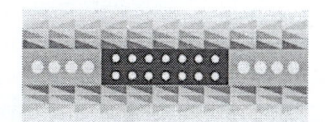

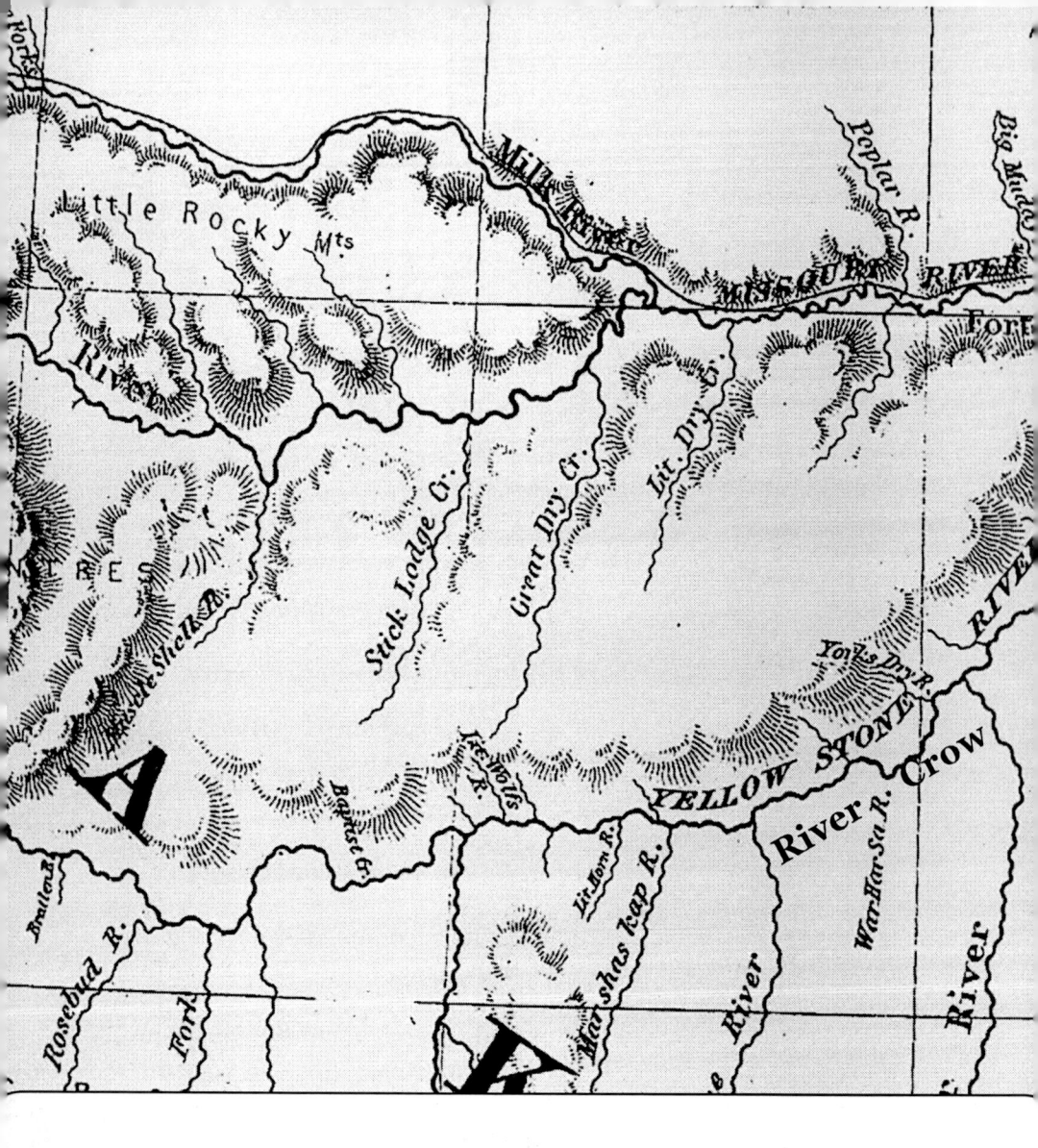

1 — 5 Knife River Earthlodge Villages, 3 Hidatsa & 2 Mandan, 1600 - 1838
2 — River Crow Earthlodge Villages, 1790s
3 — Arikara Earthlodge Villages, 1800 - 1825
4 — Fort Mandan, built by Lewis & Clark, 1804 - 1805
5 — Fort Manuel trading post, 1812 - 1813
6 — Fort Union trading post, 1829 - 1867
7 — Fort Clark trading post, 1830 - 1861
8 — Like-a-Fishhook Earthlodge Village, Hidatsa, Mandan & Arikara, 1845-188
9 — Fort Berthold trading post, 1845 - 1874
10 — Fort Buford army post, 1866 - 1895
11 — Crow Flies High Earthlodge Village, Xoshga Hidatsa, 1870 - 1884

NIBOINS
Rivière des Lacs
Mouse R.
Mouse R.
GOV STEVENS ROUTE & LINE OF THE PROPOSED
White Earth R.
Knife R.
Wintering R.
MINETARES
Rising Cr.
Ft Berthold
Snake Cr.
Ft Clark
Argalia R.
Little Missouri R.
Mina W. or Knife R.
Beaver Cr.
MANDANS &
Ta Chanta W. or Heart R.
ARICAREES
Inya Wa Karap W. or Cannon Ball R.
Shepherd Cr.
Apple C.
PLATEAU DU C
Elder R.
Pa Cham Shoka or Thick Timbered R.
Stone Idol
Ree R. Palanato W. or Grand R.
Swamp
Lr. Shyenne R.
BLACKFEET & UNKPAPA DAKOTAS
Thunder Hill
Hiha W. or Moreau R.
Cherry Cr.
Big Shyenne R.
Crow Cr.
North Fork
OHENONPA DAKOTAS
FORT PIERRE
Elder Cr.
Bear Cr.
Mato W.
1
2
3
4
5
6
7
8
9
10
11

# Our Story of Eagle Woman
## *Sacagawea*

— MHA Emblem by Dennis Fox, Jr.

Cover Illustration:

The cover depicts Eagle Woman, Sacagawea, as our vision of the teenage young woman who accompanied the Lewis and Clark Expedition. The designs used are taken from an Hidatsa/Crow style cradleboard at the Peabody Museum at Harvard University, from Mrs. Two Raven's Hidatsa dress in a painting by Catlin, and from a design on Hidatsa Chief Crow Flies High's leggings. Added are coffee beans on the oval frame, as the elders frequently bring up the fact that Eagle Woman liked coffee and its aroma. The blue belt represents the belt she acquired as a result of meeting requirements to become a woman of her Hidatsa tribe.

*This illustration was expressly designed for the cover of this book.*
— *Dennis Fox, Jr. illustration*

*End Paper Map: Hidatsa & Crow Territory during the 19th Century*
— Barry Lawrence Ruderman Antique Maps

# Our Story of Eagle Woman
## *Sacagawea*
### — *They Got It Wrong* —

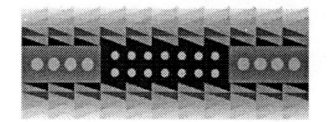

By
The *Sacagawea* Project Board
of the Mandan, Hidatsa & Arikara Nation

Dr. Gerard Baker, Yellow Wolf
Calvin Grinnell, Running Elk
Bernard (Bernie) Fox, Yellow Dog
Carol Fredericks Newman, Sweet Grass
Wanda Fox Sheppard, Plenty Sage

The Paragon Agency, Publishers
Orange, CA
2021

Library

# Our Story of Eagle Woman, *Sacagawea*
## — They Got It Wrong —

*Sacagawea* Project Board
of the Mandan, Hidatsa & Arikara Nation

Published by
The Paragon Agency, Publishers
Orange, CA
2021

1. Native American History
2. Hidatsa Indians
3. *Sacagawea*
    I. Title
    II. Author

ISBN13: 978-1-891030-80-2
ISBN10: 1-891030-80-9
Library of Congress Control Number: 2020948519

©2021 The Mandan, Hidatsa & Arikara Nation
All Rights Reserved

No part of this book may be reproduced
without the previous written consent
of the publisher.

Printed in the USA

# Dedication

This book is dedicated to all who kept this story of *Sacagawea* alive, **especially Marilyn Cross Hudson,** and to the youth as they learn the story of an extraordinary Hidatsa/Crow woman and pass it on to future generations.

*Lucy Bulls Eye Evans, great-granddaughter of Sacagawea*

# Acknowledgements

The *Sacagawea* Project Board would like to acknowledge and thank our **Tribal Chairman, Mark Fox, and the rest of the Tribal Council for supporting and funding this project.**

The *Sacagawea* Project Board would like to acknowledge three individuals, MHA Tribal members and scholars, for their contributions to the development of this book:

Jerry "Bird" Birdsbill Ford, Cornsilk
Who persisted with the goal of pursuing DNA evidence.

Quincy Baker, Rattling/Shaking Medicine
Who persisted with not accepting information without questioning it and digging further.

Claryca Mandan, Peppermint Woman
Who provided valuable historical documents and cultural information.

The *Sacagawea* Project Board would like to acknowledge and thank Drs. Dennis and Sandra Fox who coordinated the project and compiled this document.

The *Sacagawea* Project Board would like to acknowledge and thank Dr. Michael Welsh, University of Northern Colorado, for research he conducted and provided to the project.

The *Sacagawea* Project Board would like to acknowledge and thank the Welch family, Annika Johnson of the Joslyn Museum, Sarah Walker of the Historical Society of North Dakota, Royce Freeman of the MHA Interpretive Center, and others for help in securing photographs.

The *Sacagawea* Project Board would like to acknowledge and thank all those who contributed information and pictures included in this book.

# Contents

Preface .................................................................................. viii
Foreword ................................................................................. xi
Introduction ........................................................................... xiv
*Sacagawea* Project Board ..................................................... xviii

1 Who We Are – The MHA Nation ........................................... 1
2 Our Stories – The Strong Jaw Story ..................................... 19
3 Our Stories – The Bulls Eye Story ....................................... 45

   Color Section ....................................................................... 79

4 Our Voices – Recent And Back to the 1940s ...................... 103
5 Our Voices/Some Distorted – Early 1900s ......................... 121
6 Three Stories – Wyoming, Ft. Manuel, Bulls Eye ............... 149
7 Our Family Connections – *Sacagawea* and Cherry Necklace 177
8 Our Family Connections – More Relatives of *Sacagawea* ... 209
9 Our Response – *Sacagawea* Entries in the Journals .......... 233
10 Our Story – Timeline of the Life of *Maeshuwea (Sacagawea)*. 267
11 Blood Proof – DNA Study .................................................. 285

Appendix ............................................................................... 297
Other Sources ....................................................................... 297
Illustrations .......................................................................... 304
Index ..................................................................................... 312
Colophon .............................................................................. 341

# Preface

The journals of Meriwether Lewis and William Clark, and subsequent writings of others, have led millions of people to believe for more than 200 years that the woman who accompanied them, *Sacagawea*, was a Shoshone Indian. On July 16, 2015, Hidatsa descendants of *Sacagawea* and others met for a full day summit in Mandaree, North Dakota, on the Fort Berthold Indian Reservation. About 50 people were in attendance.

They shared facts and family oral stories about the woman who helped accomplish the historic 1804-1806 Corps of Discovery Expedition. After two centuries of misinterpretation, which began with speakers of at least four different languages participating in the Expedition, and in order to oppose lies and speculation of various writers which led to mythical accounts, the Mandan, Hidatsa and Arikara Nation (MHA Nation) was at last on a journey to record its stories of direct lineage to *Sacagawea,* who was Hidatsa, and to correct inaccuracies surrounding her life.

Jerome Dancing Bull, a direct descendant of *Sacagawea,* was the Master of Ceremonies. He stated to the participants that they couldn't forget this part of history (the story of *Sacagawea* being Hidatsa) and need to tell it to the young ones, including the young ones in the room. He reminded those in attendance that many tribal and community members had stories about *Sacagawea* and knew who her family was. He told that *Sacagawea* had snake medicine and that was probably why they thought she was a Snake Indian. He ended with, "They got it wrong!"

Randy Phelan, West Segment Tribal Council Representative and Tribal Vice Chairman at the time, stated that the reason he was fully behind a project to document the Hidatsa story of *Sacagawea* was that he wanted to make sure the record was set straight. He said the time was right to get the story out there. "Our young ones don't even know the story and likely believe the history books that say she is Shoshone."

Dennis Fox, Sr., tribal elder, stated that "Chief Bulls Eye and others told the Hidatsa story of *Sacagawea* to Major A.B. Welch in 1923. Major Welch documented the story and said it would eventually lead a person of research to the true light."

Calvin Grinnell, MHA Tribal Historian, read from the Bulls Eye story. He stressed that Charbonneau may have lied about his wife's heritage in order to get a job with the expedition, and that since he was the interpreter, he could maintain the lie throughout the journey. He also stated that *Sacagawea* met a "brother" (through an Indian adoption) among the Shoshones they encountered whom she had seen the year before on a trip with Charbonneau. She wanted to ensure a peaceful visit with them and so stressed the relationship which was a tribal practice.

Calvin stated that time was of the essence in regard to documenting the Hidatsa story of *Sacagawea*. He said, "We have to tell our young people that we had a role in history. If we deny our own traditions, we will have to call our ancestors liars." Mr. Grinnell had done extensive research on the *Sacagawea* story and was anxious to see his work further documented.

Bernie Fox read from Major A. B. Welch's papers where Welch stated that Bulls Eye's story was correct - Bulls Eye was the grandson of *Sacagawea,* and Ted Lone Fight III talked about how *Sacagawea's* name is Hidatsa, not Shoshone. It is an Hidatsa name meaning Bird Woman.

Gerard Baker, tribal member and former National Park Service Superintendent, told about how, when the Lewis and Clark bicentennial came in 2004-2006, he was asked to help lead the national celebration. He told the people it was not going to be a celebration. Instead it would focus on changes that occurred for the Indian people because of the visit of Lewis and Clark. He would stress the role of the Mandan and Hidatsa, for example, and how they were premier traders in Indian country.

He would stress that *Sacagawea* was an Hidatsa woman. He would note how the use of various languages led to misinterpretations. He went on to tell the Hidatsa story of Strong Jaw or Wolf Woman, one of the stories indicating that *Sacagawea* was Hidatsa.

Other participants, including Quincy Baker, Diane Hall, Claryca Mandan, Jerry Birdsbill Ford and Casey Hunts Along, added support for what had been presented. Delores Sand, Wanda Fox Sheppard and Carol Fredericks Newman were interviewed and told how they were related to *Sacagawea*.

Initial funding for a *Sacagawea* project was made available by Councilman Randy Phelan whose request was to find and present evidence for all to see: local stories, statements, articles, interviews, etc., to support the claim that *Sacagawea* was Hidatsa. A second charge that emerged was to have the information be accessible to students.

This document is an attempt to realize both. It was determined that a book would be developed, built upon the work of Calvin Grinnell, Tribal Historian and member and past president of the North Dakota State Historical Board, and be written from a tribal perspective. The book would lay out pertinent information, the evidence gathered -- including especially primary sources, and the evidence would be used toward correcting the story. It was also assumed that those interested in reading the book would probably already be familiar with the popular, but inaccurate, versions of the *Sacagawea* story.

A *Sacagawea* Project Board of tribal elders was established to gather and review information and provide oversight, and a university researcher was located to find information gathered by outside historians. Over a five year period, the group worked with funding provided by the MHA Tribal Council. Other interested tribal members joined the effort. All involved in the development of this book did research and brought findings. This book is the result of all of their efforts.

# Foreword

This is the story of Eagle Woman, *Maeshuwea,* of the Hidatsa (Awatixa) Tribe who later became *Sacagawea,* Bird Woman, whom we all know from the famed Lewis and Clark Expedition. Premiered in this publication, this story goes far beyond the commonly read and believed story regarding her. This book is a compilation of what our ancestors and elders have passed down to us about *Sacagawea*. It also includes other information that supports our claim that *Sacagawea* was Hidatsa, not a Shoshone captive of the Hidatsa.

In a chapter entitled "The Two Versions" in his book, *Sacajawea,* 1971, University of Oklahoma Press, Harold P. Howard discusses differences between the two popular versions of the story about *Sacagawea,* the Wyoming story and the Ft. Manuel story. He also mentions that there is a possible third story, the one told by the Hidatsa, Bulls Eye, speaking in a council setting. Howard states that this version of the story has never been authenticated. Fifty years from that time, and almost 100 years from the time Bulls Eye told the story in 1923, we are authenticating his story.

We have chosen to present evidence as we found it in stories, in statements and interviews, in notes and in other pertinent documents. We have chosen not to go the usual route of reading things and then interpreting them into a narrative as other books regarding *Sacagawea* have done. We wanted the readers to see what we had found so they could interpret for themselves. We have made and state our observations in regard to them.

To understand the Eagle Woman or *Sacagawea* story, one has to understand the Hidatsa/Crow tribal ways of life. The two tribes once were one tribe. One also needs to understand that we Hidatsa were a trading hub long before the coming of the Anglo fur trade. We were the center of the trading network among northern tribes, many of whom were our enemies.

We had many tribes come to our villages to trade for what we had, and later on we had many White traders come, representing various countries. This created a challenge when it came to communication between all groups, so in most cases "hand signs" were used. When they did attempt to communicate by speaking, the discussion often went through at least two to five language interpretations before a final interpreter translated and stated it or wrote it down. Each time it was possible to not only have the words change but, in some cases, it would change the entire meaning of the initial conversation. This was a big factor in keeping our story of *Sacagawea* from being heard.

Another factor was the anti-Indian bias and lack of respect the trappers and explorers had towards the Natives they encountered. The trappers themselves, usually employed by companies such as the Hudson Bay or the American Fur Company, often had limited education. These things added to the problem with recorded history. When someone wrote it on paper, it became entrenched in history as the "way it was" giving no respect for other or Native ways of thinking.

We have had the challenges of many events throughout the years, including various types of sicknesses with the loss of many during that time and relocation because of the Garrison Dam, but our stories prevailed, and our history has been kept mostly intact. This book opens up an opportunity to explore and keep our stories alive through oral history and research.

Drs. Dennis and Sandra Fox organized a group (the *Sacagawea* Project Board) to help develop a book that would once and for all explain who *Ma-eshu-weash,* Eagle Woman, was and is and explain family connections to her. The group was made up of respected elders, each a tribal historian in their own right, and each coming from very strong families with ties to tribal history.

The group consisted of Drs. Dennis and Sandra Fox, Wanda Fox Sheppard, Bernard Fox, Carol Fredericks Newman, Calvin Grinnell and Gerard Baker. Tribal members Claryca Mandan, Quincy Baker and Jerry "Bird" Birdsbill Ford joined our effort. Dr. Michael Welsh, History Department, University of Northern Colorado, was hired to help with research and assist in the exploration of this subject.

We hope young people, especially, will read and learn this story. This book is organized to contain information about the MHA Nation, our *Sacagawea* stories and connections, voices of those who have spoken of *Sacagawea*, views of other stories that have been told, our *Sacagawea* relatives, our interpretations of the Lewis and Clark Journal entries about her, a timeline of *Sacagawea's* life as we know it, and DNA evidence. Some sections will probably be more useful to the general student population than others. We have written this book in keeping with the latest approaches to teaching history by chunking some information in shorter sections and highlighting names, introductions, observations and conclusions. We hope to have the students approach their reading and learning as historians, utilizing primary sources and inquiry with questioning and critical thinking. Upon reading sections, students should determine what was included that would support *Sacagawea* being Hidatsa (Hidatsa/Crow) and how.

Finally, we want to stress how invaluable oral history is. Tribes across the country are bringing their stories to light and working to correct false historical accounts. "THEY GOT IT WRONG!" is a quote from Bulls Eye who told the *Sacagawea* story in 1923 and is deemed to be a fitting part of a title for this book.

*Sacagawea* Project Board Members
Dr. Gerard Baker
Calvin Grinnell, MHA Tribal Historian

# Introduction

In writing our own history, our tribal orators and writers represented in this book with the support of the Mandan, Hidatsa and Arikara Nation, will convey, through virtually one hundred and fifty years of oral tradition and centuries of tribal knowledge of our tribal cultures and traditions, a very different version of the life of *Maeshuwea,* Eagle Woman as she is known to us. Volumes of fact, fiction, and theory have been written about her and her role in the Lewis and Clark Expedition, but much of her real identity has been held until now by her own people. She was a Native woman of the Hidatsa/Crow.

The information contained within this document may be difficult to understand for those who do not know the history and cultures of the Three Affiliated Tribes, especially Hidatsa culture with its complicated societal and family structures and the Hidatsa/Crow relationship. But to us, our story of Eagle Woman or *Sacagawea* makes perfect sense. Every effort has been made, in the research and writing of this book, to document our cultural and historical knowledge with the oldest Fort Berthold Agency records, historical journals and notes, maps, transcripts, tape recordings, census records, photographs and even DNA.

But because Eagle Woman walked the face of this earth during the time that she did, much of the knowledge we hold today about her life and death one hundred and fifty years ago is based upon the oldest method of passing along our tribal history — Oral Tradition. This cannot be, and must not be, discounted since it is the method through which our clanships, names, language, and ceremonies still survive today, more than eight generations since *Sacagawea* died and after more than three centuries of the Hidatsa occupation from the Painted Woods region to the east, then moving to the Knife River, to Like-A-Fishhook Village, to the Confluence of the Missouri and Yellowstone Rivers, and beyond.

Our stories based on oral tradition may seem somewhat confusing at times to the reader. Stories may match in general content; however, names may be different, timelines may be off, or place names may not match. In our oral tradition, no two stories are ever told exactly the same way.

Many factors account for this difference: the age of the storyteller, the identity of the audience, the language being used for telling or interpreting, the scribe recording the story, and sometimes the need to protect sacred tribal bundles, ceremony or places.

Most often, though, the events and characters of an oral story are woven together in the same general thread. This is the case with the Hidatsa stories about the life of *Maeshuwea*. In an effort to document the oral tradition for the reader, the writing team has included, at the end, a timeline of her life with key events.

A second barrier to interpretation for the reader may be geography. When reading this book, the reader should have an appreciation of the Hidatsa/Crow relationship and the historical fact that they were once one tribe living at the Knife River. These two tribes shared a vast region, not based upon any of the contemporaneous boundaries of the United States and Canada today and certainly not based upon the current reservation boundaries of either tribe.

Those boundaries have been shaped and imposed upon both tribes in the years ensuing the Louisiana Purchase and the Lewis and Clark Expedition. Tribal history paints a much different map whereby both tribes shared a much larger territory ranging from the Knife River of the Hidatsa to the Confluence of the Missouri and Yellowstone to the Three Forks area of the Crow. Tribal place names in this vast territory are central to the writing of *Sacagawea's* story. Virtually every river or geographical feature outlined in the Lewis and Clark journals had a tribal place name, and some have been used in telling her story here.

In reading the Three Affiliated Tribes' interpretation of *Sacagawea's* life, one needs to understand that there was a high degree of interaction, visitation and shared culture between the Hidatsa and their River Crow relatives during the period of her life. Likewise her knowledge of the many plants, food sources and medicines were based upon the fact that she had both an Hidatsa and Crow upbringing and spent her younger years in both tribal territories.

A third barrier for a reader might be the lack of understanding of aspects of the Hidatsa and Crow cultures including their clanship systems and the transfer among generations of individual names.

Names of individuals were and are (Indian names of individuals today) achieved in several different ways. Names already used can be transferred by one generation to the next with permission of the clan members. This was the case in *Sacagawea's* family where her mother, her sister and her daughter were all named Otter Woman. Names might also be purchased.

Names could be used four times. Original names can be given coming from medicine or a dream of the person doing the naming. An individual can have more than one Indian name. One can be a childhood name; another can come from a war record or respected act. When names were interpreted from the Native language to English, they were interpreted differently. One of *Sacagawea's* relatives was All Moves, also called Moves Along.

The Hidatsa and Crow have functioned under highly developed clanship systems from time immemorial. A matrilineal clanship system is the method by which both the Hidatsa and Crow acknowledge their kin and clan relationships. A clanship system is very complicated and extremely hard to understand for those who did not grow up in it. Relatives are recognized in a unique way. For example, *Sacagawea* had a brother named Cherry Necklace. She also had first cousins who were called her brothers.

In fact, she would have called other male relatives "brother" in certain family configurations. Among the Hidatsa and Crow, adoption of others not related was a very serious action and was taken literally. Thus there were adopted "brothers" who were considered family members. This was the case with Cameahwait of the Shoshones who was adopted by Smoked Lodge, *Sacagawea's* father.

According to Bowers in *Hidatsa Social & Ceremonial Organization,* the practice of adoption of those from other tribes encouraged intergroup visiting and trading. This system was not understood by the Lewis and Clark party. If Charbonneau himself had an understanding of these tribal relations, he did not convey the information to Lewis and Clark.

The clanship system is a very vital part of understanding the identity of the Hidatsa and Crow. It assists in the tracing of genealogy of *Maeshuwea*.

She and her relatives, who were descendants of Crow mothers, had to be adopted into Hidatsa clans when they lived among them. This was the case described in the Naomi Foolish Bear, Black Hawk story, included herein, where she tells of the Crow women relatives of *Sacagawea* who were adopted into the Hidatsa Low Cap Clan.

A fourth barrier to interpretation is understanding the role of language. For example, some Crow and Hidatsa words are the same and mean the same thing. Others are similar sounding but mean different things. In the Hidatsa language, the slightest change in a sound makes the word mean something different. Translation from either Crow or Hidatsa to French through *Sacagawea's* husband, Charbonneau, then to another French speaker, then to English for the understanding of Lewis and Clark would have been an exhaustive process with many opportunities for corruption.

The one common language used by most tribes of the Northern Plains for the purpose of communication and trade would have been sign language. Most likely, because of her background and the fact that she lived at the Five Villages which was a continental trade center of that era, *Maeshuwea* was fluent in sign language and used it as a primary means of communication on the Expedition. This is evidenced in the Lewis and Clark journals and in our own oral stories and traditions.

We also want to explain that *Sacagawea's* true name was Eagle Woman, *Maeshuwea* or *Maeshuweash* in Hidatsa. Her name was changed to *Sacagawea,* Bird Woman in Hidatsa, because that was easier for the nonIndians to say or was a misinterpretation that stuck. It was, however, spelled *Sakakawea* before it was officially changed to *Sacagawea,* the correct pronunciation of Bird Woman, by the MHA Nation. *Sacajawea* is a Shoshone word meaning "one who pulls the boat." At no time did the captains ever use that term for *Sacagawea*. The authors and other contributors to this book have utilized the various spellings or names for her.

Not recognizing and understanding this information provided for the reader can lead to misinterpretation and misinformation, as it did in the past.

Claryca Mandan, Executive Director<br>Hidatsa Heritage Center

# *Sacagawea* Project Board

Back Row, L to R:
Calvin Grinnell or Running Elk, Bernie Fox or Yellow Dog,
Dr. Gerard Baker or Yellow Wolf
Front Row, L to R:
Carol Newman or Sweet Grass, Wanda Sheppard or Plenty Sage

All are relatives of *Sacagawea*.

*Photo by Bernie Fox*

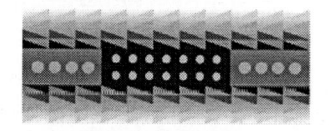

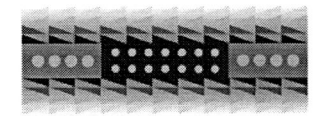

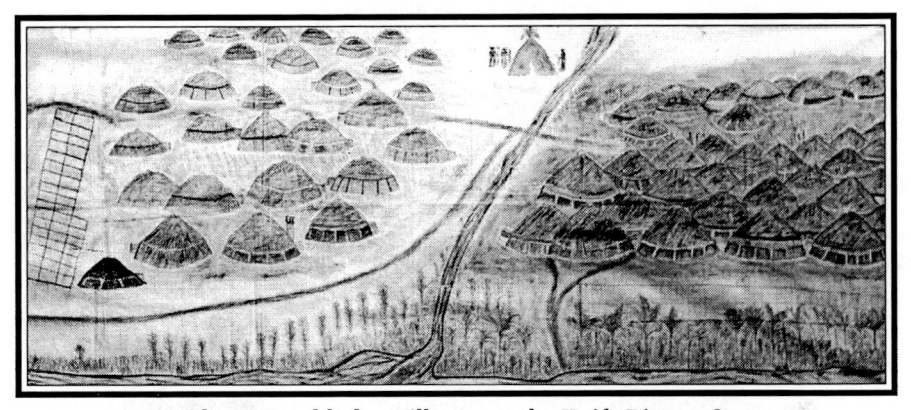

*Hidatsa Earthlodge Villages on the Knife River, 1810*
*Awatixa Village, where Sacagawea lived, is at the left.*
Sitting Rabbit, Mandan, 1905 — State Historical Society of North Dakota

# Chapter 1
## *WHO WE ARE*

*The Mandan, Hidatsa, and Arikara Nation*

**We, the people of the MHA Nation (Mandan, Hidatsa and Arikara — the Three Affiliated Tribes), live along the Missouri River in the northwestern part of North Dakota. Our reservation, Fort Berthold, includes 988,000 acres with approximately half in Indian ownership. We had 16,500 members in 2020, with about a third of them residing on the reservation. Our MHA website includes detailed information about our tribes. Aspects of our history and culture set us apart from other Plains tribes in several ways.**

First of all, our nation is made up of three tribes who came together out of necessity in the 1800s. The Mandan joined the Hidatsa after the devastation of the smallpox epidemic of 1837, and the Arikara joined the Hidatsa and Mandan in 1862, mainly because of constant attacks by the Sioux. Joined together, the three groups became known as the Three Affiliated Tribes and today are one nation.

## Our Story of Eagle Woman, Sacagawea

The Hidatsa are a Siouan-speaking people who had once been one tribe with the Crow people. They separated from the Crow but have maintained a closeness over the years that has lasted to the present, with there being Hidatsa/Crow relatives and a similar language. The Hidatsa were misnamed "Gros Ventre" by early French traders. The proper name, Hidatsa, was starting to be used in the early 1900s. It was made the official name in 1943. Hidatsa means "People of the Willows." Some of their creation stories say that they emerged from Devils Lake — present Spirit Lake — in northeastern North Dakota.

The Mandan are also a Siouan-speaking people. They were almost taken to extinction by smallpox, but the tribe survived and exists today. The Mandan deny the story, promoted by some in the 19th century, that they are descendants of Welsh people. Their traditional name is the *Nueta*, "Our People." Some accounts of the origin of the Mandan say that they were created by First Creator and Lone Man at the Heart River in the North Dakota area, while others tell of a migration from the Gulf of Mexico with Lone Man.

The Arikara people are said to have come from the South up the Missouri River, first to the Nebraska area, then to what is now South Dakota, and then on to the North Dakota area. Their traditional name is *Sahnish*, "The Original People." Their language is Caddoan, and they are related to the Pawnee. The Arikara and the Pawnee from Oklahoma regularly meet to acknowledge their relationship. The history of the Arikara is held within their sacred bundles and was directed by Chief Above and Mother Corn.

Each of the three tribes brought their own language, cultural ways, and traditions, making it more complicated as we try to maintain and revive our cultures and languages. The Three Tribes have intermarried and have shared and adopted some aspects of culture across all three. There is, however, an honoring of original ways specific to each tribe. There are traditional clan systems among the Hidatsa and Mandan. Separate language revitalization efforts are underway for all three tribes.

Attention to spirituality is evident for all, and tribal specific ceremonies still take place. There is a Native American Church in addition to other church denominations such as Roman Catholic and the United Church of Christ.

Some traditional tribal societies are still active. The values of humility, generosity, honesty, and integrity are prized across the tribes. Members of the MHA Nation are highly patriotic, especially in regard to honoring the service of soldiers and veterans.

Although there is intermarriage across the tribes, with people being of all three groups, the Hidatsa live mainly in the western part of the reservation, the Arikara in the eastern part, and the Mandan in the southern part. There is one tribal council and government that serves all three groups, with representatives from six segments of the reservation. Our tribal headquarters is in New Town, North Dakota, where members of all three tribes live and work.

Significant events in our history have impacted us. For example, all three of the tribes were devastated by smallpox brought by outsiders in 1781-1782, 1837 and 1866. It is estimated that fifty percent of the Hidatsa died, sixty percent of the Arikara, and as many as ninety percent of the Mandan passed in 1837. Mandan chief Four Bears was among the victims.

Nation to nation treaties in 1851 and 1868, executive orders in 1870 and 1880, and the Allotment Act in 1891 established our tribe's land base and then systematically reduced it. In 1910, 320,000 acres of prime grasslands on the reservation were opened to homesteaders. From 1949-1954, the Garrison Dam was built and flooded 154,911 acres of reservation land. Our land base has been diminished by over ninety percent since the 1851 Treaty of Fort Laramie.

The three tribes were premier traders of the Northern Plains. Our ancestors traded with other tribes, with French fur traders, and others. In 1825, the U.S. Government ratified the Atkinson and O'Fallon treaty with the Mandan, Hidatsa and Arikara. The treaty was to secure the friendship of the tribes and to control trade with them. The tribes especially traded their agricultural produce and Knife River flint, prized for making tools and weapons.

## Our Story of Eagle Woman, Sacagawea

The Mandan, Hidatsa and Arikara were all highly-skilled agriculturalists who domesticated many strains of corn. Our people also grew beans, squash, sunflowers, pumpkins, and tobacco. In 1882, Oscar Will, of the Will agricultural seed company, secured his first stocks from the Mandan, Hidatsa and Arikara at Like-A-Fishhook Village. These crops now feed the people of the United States. The men hunted buffalo and other game to supplement agricultural products while women tended the gardens. There were times when the environment made gardening difficult, and our people had to rely on natural plants.

As part of a trading network, our tribes were visited by many outsiders including other tribal people, white traders, and explorers. German Prince Maximilian and artists George Catlin and Karl Bodmer were among them during the 1830s. They studied the three tribes, wrote about them, and captured their likenesses through drawing and painting.

Other visitors were the U.S. Army captains Meriwether Lewis and William Clark. President Jefferson sent them to lead the Corps of Discovery into western lands acquired by the Louisiana Purchase.

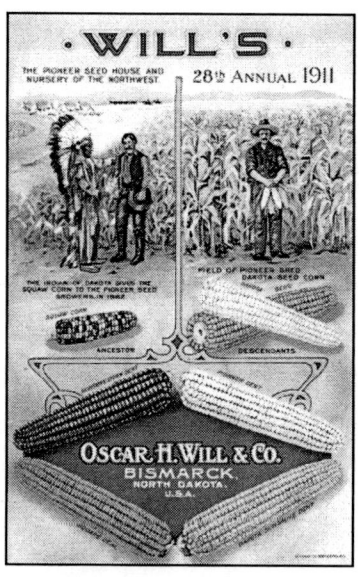

Oscar H. Will Company Seed Catalog. 1908 — North Dakota State Archives

## The Mandan, Hidatsa, and Arikara Nation

*William Clark, 1810, and Meriwether Lewis, 1807 — Charles Willson Peale, National Park Service*

Much has been written about the expedition of Lewis and Clark who spent the winter of 1804-1805 among the Mandan en route to the Pacific Coast. The Mandans' presence in the Knife River region, their knowledge of the western lands, and their abundant supplies of food were all of great benefit to Lewis and Clark.

Also helpful to Lewis and Clark was information provided by prominent tribal leaders like Sheheke, White Coyote, pronounced "Shahegshote." He was a compassionate, generous, traditional man and an excellent orator.

*Lewis and Clark meeting Sacagawea and Charbonneau at Mandan Village, 1804 — Vernon Erickson, State Historical Society of North Dakota.*

## Our Story of Eagle Woman, Sacagawea

*Mandan Chief Sheheke (White Coyote), 1807* — Charles Balthazar de Saint Memin, copy by Charles Bird King, 1837, McKenny & Hall

Sheheke traveled to the Pacific Coast as a youth, an experience that allowed him to draw a map of the upper Missouri River basin that Lewis and Clark found most helpful. The explorers never went hungry while spending a winter on the Missouri River. Sheheke promised "If we eat, you shall eat." Sheheke and his wife were later invited to visit the East Coast. They saw American cities and visited President Jefferson at the White House. The good experience that Lewis and Clark had at Fort Mandan prepared them well as they departed in April, 1805, to seek the Northwest Passage.

The expedition was aided by our relative, a young Hidatsa/Crow woman, known to the explorers as the Bird Woman, *Sacagawea* in Hidatsa. She had knowledge of the river and of the tribes whom the party would meet because of her prior experiences. *Sacagawea*, Eagle Woman, came from the Awatixa Hidatsa village on Knife River that is today referred to as "*Sakakawea* Village" in her honor. This book presents our understanding of her family and our knowledge and understanding of her life.

## Life in the 1800s

*In order to better comprehend the story of Sacagawea, one must have a general understanding of her world in the 1800s.*

In the early 1800s, the Mandan, Hidatsa and Arikara Tribes lived near one another along the waterways in what is now North Dakota, in the northern part of the political division of the Louisiana Purchase. Each tribe had several different villages. As was previously stated, the Mandan and Hidatsa joined together in 1837. They lived together in Like-A-Fishhook Village, established in 1845 after the smallpox pandemic. The Arikara did not join these tribes until 1862; therefore, the description of life between 1800 and 1862 is mainly from the Hidatsa and Mandan perspective.

The two tribes each had their own chiefs. The Hidatsa had multiple chiefs who were recognized as leaders among the people. The leaders were expected to give and receive respect and to have learned to represent and be of service to all of the people. Later, the Hidatsa formed a council of war leaders of each of their villages. The Mandan had a "war chief" and a "village chief" for each of their villages. They viewed leadership in regard to ownership of sacred bundles. For both tribes, the chiefs decided tribal matters, sometimes after a consultation process. There were two famous chiefs named Four Bears, one Hidatsa and one Mandan.

The people lived in villages of earth lodges, large rounded structures that held extended families, and some even had room for horses. They were built of heavy timbers and covered with dirt. They provided warmth in the harsh winters. They were designed and built by the women with help from the men. The lodges belonged to the women and included everything else associated with the lodge except for geldings and stallions that belonged to the men.

The very important garden plots were nearby. The experience of Buffalo Bird Woman, Hidatsa, with her gardening has been documented extensively. The Hidatsa had nine distinct varieties of corn, five varieties of beans, and several varieties of squash.

## Our Story of Eagle Woman, Sacagawea

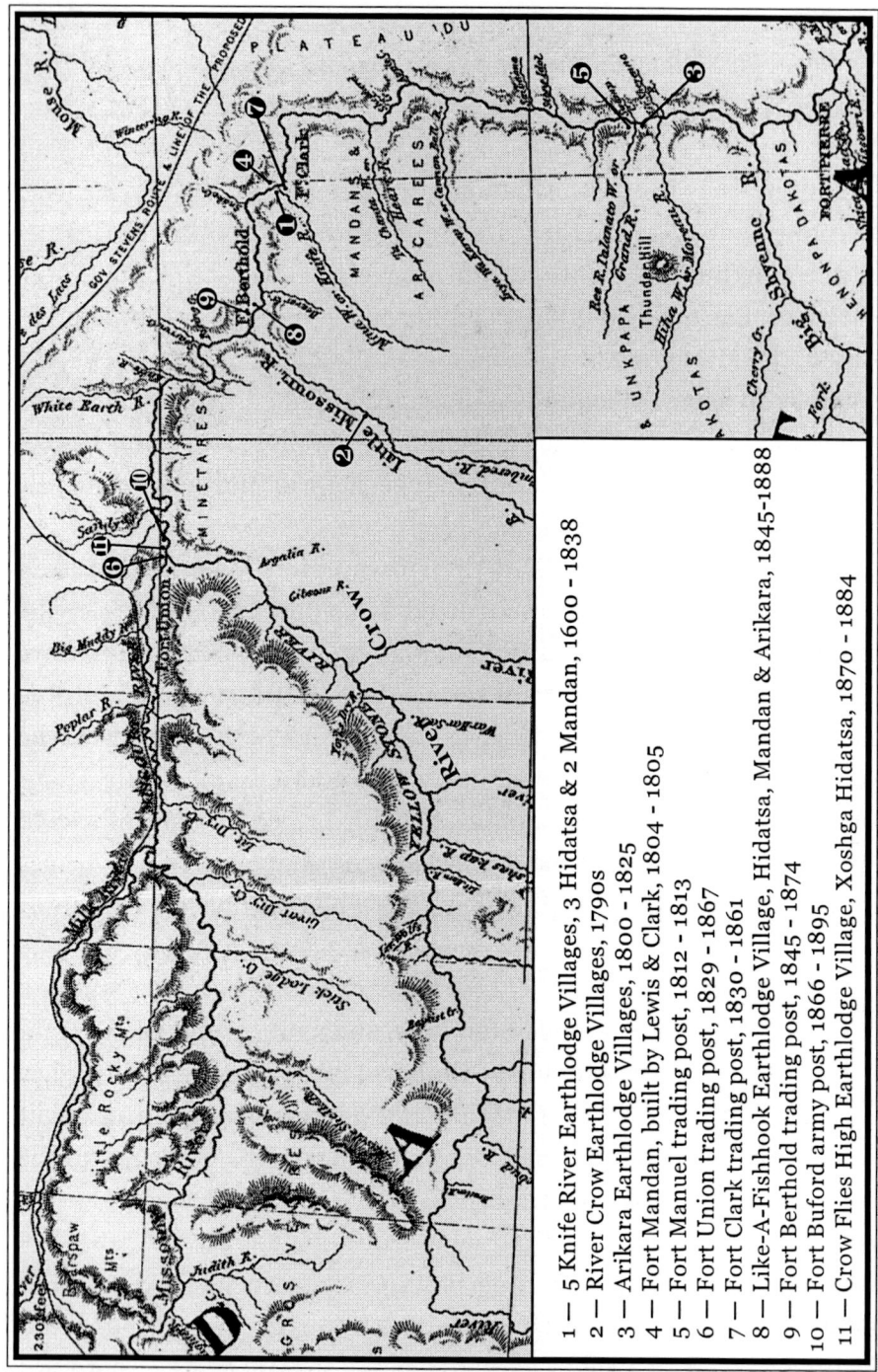

1 — 5 Knife River Earthlodge Villages, 3 Hidatsa & 2 Mandan, 1600 - 1838
2 — River Crow Earthlodge Villages, 1790s
3 — Arikara Earthlodge Villages, 1800 - 1825
4 — Fort Mandan, built by Lewis & Clark, 1804 - 1805
5 — Fort Manuel trading post, 1812 - 1813
6 — Fort Union trading post, 1829 - 1867
7 — Fort Clark trading post, 1830 - 1861
8 — Like-A-Fishhook Earthlodge Village, Hidatsa, Mandan & Arikara, 1845-1888
9 — Fort Berthold trading post, 1845 - 1874
10 — Fort Buford army post, 1866 - 1895
11 — Crow Flies High Earthlodge Village, Xoshga Hidatsa, 1870 - 1884

*Hidatsa & Crow Territory during the 19th Century*
— Barry Lawrence Ruderman Antique Maps

Food was dried for consumption in the winter. Outsiders traded for foodstuffs and beautiful items made by tribal members.

Both Mandan and Hidatsa women made pottery and baskets. Men and women painted to decorate items with designs, and they utilized certain blue beads to make adornments. Decorations were also insignias of achievements, of age-grade societies, or the like. Various necessary items were made from all parts of the buffalo. Bull boats, made from buffalo hides, were constructed and used to cross streams.

Both tribes were matrilineal. The tribes had sophisticated and unique clan systems and ways of determining kinship. Relatives addressed each other by terms of relationship instead of by proper names. Children were born as members of the mother's clan. If someone passed away, they were to be buried by someone of their father's clan. Clan members took care of one another. There were adoptions of individuals into clans and into tribes. Sometimes there were adoptions of individuals from adversarial tribes in order to make them indebted, instead of bringing harm or cheating while trading.

There were arranged marriages. It was common for a man to have several wives because of the work that had to be done. Co-wives were usually biological sisters or cousins. If a man died and left behind children, his brother would marry the widow in order to take care of the children.

Education was provided by old men teaching boys by stories and lectures and by mothers, aunts and grandmothers teaching the girls skills they would need to know. The first "day school" was opened at Fort Berthold in 1870. In the mid 1870s, the government agent declared that families who did not send their children to school would have rations withheld. Children attended school at Ft. Stevenson Boarding School or the Congregational Mission school. Many were taken to far off schools in Carlisle, Pennsylvania, or Hampton, Virginia. Discipline of children was provided by the mother's brother for boys and by older sisters or by the mother's older sisters for girls.

## Our Story of Eagle Woman, Sacagawea

*Yellow Cloud Woman, Hidatsa, in a Bull Boat on the Missouri River, 1911* — G.L Wilson & *Bull Boat and carved paddle, 1879* — Orlando Scott Goff, both State Historical Society of North Dakota

The tribes maintained societies that held their members to certain values or behaviors such as bravery or chastity. There were women's societies and men's societies. The tribes held ceremonies like the *Okipa* (Mandan ceremony) and the *Naxpike* (Hidatsa ceremony). These were outlawed by government order in 1886. The Catholic and Congregational churches were first to impact the people at Ft. Berthold.

Health issues were addressed. Individuals and/or families were keepers of various medicines, often divinely ordained, and tribal members went to them for help depending upon their ailments. Some medicine people, such as *Sacagawea*'s brother Cherry Necklace, had very powerful snake medicine.

Because the land of the Mandan and Hidatsa was a trading center, tribal members interacted with people from other tribes and non-Indians. Accordingly, the Mandan and Hidatsa knew those two languages and at least some of many other languages. They also used sign language to communicate in order to trade with the outsiders.

In 1845, when smallpox had forced the people to move from their Knife River villages about 40 miles further up the Missouri, they built one large community together on a sharp bend of the river, accordingly named Like-A-Fishhook Village. The first trading post nearby was built by James Kipp and was called Fort James. The name was later changed to Fort Berthold.

Although the three tribes warred with other tribes, the Sioux tribe was their principal foe. Sioux raiding parties hit the three tribes often. In 1862, Four Bears, Village Chief of the Hidatsa, was killed by the Sioux while bathing in a creek near Like-A-Fishhook Village. When Sioux threats forced the Arikara to join the Hidatsa and Mandan at Like-A-Fishhook Village in 1862, they fit in because they were also agriculturalists and lived in earth lodges.

*Our Story of Eagle Woman, Sacagawea*

*Like-A-Fishhook Village, 1871-72 — Stanley J. Morrow / State Historical Society of North Dakota*

## The Mandan, Hidatsa, and Arikara Nation

Their chiefs were chosen from among their spiritual leaders. The Arikara did not have a clan system. They had their own societies and ceremonies.

The Hidatsa, especially, traveled to the west often to visit their Crow relatives in Montana, living closer to the Hidatsa than they do now. The mother of Eagle Woman or *Sacagawea* was Crow. The Crow had separated from the Hidatsa, and some of them lived near the Bighorn Mountains of Montana and were referred to as the Mountain Crow. Other Crow people lived along the Missouri and Yellowstone Rivers and were called the River Crow.

The Hidatsa also went to acquire goods from traders in the Fort Union and Fort Buford area or to seek protection from their enemies. The area around Ft. Buford was better suited to providing for the people, also, as drought occurred in the 1860s at Like-A-Fishhook Village.

In 1870, a group of Hidatsa under chiefs Crow Flies High and Bobtail Bull moved to an area near Fort Buford at the mouth of the Yellowstone River because of a dispute with other chiefs, Poor Wolf and Crows Paunch, over matters of practices and protocols. This group was called the Xoshgas. They remained there for 25 years before being returned by the U.S. Army to the Shell Creek area of the Fort Berthold reservation. They are credited with maintaining aspects of the Hidatsa culture such as songs, dances, stories, and other cultural activities.

In 1886, Like-A-Fishhook Village was abandoned, and eight communities along the river were established: Red Butte and Charging Eagle (Mandan), Nishu and Beaver Creek (Arikara), Independence (Mandan & Hidatsa), Lucky Mound and Shell Creek (Hidatsa). The eighth, Elbowoods, was settled by a combination of the tribes and became the center of government for the reservation. In 1891, the Allotment Act gave parcels of land to individuals on Fort Berthold.

*Our Story of Eagle Woman, Sacagawea*

*Xoshga Hidatsa Chief Crow Flies High*, 1879,
— Orlando Scott Goff, Smithsonian Institution

## The 1900s to 2020

The most significant event to affect our people in the 1900s was the construction of the Garrison Dam and the taking of the reservation bottomland in the 1950s. People had to move from their homes and gardens along the Missouri River to less fertile areas. There were community meetings regarding the move.

In an account in *Fort Berthold and the Garrison Dam* by Roy Meyer, James [Jim] Driver of the Shell Creek area of the reservation stated, "the Army's job is to fight wars, not build dams to flood out people like us. This land is our home, our people are buried in the hills of our lands. We are opposed to leaving our homes." Our people had been living where most had been self-sufficient then had to move to other, less-desirable parts of the reservation where the statistic for self-sufficiency was reversed.

New communities were established at Mandaree, White Shield, Twin Buttes, and New Town. In an article in a Minot, ND, newspaper on March 14, 1955, tribal member Jefferson B. Smith stated, "Having to move to new surroundings, their home life and economy shattered, the Fort Berthold Indian is confused in mind as to his actual status, and is very much in the dark as to Uncle Sam's ultimate purpose he has in store for him."

The Three Affiliated Tribes had adopted the 1934 Indian Reorganization Act's government structure. A Tribal Council, under this structure, attempted to stop the building of the dam but to no avail. Tribal Chairman, Carl Whitman, before a U.S. House committee in 1949, in regard to the 1851 treaty, stated:

> We kept our promise and have worked to build up a strong and growing cattle industry and steadily expanding agricultural program. Just as we were in sight of economic independence you began to build a reservoir and take away the heart of our reservation… The homes which we built, the bottom lands on which 85% of our people lived and on which our cattle industry depended, our churches, our schools [will be destroyed.] Our government, and our social life will be disrupted.

*Our Story of Eagle Woman, Sacagawea*

**Signing of the Garrison Dam Project with
George Gillette, Chairman Tribal Business Council, in tears.**

*(L-R) Lieutenant General George A. Wheeler, Chief of Corps of Engineers, US Army; Leo Young Wolf, Tribal Councilman, Mandan Tribe, Shell Creek District; Ben Reifel, Sioux Indian Superintendent at Ft. Berthold; George Gillette, Chairman Tribal Business Council, Arikara Tribe, Beaver Creek District; Joseph Packineau, Councilman, Arikara and Gros Ventre Tribes, Elbowoods District; James Hall, Vice-Chairman, Gros Ventre Tribe, Independence District; Levi Waters, Councilman, Arikara Tribe, Nishu District; Mark Mahto, Secretary Tribal Business Council, Mandan Tribe, Red Butte & Charging Eagle Districts; George Charging, Treasurer Tribal Business Council, Mandan Tribe, Lucky Mound District; Earl Bateman, Councilman, Arikara Tribe, Nishu District; Ralph Hoyt Case, Tribal Attorney; James Baker, Councilman, Mandan Tribe, Independence District; Allan Harper, US Assistant Director Missouri River Basin Investigating Unit; Jefferson B. Smith, Tribal Delegate, Gros Ventre Tribe; Julius Krug, US Secretary of the Interior (seated).*

— 1948, National Archives and Records Administration

*The Mandan, Hidatsa, and Arikara Nation*

Since the building of the dam, the Tribal Council has evolved with self-determination and changes to the constitution. Our people have worked to rebuild the economy and social structure.

Today the people of the MHA Nation who live on the reservation work as farmers or ranchers, work in tribal government in many different program areas, work in the communities in various service areas, work in the oil fields, or have their own businesses. Our people are lay persons and professionals in all areas.

The MHA Nation has a tribal casino and resort, a tribal ranch and buffalo herd, and other enterprises and investments. They have a tribal college, a cultural center, a clinic, and a tribal treatment center. They have housing developments, new schools, and other new tribal buildings including a veterans center. They continue to enhance the infrastructure.

In the early 21st century, our tribe began to extract oil and gas from the Bakken/Bird Bear Geological Formations, among the most abundant sources in the country. The drilling for oil and extraction of gas at Fort Berthold has been viewed as a blessing and/or a curse. History will determine the impact.

**Our history is unique and our culture is rich. Our history includes the fact that Eagle Woman, *Sacagawea*, the woman who accompanied Lewis and Clark to the West, was Hidatsa/Crow and not a Shoshone captive of the Hidatsa. We hope the reader will be enlightened by the information in this book and come away with a new appreciation of the identity of *Sacagawea* or *Maeshuwea*/Eagle Woman and her rightful place in Tribal and American history. The next sections include transcripts of oral stories passed down from generation to generation, gathered herein to pass on to others and tell her story, *our* story.**

**Sources Authored or Provided by MHA Tribal Members:**

Mandan, Hidatsa & Arikara Nation. *Reunion at the home of Sakakawea*. Lewis and Clark Signature Event, August 17-20, 2006, New Town, ND.

MHA Nation History. http://www.MHAnation.com/history

North Dakota Department of Public Instruction. *The History and Culture of the Mandan, Hidatsa, Sahnish (Arikara)*. Bismarck, ND: 2002.

*Sacagawea* Project Board Members, MHA Nation, 2015-2020.

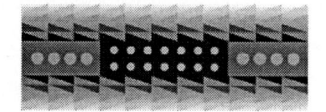

*The Little Missouri River* — National Park Service

## Chapter 2
### *OUR STORIES*

*The Strong Jaw Story*

People of the Mandan, Hidatsa and Arikara Nation have always held that *Sacagawea* of the Lewis and Clark journey was Hidatsa, not Shoshone. We have traditional stories that support this claim.

There are two main stories, one the Hidatsa Strong Jaw Story or Wolf Woman Story, and the other, the Bulls Eye Story, told to Army Major A. B. Welch in 1923.

Whether our people told one or both stories, they agreed, and still agree, that *Sacagawea* was Hidatsa.

*Our Story of Eagle Woman, Sacagawea*

# The Strong Jaw Story documented by Alfred Bowers in the early 1930s

*Some believe that Strong Jaw's daughter was Sacagawea.* This [story] has its origin with the Hidatsa who were living at the mouth of the Knife River on the north bank. A very holy man named Strong Jaw lived in this village. He had grown holy because he fasted nine days and nights and had dreamed of all the different kinds of wolves.

The wolves told Strong Jaw to stuff a wolf hide with sage and take it outside of the lodge whenever the wolves howled and they would reveal what news they were sending him. Because he could predict the future this way with the help of the wolves, he was of great assistance to the village. The other holy men were jealous of Strong Jaw's supernatural powers and a friend warned him that it would be best to leave the village and take the friendly families with him.

*Big Hidatsa Village site on the north side of Knife River, near the mouth. Across the river is seen the smaller Awatixa village, where Sakakawea lived. The "Strong Jaw" story tradition came from the people at Big Hidatsa Village.*
— National Park Service

## The Strong Jaw Story

Thirty-five families broke away and traveled westward towards the Killdeer Mountains until they reached a place on the Little Missouri where they built a new village. They hunted afoot, for there were few horses in those days. They lived there three years. Strong Jaw had a son named Walks-at-Dusk and a daughter who was eight years of age.

Farther west the Snake [Shoshone] Indians lived. One of their men was very holy so he was looking around to find someone suitable to buy [transfer] his sacred rites. His power was a sacred hoop through which he could look and see every tribe on the earth. He would take up his hoop and point it towards tribe after tribe, looking for the right man, but he could not find anyone who was strong as he was. He looked through all the tribes until he saw Strong Jaw and his party traveling towards the Killdeer Mountains. He saw a man in the camp with something powerful looking back at him.

The Snake Indian called the people together and announced that he was getting old and wanted someone to take over his medicine powers. The only one fit to do so was Strong Jaw's son, Walks-at-Dusk. The Snake Indians did not approve the idea but agreed to assist in the transfer.

His tribesman inquired how he would handle it and the Snake holy man said, "We will go after that little boy in the middle of the summer. I do not know whether we can get him or not for his father keeps a pack of wolves watching over him all the time. The only way I can get them off their guard is to feed them something. We will drive a large herd of buffaloes into their camp. When they go out to hunt them, we will have our chance. The men will be out hunting, leaving the women and children alone in camp. Do not kill any of the children."

The Snakes, 200 in number, started for the Hidatsa village, driving the buffaloes before them. One night the leader announced that he was to pray to his hoop that evening and then camp four times before reaching the Hidatsa. They moved one more camp towards the village. Strong Jaw's daughter had a dream which she related to her parents in the morning saying, "I saw a big smoke in my dream. I was carrying my little brother on my back and did not know where to go." The old people said it was surely a bad dream but did nothing about it.

The second morning she told the same story saying that things were so clear she could not get it out of her mind. The third night her dream was even more vivid. Strong Jaw's wife said to her husband, "You should pay attention to what she is saying." He thought it was only a child's dream for no enemies were near or the wolves would have told him.

She had a fourth dream. By that time the Snake Indians were on the opposite side of the hills. Again she said, "I had my little brother, Walks-at-Dusk, on my back. The lodges were burning and all the dogs were howling."

This time Strong Jaw's wife convinced him that something should be done. He brought out his sacred pipe and the wolf skin. He burned sage before the skin and it turned into a live wolf. When the wolf went out of the door, the dogs rushed at him and drove him back into the lodge, just as the Snake holy man had planned it. The people told of a large buffalo herd near the village; Strong Jaw was uneasy and could not decide at first what to do.

At last he decided to go after the herd and the men were soon killing the buffaloes. The Snake Indians killed the women, captured the children, and burned the lodges.

Four days later the Snake holy man took the little girl and boy, giving the other children to his tribesmen to raise. He said of the little boy, "This is the young man who will some day be your strong man."

When they reached the main camp, the little girl was given to another woman who was very kind. One day this old woman said, "I pity you. Do you think you could reach home if I showed you the way? I will take you away from the camp."

She drew a map of the Missouri and the Little Missouri Rivers on the ground and showed her where the Knife River villages were situated. She said to the girl, "We will start tomorrow evening. I will take you part way. Tell your people what happened but do not urge your brother to go for he has a good home here. Some day when he is strong enough, he may come back to visit you."

## The Strong Jaw Story

*Wolf with the leg of a deer* — National Park Service

Before leaving the girl, the old woman gave her advice on conserving the food and warned her not to travel during the daytime. She traveled night after night until her food was gone. She was very hungry but still she traveled. One moonlight night she saw something ahead of her. At first she thought it was a white rock but when she was nearer, she saw that it was a large wolf.

The wolf wagged its tail like a friendly dog and walked up to her. Then the wolf walked on, showing her the way. When it was daylight she stopped and the wolf brought her an animal leg bone with some meat on it. She broke the bone and ate the marrow.

That night the wolf came again to lead her and when she was hungry, the wolf brought her tallow from around the animal's kidneys. The fourth night the wolf said, "I know all about you. I did not come to you until you lost your way. When we get to Butte-with-Grass I will call all the wolves to you and they will tell you what to do when you get home."

They walked all night until light appeared in the east. Then the wolf said, "This is the place." Wolf faced toward the south and howled. Soon wolves were coming from that direction. Then she faced the west and howled and the west wolves came. Then she faced to the north and to the east to howl and the wolves of those directions came also. She listened to their conversation and could understand everything they said.

The "leader of the wolves" kept repeating, "We must finish what we have to say before sunrise." The wolves selected the north wolves to speak to her as that was the most numerous group. Their leader said, "Whenever she goes anywhere alone, she will turn into a wolf and have powers like we have. And one thing more, she must make a ceremony to the wolves. When making the ceremony, you should give offerings and call the name 'prairie people' because the wolves are the people of the flats."

The wolves decided that the wolf who had taken her this far should lead her to the village. The wolf led her to a high hill back of the village and then said, "Your fathers will come to look for you because they know you are coming toward the village. You stay here until they find you." While she sat there, it became light and she could see people walking in the distance. They were her father and brothers.

She scolded them saying, "Look at all the trouble we have had just because you would not listen to my dreams. My brother is with the Snake people whose holy man gives him good care.

The older women were killed. I promised the wolves to give their ceremony as soon as I reached home." Her father knew what she meant. Soon the criers were calling that Strong Jaw's daughter had returned from the enemy and that the wolves had led her all the way back.

A few days later she resolved to give the ceremony to the wolves. She carried robes and corn balls onto the earth lodge and wore ceremonial clothing such as the wolves told her she must wear. The wolves had said, "Take the skin off of a wolf's head and with the head and nose on to make the headdress of. Wear twelve eagle tails fastened to a band made of porcupine quills. Wear wolf claws around your ankles and wrists." Then she went onto the lodge and called, "People of the Prairies." Since she was too young to fast, her father and his seven brothers fasted and performed the dances for her as the wolves had instructed her. Each called for arrows to record his exploits in warfare.

In this way the men tried to outdo each other. Afterwards others wanted to perform the ceremony and she would tell them when the proper time had come to give it again. She grew up like other girls only all knew her to be holy. She learned to plant and harvest corn like the other women. People praised her for discovering the wolf dance and said that it was good for the tribe.

*Wolf Headdress*
— National Museum of Natural History

When men wanted to go on the warpath, they would give her elkskin dresses, robes and moccasins to bring them good luck and she would say, "I will pray for you to get many horses without being seen." Everything would happen just as she predicted. One time a large war party was going out and the leader came to her and asked for good luck. She said, "Go on your way. Start tonight. On the fourth night I will come to you. Have a fat cow butchered and camp in the timber near good water. Roast the ribs and at sundown I will be there. Just on the other side of the hill you will hear a wolf howl so you will know I have come."

They did what she said. Just as the full moon was coming up she howled and the leader said, "The Wolf Woman is here." She had been working in her gardens for four days but on the last day she sang the war party songs saying, "I will be there when the ribs are cooked." Suddenly she changed into a wolf and all the people of the village saw her run away. She reached the war party that night and asked for the short ribs. Others brought her roasted ribs, asking for luck. She said to the leader, "I told you I would be here to tell you what to do. Move your camp three times. The fourth time you will be near your enemies. Run a little and they will chase you; turn and you will kill many. Doing that several times and you can take the whole camp. You will find the chief's lodge in the middle of the camp. Save everything in that lodge for those things belong to me. Now I am going home."

They did as she instructed. They killed the men and took the women and children prisoners. Meanwhile her brother, Walks-at-Dusk, had grown up and was quite prominent for he had a full knowledge of the Snake Indian medicine rites but he often dreamed of his own father's Wolf bundle. He was the leader of many war expeditions. In his dreams the wolves had told him to go east towards the Killdeer Mountains where he could kill seven men. He knew he was Hidatsa so he was afraid they might be his own people. The wolves sent him dreams every night until he decided to go. Each time he dreamed of seven men and one spotted horse.

## *The Strong Jaw Story*

At the same time an Hidatsa living on the Knife River dreamed that he should go toward the Killdeer Mountains where he would find seven men and a spotted horse. The Knife River party started out with seven men and a pinto horse at the same time Walks-at-Dusk came east with six men and a pinto. The Hidatsa sent two men ahead as scouts and the Snakes did likewise. The Snake Indians were run onto a high butte and were surrounded.

One Hidatsa was sent back on the spotted horse to bring warriors from the village. Before the warriors arrived, one of the Hidatsa said, "I am going to talk to them and see if they know what I say. Are you up there, Walks-at-Dusk? If you are, you better be brave because we sent for a large force. We are about to kill all of you." Walks-at-Dusk replied, "Come along" and he sang the wolf songs. The Hidatsa heard a wolf howling to the west.

That night the Snake Indians went out between the Hidatsa sentinels but they were not seen. The war party arrived from Knife River the next day but none of the enemies could be found. When Walks-at-Dusk returned he told how he had nearly lost his life because of the great super-natural powers of the Hidatsa wolf leaders. After that, the Snake Indians never led war parties against the Hidatsa.

**Alfred Bowers** documented the Strong Jaw story from informants **Joe Ward** and **Bears Arm** in his book, *Hidatsa Social and Ceremonial Organization,* published in 1963 as Bulletin 194 of the Smithsonian Institution, Bureau of American Ethnology. The story is taken from that book.

**Bowers did not tie the story to *Sacagawea* of Lewis and Clark, but the story does establish interactions between the Shoshone and Hidatsa, explains *Sacagawea* being Hidatsa, supports the story that the leader of the Shoshone was her brother, but makes a case for *Sacagawea* being captured by the Shoshone instead of the other way around as in the popular story.**

## Our Story of Eagle Woman, Sacagawea

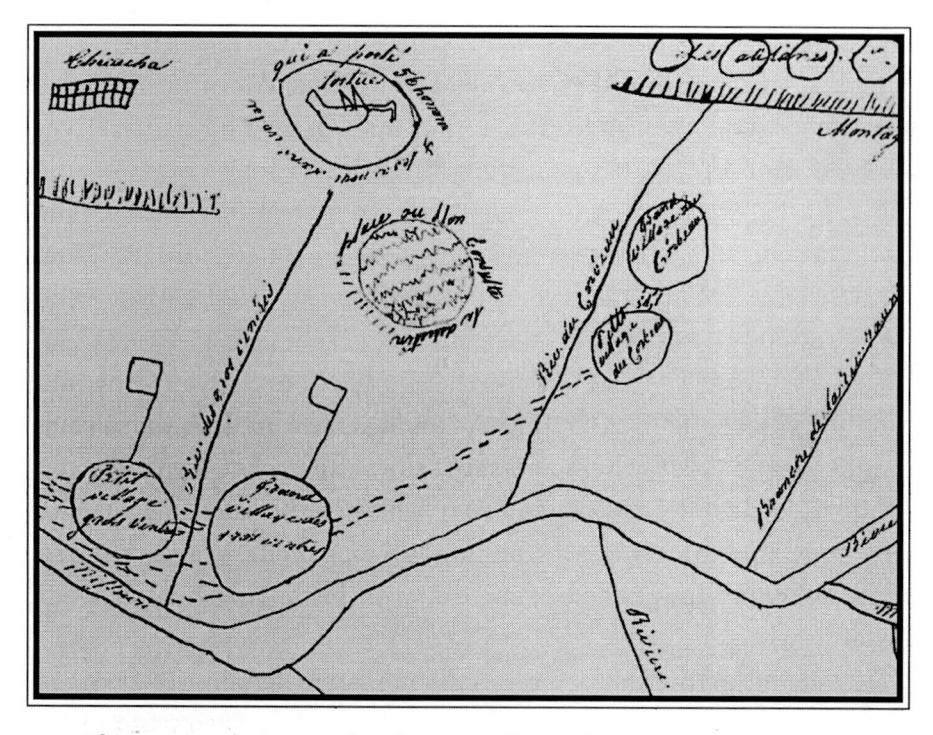

This map made in 1806 for Thomas Jefferson by the Arikara leader Inquida Necharo (Riding Chief), also called Too Ne (Whipporwill), with identifications in French added by the trader, Joseph Gravelines. Rediscovered only within the past five years in a French archive, the detail shown here confirms part of the Strong Jaw/ "Wolf Woman" oral history recalled by Hidatsa and Mandan descendants.

The Missouri River is shown at bottom. At lower left, Big Hidatsa Village (Grand village des Gros Ventres) and Awatixa Village (Petite Village Gros Ventres) are shown on opposite sides at the mouth of Knife River (Riv. des Gros Ventres). Further west, the next stream entering the Missouri is the Little Missouri River (Riv. du Corbeau-"River of the Crow"). Two earthlodge villages are shown on this stream, precisely in the area where the Nightwalker Butte Village is located. The Arikara referred to them as the Big Crow Village-"Grand Village du Corbeau;" and the Little Crow Village-"Petit Village du Corbeau."

Throughout the 18th century, small groups were splintering off from the Hidatsa villages and moving west in short stages toward the Yellowstone Valley, where by the 19th century they were referred to as the "River Crows." This is precisely what the map shows: a large trail of footprints leaving the Hidatsa villages on Knife River to found new villages on the Little Missouri. This 1806 map confirms the historical memories of the Joe Ward, Bear's Arm, and Paige Baker, Sr., families, 1806. — Bibliotheque national de France, Paris.

## The Strong Jaw Story

**Gerard Baker**, Yellow Wolf, retired from the National Park Service where he was Assistant Director for American Indian Relations and Superintendent of the Lewis and Clark Trail and Corps of Discovery II (2003-2005).

An MHA tribal member, he stated in "Mandan and Hidatsa of the Upper Missouri: The Corps of Discovery...One of Many" in *Lewis and Clark through Indian Eyes* edited by Alvin M. Josephy, Jr. , 2006, that a version of the Strong Jaw story was told in his home:

> When I think back to my early days on our ranch about nine miles northwest of Mandaree, North Dakota, I remember the visits of many elders from the Fort Berthold Indian Reservation from both sides of my family, Mandan and Hidatsa.
>
> My mother's side were descendants of the Hidatsa villages and matrilineal, whereas my father's side were descendants of the Mandan villages. I heard many stories of our people and the villages when we lived on the mouth of the Knife River and the Big Missouri River near what is today the small village of Stanton, North Dakota.
>
> In remembering the stories I heard and the many people who visited our villages, I remember not hearing much about the famed trip of Lewis and Clark. As some would say later, they were no big deal to our people, as our tribes had dealt with white trappers and traders for many, many years, and I was told that "we were used to the speeches."
>
> What was remembered and told to me was the story of the first Black man our people ever saw and of course the young woman who was married to the French trapper, Charbonneau. The Black man was of course the slave York, and the young woman we Hidatsa know as *Sakakawea*. There are many stories about this *Sakakawea* and who she was. I will tell one that I remember. I remember hearing this in different parts from several different people, but I remember this version from my father, the late Paige Baker, Sr.

He told me that our people, now called the Mandan and Hidatsa (he was almost a full-blood Mandan, and Mandan was his first language), were known to have lived in five villages on the Knife and Missouri Rivers.

Our creation stories tell us that we had three subtribes of Hidatsas and two subtribes of Mandan. From north to south, the villages were the homes of the Hidatsa, Awatxia [*Awatixa*], and Awaxixa [*Awaxawi*] (now these groups are all called under the general name of Hidatsa). The Mandan, he said, had lived in two villages.

He said there were more villages in the old, old days, but he always heard only of the two where he said the bands called the *Nuptadi* and the *Nuitadi* (the languages spoken by these were later classified as dialects) had lived, and it was the people of these villages who had pretty much kept the Corps of Discovery alive, given them information regarding the tribes upstream, and shown them the "lay of the land."

*Remains of the Awatixa Hidatsa village on Knife River, where Sacagawea lived prior to 1837. Impressions of the circular earthlodges are still visible.*
— National Park Service

## The Strong Jaw Story

*Aerial view of Night Walker's Butte Village. A number of houses have been excavated, and the remains of a defensive stockade, encircling the site at the edge of the Butte top, have been exposed.* — Missouri Basin Project, Smithsonian

Each of these tribes had their own creation stories, and each would live in different areas in and around the Missouri River, and not just in the village locations that are outlined today.

It was one of these peoples, the Awatxia [*Awatixa*], he said, where *Sakakawea* came from. When she was born, her group had been away from the Missouri River, which was common in that time, and had lived in a fortified village that was located on a high bluff, but several miles up the Little Missouri River, in the Badlands of what is now North Dakota.

The leader of the village went by the name of Twilight Walker or Nightwalker. My father said he had this name due to the fact that he would use the evening time to pray, as that "time" was his medicine.

The area today is called Nightwalker's Butte, and one can still find remains of the village, including the cottonwood posts that were part of the lodges and the palisades.

What made this village unique is that it was built on a very steep plateau with only one way to enter, so it had a natural fortification made from cottonwood trees and a ditch that was dug around the village.

The dirt from this ditch was used for the earth-lodge construction, so it served several purposes, including providing a defense around the village. It was here that my father and other elders say *Sakakawea* was born. I never heard a date, as the people never had actual dates, but seasons, and they never mentioned what season *Sakakawea* was born in. I never heard who her parents were, but they did say that she was one of several children.

She grew up in the Awatxia [*Awatixa*] world of clans and societies, being taught by her elder clan relatives. The clan system is matrilineal, meaning your mother's side had many responsibilities as the teachers.

The societies are age-grade organizations, and you would change societies as you got older, many times following your family's line of societies. The people of the village, like many others, would have lived an agriculture-based life, but in those early days, they had subsisted on hunting and gathering as well.

It was the responsibility of the men to hunt and protect the village and, as was the custom, when the men went out hunting they would usually leave behind some younger boys to defend the people, and of course the old men would always stay, so they too would protect the village. It was at these times that the village was the most vulnerable to the tribes that were considered enemies.

One of these tribes was the Shoshone, whose name means "from the west." As my father's version of the story goes, the Hidatsa men were all out hunting when the Shoshone attacked the village, not only killing the defenders left behind, but also taking some of the children and women, *Sakakawea* and her brother being among those taken.

They were taken back to Shoshone territory in the mountains, and the young ones were then raised as Shoshone. It was told that *Sakakawea* was old enough to remember where she came from, and, as time went on, she would look to the east, toward the way she had come, and remember her village and cry for her family.

She was noticed by an old woman of the Shoshone, and that old lady, it is said, took pity on her. One day she told *Sakakawea* that she knew she missed her people and that she would help her get home. She told her to prepare for her journey and that, as the sun set the next day, she should go once again and look toward the east, but this time she would see a wolf, as this was the old lady's helper.

The young girl was to follow that wolf each night; when morning came, the wolf would go away, and it was at that time that *Sakakawea* should hide. She told her that four wolves would lead her back to her people. *Sakakawea* then went to her brother and told him what this old lady had said.

He replied that if it was true that they came from the villages to the east, he did not remember, as he was very young when they brought him to this village, and because of that, he considered this to be his village and his people, and that someday he would be a leader among them.

She did not argue, but said her good-bye and got her things ready for the next night when she would sneak out of the village. The next evening, she sneaked away from the village and as she stood looking to the east, just as the old lady had said, a wolf appeared. The wolf would trot ahead, then look back; on the fourth time it did this, she followed.

As the old lady said, each wolf would stay just far enough ahead so *Sakakawea* could follow; she did this for four nights. Now, as I mentioned, the people at that time had no concept of "time" in the modern sense, so the "four" could be translated to mean four days, or four weeks. The number four also represents the four sacred directions of the Earth.

*Awatixa Hidatsa Village on the Knife River* — National Park Service

It was told to me that *Sakakawea* not only lived off the fruits and berries of the land, meaning her journey took place in the time when the berries were ripe, early summer perhaps. Each wolf also killed game for her and would leave it on the trail so that she could cook and eat meat as well.

This is the way that *Sakakawea* made it back to the village of her people, the Hidatsa, according to my father, who heard this story as a young man himself. There are many stories and many claims as to who *Sakakawea* was... Some things to consider as we discuss this famed lady and who her "family" and tribe really were — Hidatsa or Shoshone: If she really was born and raised among the Shoshone, why did she not run away from her husband, as he was supposed to be very mean and would beat her?

Why did she not stay with her people, the Shoshone, and why did she come back to the Hidatsa village? Or did she know that the Hidatsa were the people she was born into? Another thought, regarding her brother — we all know the story of how excited she got when she realized that she was meeting him, as in the story I heard told.

*The Strong Jaw Story*

Was he too an Hidatsa, but preferred to stay behind, or could he have been an "adopted" brother from her trip out west? I can remember the elders, including my father, talking about this and, of course, we say she is one of us.

**Following are pieces of information and thoughts regarding the Strong Jaw Story.**

**Alfred Bowers'** book, *Hidatsa Social & Ceremonial Organization,* in which he recorded the Strong Jaw story, also contains the following which lends support to the Strong Jaw Story:

> It was at this time, according to traditions largely substantiated by recent tree ring studies, that one group under Strong Jaw moved out of the Hidatsa village to build on the Little Missouri near the mouth of Cherry Creek (Will, 1946).

Concerning the *Awaxawi,* Bradbury (1904) wrote — On our way to the Mandans we passed through the small village belonging to the Ahwahhaways... This nation can scarcely muster fifty warriors, and yet they carry on an offensive war against the Snake and Flathead Indians.

*Our Story of Eagle Woman, Sacagawea*

**Some historians in North Dakota became interested in the Hidatsa claiming *Sacagawea* as their tribal member and in the Strong Jaw story.**

From an article by James B. Connolly, Historian, in *North Dakota Motorist,* July-August, 1975, Vol. 21, No. 1 "One small segment of the Indian population — the Hidatsa of the Fort Berthold Indian Reservation in North Dakota — for years have been trying to correct history... and no one pays a bit of attention... What the Hidatsa have been saying, and still claim, is that *Sakakawea* was Hidatsa."

"This is a very serious tradition," wrote Paul A. Ewald, New Town, who has spent several years at Fort Berthold... and is an adopted Hidatsa... charged with the responsibility of keeping family records, including the history of Strong Jaw and his progeny.

[Regarding the dispute about her name:]
"*Sacajawea*" is a Shoshone word meaning Boat Launcher. *Sakakawea* is a Hidatsa word meaning Bird woman, and that is the name by which she was known...

Part of the confusion on the spelling of the name comes from relying on notes of the two leaders, and while Lewis and Clark are among the country's great heroes, they were notoriously bad spellers... They also are the authorities for the *Sakakawea* story.

Is it significant that *Sakakawea* had a good Hidatsa name? Indians weren't inclined to bestow names on women captives. For example, in a grave near New Town, Ewald noted three graves with no names but just a title: Assiniboine Woman...

[Regarding the use of languages during the Expedition:]
*Sakakawea* spoke two languages, Shoshone and Hidatsa. Charbonneau, whose employment was strictly as an interpreter, was fluent in French, spoke "a few English," was familiar with the Hidatsa tongue and some other Indian dialects, plus the universal sign language of the Plains Indians.

York, Clark's Negro servant, knew French and so was able to help in the transmission. In obtaining *Sakakawea's* story, it's just possible there could have been some alterations en route. (If Charbonneau was aware of any misconceptions, he would hesitate to make corrections inasmuch as his value to the Expedition was enhanced by his wife's identity as a Shoshone.)

[Regarding *Sacagawea's* response when she came to the Shoshone's camp with Lewis and Clark:]

With the Party of Exploration deep in the Rockies, Meriwether Lewis thought *Sakakawea* most insensitive when he wrote: "Our present camp is precisely on the spot that the Snake Indians were encamped at the time the *Minnetaree* (Hidatsa) of the Knife river first came in sight of them five years since, from hence they retreated about three miles up Jefferson River and concealed themselves in the woods.

The *Minnetaree* pursued, attacked, then killed four men, four women, a number of boys and made prisoners of the females and four boys. *Sakakawea*, our Indian woman, was one of the female prisoners taken at that time though I cannot discover that she shows any emotion of sorrow in recollecting this event or of joy in being again restored to her native country.

However, when *Sakakawea* actually met the Shoshone, she was observed sucking her fingers in joy and the meeting was "really affecting," said Lewis, "particularly between *Sakakawea* and an Indian woman, who had been taken prisoner at the same time with her and who had afterwards escaped from the Hidatsa and rejoined her nation."

Instead of having been captive, could this have been the woman who befriended her? The most moving moment came when *Sakakawea* was sitting to interpret at a council and recognized the Shoshone chief. She jumped up, ran to him, threw her blanket around him and wept. Here was her brother, *Cameahwait* (Walks-at-Dusk?), whom she had not seen for five years.

Purportedly here was *Sakakawea* in her homeland with her own people and where her brother was a man of power. She had a husband but, if historical reports are correct, Charbonneau was no great bargain as a mate. What would have been more natural than for *Sakakawea* to elect to stay with the Shoshone? There is no hint that such action was even contemplated...

The attack on Strong Jaw's village — the last battle between the Shoshone and Hidatsa — came historically at just the right time, as far as *Sakakawea*'s story is concerned. And that was about the time according to Lewis' report, that Hidatsa were attacking the Shoshone, deep in the Rocky Mountains...

Several years ago I was plugging to have North Dakota represented in National Statuary Hall be a Mandan chief, Four Bears. A Mandan friend, **Carl Whitman** of Parshall was asked if he was related to Four Bears. "No, but I'm related to *Sakakawea*," was his answer, I believe him.

**Connolly seemed to believe:**
- that the Strong Jaw story was historically at the right time.
- that, if the young girl in the story was *Sacagawea*, *Cameahwait* of the Lewis and Clark Journals could have been her brother Walks-at-Dusk. The Journals state that *Sacagawea* found her brother at the Shoshone camp.
- that the Indian woman at the Shoshone in the Journals who was glad to see *Sacagawea* could have also been the one who befriended Wolf Woman (*Sacagawea*) and helped her get home in the Strong Jaw story. The Journals state that a woman was very glad to see her when the party reached the Shoshone camp.

Connolly questioned:
- the use of the name *Sacajawea* rather than *Sacagawea*, her Hidatsa name which means Bird Woman, the known interpretation of her name.

- the fact that *Sacagawea* had an Hidatsa name, and he believed that the Hidatsa did not name captives.
- the fact that language misinterpretations would likely have occurred and the fact that Charbonneau would not have corrected misconceptions since his employment relied on his wife's being Shoshone.
- the fact that *Sacagawea* did not show much emotion when the party reached what was supposed to be her home, and she did not attempt to stay there.

### From *SAKAKAWEA*, HIDATSA OR SHOSHONE?
by Doris Eastman, *Fargo Forum*, October, 1975

Until lately, there hasn't been much question of the "Shoshone" part of the [Lewis and Clark and *Sacagawea*] story. But in the July-August issue of the *North Dakota Motorist*, [James] Connolly disputes that, too. He has gone to great lengths and great heights, too, in his research on the subject, and his article goes into much detail on his theory that *Sakakawea* was not Shoshone, but a member of the Hidatsa tribe, making her a North Dakotan.

Hidatsas have been saying it for years, but not much attention has been paid to their claims. Now Connolly has told what he believes is the story of *Sakakawea*, advancing a number of well researched arguments. [He promoted the Strong Jaw story.]

Connolly writes that part of the confusion in the spelling of the names (of *Sacagawea*) comes from relying on notes of the two leaders, Lewis and Clark, of whom he says, "while they are among the country's great heroes, they were notoriously bad spellers."

He quotes a number of historians who are inclined to support his theory. Shortly after the *Motorist* article appeared, Rev. Louis Pfaller, O. S. B., Assumption Abbey, Richardton, N. D., a teacher and historian, wrote Connolly: "Nice job on the *Sakakawea* article. It makes a good feature and should stir up lots of speculation.

**Buzz Fredericks**, (a former director of the United Tribes office in Bismarck) [and a MHA tribal member] tried to tell me that she was Hidatsa, but I discounted it. Your article makes it sound plausible."

Erling N. Rolfsrud, Alexandria, Minn., historian and author, who has done most of his writing about his native North Dakota, commented: "I found your article on *Sakakawea* very interesting and am intrigued with this new angle about *Sakakawea* being a Hidatsa; it makes sense to me."

Edna LaMoore Waldo, North Dakota historical writer, living in Palo Alto, Calif., wrote "The Hidatsa story about *Sakakawea* makes a great deal of sense. What I'd like to know is, where was it all these years? Known? Suppressed? If our state people had the information, however sketchy, they should have let us know so that writers like me would not have stayed with the Shoshone story. We'll probably never get the rest of the country to believe it or to accept our spelling, but at least, responsible Dakotans should know."

A letter from **Alfred W. Bowers** [notable Hidatsa researcher] of the University of Idaho, wrote: "When time permits I am going to re-examine my field notes on Strong Jaw and his daughter who came back from the Snake Indians and see if there was something I overlooked. Offhand, it does seem that there might be a time lag there, but certainly the Wyoming studies [the story that she was Shoshone and buried in Wyoming put forth by Grace Hebard and Charles Eastman] are open to severe criticism at this time."

**Juanita J. Helphrey**, executive director of the North Dakota Indian Affairs Commission, Bismarck, and a member of the Hidatsa nation, wrote: "I read with great interest your article in the *Motorist* and I think it is excellent. I sincerely hope that it can be a proven fact that *Sakakawea* is of the Hidatsa tribe.

I have been associated with the Lewis and Clark Trail Council and from time to time have heard arguments as to her history and tribal affiliation. It would be a great day indeed for the history of North Dakota and for the history of our Hidatsa tribe to reach a final consensus as to the background and tribal affiliation of *Sakakawea*.

*The Strong Jaw Story*

My grandfather, **J. B. Smith [Jefferson Bird Smith],** who passed away in the spring this year, very strongly supported the fact that *Sakakawea* was one of the Hidatsa tribe."

In *Hidatsa Place Names* by Louis Garcia, unpublished paper, 2006, it states:

> Shoshone Butte: *Maabuksha Nuxpaga*. The Shoshone are known as Snake People. This butte is located in... Dunn County.
>
> The story of Wolf Woman occurred at this butte. In about 1799, the Shoshone attacked an Hidatsa hunting camp while the men were away. They killed the women and children, except a few who escaped to the top of this butte and successfully defended the only path to the top. Some say this is where *Sagagawiash* (*Sakakawia*) was captured by the Shoshone.

Garcia's informants were tribal members from Fort Berthold.

**Some tribal members, however, have discounted the Strong Jaw story as being about *Sacagawea*:**

**Helen Wolf Wilkinson** in *Earth Lodge Tales from the Upper Missouri,* University of Mary, recorded in the 1980s, tells a version of the Strong Jaw or Wolf Woman story. She says, however, "This is a story which they often add to the tale of Bird Woman. I want to straighten out the true story of this... Those are the ones who perform the wolf ceremony. This is a different story than the one about Bird Woman. This is the story of the Shoshone raid."

**Gerald Tex Fox** recorded **Pat Fredericks** in 2004 at Mandaree. Pat said, "That story, that (Wolf Woman), they said she was stolen from here with her brother, but he never came back. She came back. Somebody told that story and put it like *Sacagawea*. That happened before *Sacagawea*. They tied it in like it was the same story. That was a different story altogether."

*Our Story of Eagle Woman, Sacagawea*

*The Little Missouri River* — National Park Service

Although some tribal members have discounted the Strong Jaw story, to other tribal members, the Strong Jaw or Wolf Woman story explained how *Sacagawea* was Hidatsa, how she knew the route to the West, how she knew the Shoshones, and especially explained the Lewis and Clark Journal report that *Sacagawea* saw her brother, a chief among the Shoshone.

However, if *Sacagawea* was in her teens at the time of the expedition, her brother would have been a young boy, and this fact would probably have been noted if he was a chief. Further, *Sacagawea* had snake medicine according to oral history. Wolf Woman had wolf medicine.

In any case, those who believed the Strong Jaw story believed *Sacagawea* was Hidatsa. The next section presents another *Sacagawea* story told at Ft. Berthold, the Bulls Eye Story, told to Major A. B. Welch by Bulls Eye in 1923.

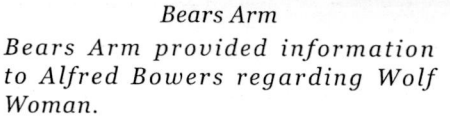

## The Strong Jaw Story

*Bears Arm*

Bears Arm provided information to Alfred Bowers regarding Wolf Woman.
— Everett R Cox/Welch Dakota Papers

*Gerard Baker*

Gerard Baker holds an honorary doctorate from the School of Mines in Rapid City, SD.
— MHA Interpretive Center

*Our Story of Eagle Woman, Sacagawea*

## Sources Authored or Provided by MHA Tribal Members:

Baker, Gerard. "The Corps of Discovery... One of Many" in *Lewis and Clark through Indian Eyes,* edited by Alvin Josephy Jr. New York: Alfred A. Knopf, 2006.

Fredericks, Pat. Personal Interview. Conducted by Gerald Tex Fox, 2004.

Wilkinson, Helen Wolf. "The Return of Wolf Woman" in *Earth Lodge Tales from the Upper Missouri,* edited by Douglas R. Parks, A. Wesley Jones and Robert C. Hollow. Bismarck, ND: Mary College, 1978.

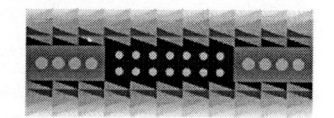

*Reconstructed Fort Mandan, built by the Lewis & Clark expediton in Nov. 1804. It was here that Toussaint Charbonneau was hired and where 18-year-old Sacagawea gave birth to their first child named Jean Baptiste, Feb. 11, 1805.*
— National Park Service

# Chapter 3
## *OUR STORIES*

*The Bulls Eye Story*

Another story about Sacagawea told at Ft. Berthold is the Bulls Eye story. This story was documented by Major A. B. Welch and printed in the *Van Hook Reporter* of April 2, 1925.

*The following documents are from Major Welch's unpublished papers.*

This story I [A. B. Welch] obtained while on a trip to the Fort Berthold Reservation to make addresses at Van Hook, and at the Antelopes Dance Hall at Crows Breast Village of the Mandans at the mouth of the Little Missouri river. They arrived at Van Hook on the 28th of May, 1923, and the last day went down to the village of the Gros Ventre [Hidatsa], Shell Village, where I made a Memorial address at the graveyard by the Catholic Church.

*Major A. B. Welch giving the Memorial Day address at Shell Village, N.D., May 1923. The Old Scouts Society members decorating graves.—* Everett R Cox

There were many whites gathered there and most of the Gros Ventre people, from miles around. The members of the Van Hook American Legion Post were there also to perform the usual services at the graves of ex-service men. When I arrived and the crier shouted the news, there was a great rush of the men for their horses, and soon the tribal Old Scouts who served with the United States Army at Fort Lincoln and at the mouth of the Yellowstone, were mounted and we started for the cemetery. I rode the tallest horse I ever saw. The Legion boys fell into line behind, followed by the church societies, with their banners. The programs consisted of prayer by the Legion Chaplain; songs by six old Indians in the Gros Ventre tongue; my address and presentation of a poppy wreath from the "Poppy Lady of France;" decoration of the graves of twenty-six old volunteer scouts and also that of one man killed in the World War (Rabbit Head). Then followed the placing of flowers and other decorations by the Indian women, on all the other graves there.

During the ceremonies, four Indians sat apart upon the grass. There was the father and mother of the soldier, Rabbit Head, and two women relatives.

## The Bulls Eye Story

During my address, one of these women wailed continually. When the time came for the decorations of this soldier's grave, the women placed many very bright artificial flowers all over the grave and also stuck several small flags upon the mound; then the old man placed a very wonderful war bonnet there. It had the long back feathers of a chief.

An old scout named Black Bear (This is the Rain Maker Medicine Man) walked over and picked it up. He had buried a nephew that same day upon the hill to the west, and the old father of Rabbit Head said he would give it to him "to wipe away his tears." After the flowers were all in position, the three volleys were fired and taps sounded by Birds Bill, a German War Veteran, and the soldiers marched away. I led the Old Scouts back to the ceremonial lodge, where they were dismissed.

I was invited to enter the ceremonial lodge and about ten men entered with me. I took the place inside the entrance and sat down. Some women brought in coffee, meat and hard tack. After we had eaten of the feast, Bulls Eye, one of the Scouts, said:

I want to talk with you now. We have heard about some white men who wrote about my Grandmother. Her name was *T(Sakakawea)ish*. These white men came along here about a hundred years ago. They made a mistake with the interpreter. He could not speak the Indian well and told it wrong. He could not talk English either. He talked French. It has been wrong ever since that time. *T(Sakakawea)ish* was not a Shoshoni. She was a Hidatsa (Gros Ventre). I will tell you about that now.

I sensed a good story and said that I would be glad to listen to it, but that it was an important thing which he was going to tell me, and there should be many people to listen when he told it to me. If he made a mistake he should be corrected by someone; if he forgot anything, they should bring it to his attention. I wanted a regular council called.

So the Chief of the Old Scout Society gave instructions to the village crier, who went out and called around the camp circle of tepees and tents. Soon the old men were present and Bulls Eye began his story.

*Our Story of Eagle Woman, Sacagawea*

## The Story

My name is Bulls Eye. I am of the Hidatsa. I have seen fifty eight winters. I was a volunteer scout. I was with the soldiers at the mouth of the Yellowstone. I was with Custer at Fort Abraham Lincoln. I was young. My father's name was Lean Bull. He was Hidatsa. He was a brave man. My mother's name was Otter Woman. She was of the Hidatsa too. I was four years old when she was killed by an enemy. She died sitting up against a wagon wheel. The name of my mother's mother was *Sakakawea*. She was my grandmother. (The two fingers to the mouth sign was given — blood relationship sign).

The father of my grandmother was Smoked Lodge [Black Lodge, Bad Lodge]. He was Hidatsa. He signed the treaty of 1825. The mother of my grandmother was Otter Woman. She was Hidatsa too. My grandmother, *Sakakawea*, had a brother whose name was Cherry Necklace. He lived with our relatives in Montana. These people are called Absarokee or the Crows, sometimes. But they were Hidatsa a long time ago. They went away from us once. She had a half brother too. His name was One Buffalo. My grandmother was married to a white man.

When my grandmother was seventeen years old, her father gave her to a white man. This white man was my grandfather. His name was Sharbonish (Charbonneau). He lived among the Mandans and Hidatsa, then — that was by the Knife River.

This white man and *Sakakawea* had several children. The first one was a man child. The second was a woman child. They named her Otter Woman. She was my mother (Here the sign for birth was given). The third child was a woman child also. Her name was Cedar Woman. The fourth child was a woman child. They gave her the name of Different Breast.

The father of all these children was Sharbonish. You have called it a little different. It is the same man. None of these [named] descendants are alive now except myself. They are all dead from the enemy or sickness. [George Parshall, a direct descendant of *Sacagawea*, was also alive.]

The same year when my grandfather took *Sakakawea* from Smoked Lodge, they went away. They went toward the west.

*Toussaint Charbonneau (left), Prince Maximilian (center), and Karl Bodmer at Fort Clark, 1833.* — Lithograph detail by Karl Bodmer/Denver Art Museum

They were gone a long time and traveled far away. They went so far that they were among people who sometimes went to the ocean out there beyond. They had shells from the ocean and other things from there. This was on the other side of the mountains, beyond the three rivers of the Missouri.

They went past these three rivers, where they flow together. Then they went on over the mountains to another river which flowed west. All the rivers and streams there flowed that way. When they came to a very bad river (Salmon River) they turned back.

## Our Story of Eagle Woman, Sacagawea

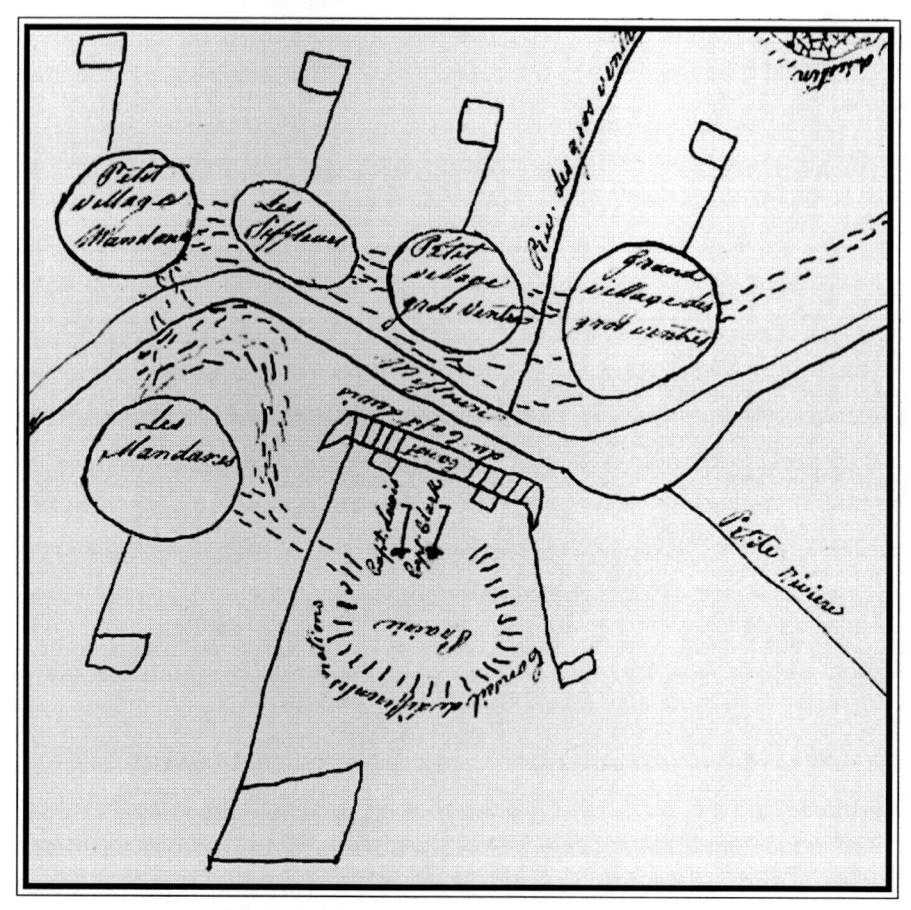

The Keelboat of the Lewis & Clark Expedition, with its large flags, at the Knife River Villages. Ink drawing from memory by the Arikara leader Inquida Necharo (Riding Chief) also called Too Ne (Whipporwill). Detail from a map made for Thomas Jefferson, 1806. — Bibliotheque national de France, Paris.

    They came back to the Knife River then. So she knew that country they went over. This was a year before this white party came. They stayed through the winter. (This was Lewis and Clark and party.)

    When these people came, they selected Sharbonish and *Tsakakaweaish*, my grandmother, to guide them into that country then. They had gone over it the year before. We have heard that they wrote it that she was not a Hidatsa, that she was a Shoshoni prisoner among us. But she was not a Shoshoni. She was Hidatsa. Everybody knew them. They knew her father and mother too.

## The Bulls Eye Story

The interpreter is not very good in both languages, they sometimes talk the easiest way. These white men were told that my grandmother knew the country well. **She had been there and traveled across the mountains. They had been among the Shoshoni people. They were told that she had a brother there. Indian relationship is not like the white tell it. When an Indian makes a friend of a stranger, they sometimes call them "brothers."**

So I think this interpreter told the whites that she had a brother there among the Shoshoni. It did not mean the Gros Ventre had her captive from the Shoshoni. Perhaps her father, Smoked Lodge, went out there on that trip, too. So they thought he had captured her and brought her back to live with the Hidatsa. But she was Hidatsa. We are sorry that **they got it wrong**. It has been wrong ever since then.

They started in boats. They pulled the boats to places. Where the banks were good, they used a small pole which the whites had on board the boat, to pull them along the shores. Then they would put the mule back on the boat. They went to these three rivers and over the mountains to the ocean.

While there my grandmother got many good shell ornaments from that place. When they came back (in 1806) they were on a large raft in the Yellowstone river. They passed through the country of our relatives, the Crows. They passed a large camp of these Absarokee at Sitting Bear Hill. *Sakakawea* called out to the people. She asked if her brother was in the camp. She said for him to go down the river, beyond the next bend. She would have the white boat land there. His name was Cherry Necklace.

So he wanted to make her a good gift then. He had a very fine white trained buffalo horse. This is a very good gift. He gave this white buffalo horse to Sharbonish. They loaded it upon the raft and brought it to our village. *Sakakawea* gave him some fine shell ornaments to wear. The Crows had good horses. This Cherry Necklace was a son of First, a Crow woman and his father was Looks Down (Indian relationship). That is all.

## Our Story of Eagle Woman, Sacagawea

While telling this story, Bulls Eye was frequently interrupted by some member of the council, who told him that he had forgotten something. They were all agreed as to the main points of the story. They paid very close attention as he related it. I [A. B. Welch] mentioned the name of Charbonneau and when they told us his name, there could be no doubt that it was a corruption of this French man's name.

Those present were:

**Birds Bill**, Chief of the US Volunteer Scouts Society

**Bulls Eye**, Son of Otter Woman, Daughter of *Sakakawea* and Charbonneau

**Dog (George Parshall),** a white scout at Ft. Buford was his father [Also a descendant of *Sacagawea*]

**Stanley Deane**, Educated Indian

**Henry Bad Gun**, Son of Charging Eagle, who was the son of Four Bears

**Black Chest**, Old US Volunteer Scout

**Thad Mason**, Indian names are Looking and Hunts Along

**Arthur Mandan**, Interpreter, grandson of Chief Red Cow, son of Scarred Face

## Bulls Eye's Account of *Sakakawea*'s Death documented by A. B. Welch, Welch Papers

The same men told me the Gros Ventre story of her death. This story rings true and is the most plausible account of the death of this Indian woman of Lewis and Clark's time. The same council of men were present and I [A.B. Welch] used the same interpreter. This story is accepted by the writer as the true one, as all other accounts are surrounded by too many doubts and weak places in the stories.

Bulls Eye said:

I will tell you how my grandmother, *Sakakawea*, died; my mother, Otter Woman, died at the same time nearly. This place was in Montana.

# The Bulls Eye Story

*Ceremonial earthlodge of Hairy Coat, at Shell Creek, ca. 1910. This is probably the site where Bulls Eye related the history of his grandmother, Sacagawea.* — State Historical Society of North Dakota

It is near where Glasgow is now, on a creek which we called Sand Creek place. My grandmother was married to this man, Sharbonneau. She had learned to like coffee terribly well. She could not get along without coffee. When she got out of coffee she would travel long distances in order to get a new supply. She saved the coffee from the pots and would put it on her head so it would smell like coffee.

During one of these trips to the trader's post to get coffee, the party she was with had two wagons with oxen hitched to them. My grandmother and my own mother, Otter Woman, and myself were in this party. I was only four years old, so do not remember who the rest were.

We were on Sand Creek, near Glasgow one night, and camped there. There was a trader's place not many miles away and we were going there to trade.

I was asleep on the ground between the wheels of one of the wagons, by the side of my grandmother; my mother was under the front wagon wheels. During the night some time, I was wakened by shooting; the camp was attacked by some enemy. The men were firing between the spokes of the wheels.

## Our Story of Eagle Woman, Sacagawea

*Major Welch, Bulls Eye and Interpreter Stanley Deane at Sanish N.D., 1927.*
— Welch Family

My mother said to Grandmother "Take the child to the willow gulch." So *Sakakawea* took me by the arm and ran into the brush of a gully close by. The firing of guns kept on for a while and then quit. All the yelling had ceased. My grandmother took me out then and we went back to the wagons. It was early in the morning when we left the coulee. I can remember it well. I have never forgotten. Several dead people lay around and under the wagons.

My mother was sitting up against a wheel of one of the wagons. She was covered with blood. She had been struck and was badly wounded there. Grandmother did not cry. She was also hit in the side by a bullet but had not said anything about that.

My mother said, "Take the boy to the trader's place. I am dying now. The boy is young to look after now." She died there against the wheel, then, that was the last I heard her speak. But she pointed to her mother's side and signed for her to go away. **So we walked over the hills and prairie to the trader's store. I got well and lived. *Sakakawea*, my grandmother, died at the trader's place, seven days after that.**

*The Bulls Eye Story*

Major Welch: This, we believe, is the true story of the death of *Sakakawea*, the Bird Woman, and is but one of the tragic stories which the Gros Ventre Indians have kept secret, but it is well known to all the old people of that tribe.

# MEMORIAL DAY
## For Old Scouts and Catholics
### AT
## Shell Village
# May 29, 5 P. M.

### PROGRAM

Grand Marching of Charley Beck Post, American Legion and of U. S. Old Scouts at Shell Village.

Cemetery—5:30. Prayer by Chaplain Rev. Father Peter.

Address by Captain A. B. Welch.

Speakers at Cemetery—Bulls Eyes, Foolish Bear.

Singing---English Songs, The Star Spangled Banner and America, by Audience.

Indian Songs---By the Old Scouts, Fort Buford.

By Order of Commanding Scout
**BIRDS BILL**

**JAMES W. HORN**
Recording Secretary

## Everybody Invited

*Shell Village Announcement, 1923*
— Everett R Cox/Welch Dakota Papers

*Our Story of Eagle Woman, Sacagawea*

On **October 14th, 1925, Horn and son, Four Dances**, and **Bulls Eye**, all Gros Ventres from Berthold Reserve, called at my (Major Welch's) office in Mandan today. They were ceremonious, so we sat and smoked my cigarettes for a time. At last Horn said (in English), "We want to tell you something about Bulls Eye's Grandmother, *Sakakawea*. That man Dr. Eastman who came out has made a bad mistake." [Eastman had been commissioned by the government to determine where *Sacajawea* or *Sacagawea* had been buried, in Wyoming, South Dakota, or North Dakota.]

After a time Bulls Eye said:

Thirty years ago, I began to hear many stories about my grandmother. Some of them were wrong. I was a Police on the Indian force then. I kept still because I thought that the truth would live. The third child of my grandmother, was a woman child and her name was "Cedar Woman." She was my aunt and the sister of my mother. My mother's name was "Otter Woman." Cedar Woman told me all the stories about my grandmother. She told the truth.

She said to remember them and when white people would hear, they would know them to be true. Cedar Woman died about thirty years ago. She was eighty six years old when she died. (Therefore: born 1809) [Census records for 1889 show Cedar Woman living in the home of Bulls Eye and that she was 52 years old at the time. She would have been born in about 1837 and died about 1895 at 58 years of age. Perhaps he was speaking of *Sacagawea* when he said she was eighty six years old when she died. She was 82.]

My mother Otter Woman was killed in the wagons in Montana. I was about four years old then. My grandmother often went to Sand Creek. They would pull out their boats there and build log houses for the winter time. She liked it there.

There were thirty four men that time. (Lewis and Clark Expedition was meant.) The way she prevented the Blackfeet from fighting was this way. **Her father had an adopted brother among them**.

## The Bulls Eye Story

*Interpreter Burr, Chief Birds Bill, Foolish Bear and Coffee, July 4, 1924 Birds Bill was the chief of the Old Scouts Society at Shell Creek when Bulls Eye told his story.*
— B. L. Brigham

(This probably referred to the Shoshones and not the Blackfeet.) When those Indians came she saw this man. She called him brother, this enemy.

Then they went to Helena. They struck a big river there. They followed it to the ocean then. She saw a big fish and got some shells there. They were gone two trips. The first one took one summer time. (The journey to the Pacific) [The journey to the Pacific was the second trip.] The second one was in the summer. They got back to *Hidatsaati*. (Village of the Gros Ventres on the Knife River, above the Mandan villages) That is what Cedar Woman told me about it.

I tell you what the old people have said. North Dakota people are friends by *Sacacawea*. Because of that thing we are always friends to the whites. I am a Catholic and I respect soldiers. They are the best people. I want them to lie well when they die.

Because my grandfather was a Frenchman, I have white blood in me. I always try to be a good American. All my folks have white blood. I try to do the best I can. We have talked much about this since I told you the story of my grandmother. We remember some things we did not say before to you.

*Major Welch with Ft. Berthold men: George Parshall, Four Dance, Ben Benson, Foolish Bear, Spotted Horn, Drags Wolf,* — Everett R Cox/Welch Dakota Papers

Dr. Eastman said he had been put in Major McLaughlin's place [Ft. Manuel]. He had the story in his bag. This is what we remember now, we say it to you.

There is a place named Wolf Point. Across the Missouri is a place called Sand Creek. It comes in from the south side. Wolf Point is on the north side there. Across from Wolf Point is a mountain called "Bear Sits." Wolf Point is the place where that trader was. Across from Sand Creek. The hills come down at that place. The store was about one half mile from the water. That is where my grandmother died.

He shook hands and sat down.

Question by Welch: Were you ever back to that trading store after your grandmother died?

Answer by Bulls Eye: Yes. I was there when I was nine years old.

Q — Was the store still there?

A — Yes. The trader was called "Yellow Hair" by the Gros Ventres.

## The Bulls Eye Story

Q — What happened while you were there?
A — The fur trader came from the Yellowstone then. He had oxen and wagons with trade goods.

I saw this when I was six [nine] years old that time. He made two trips. The Sioux fought them that year.

The Sioux did not kill anyone but took goods away with them. He came the second trip then. This was the same year. When he came that second trip he had soldiers with him. He had some Indian scouts and hunters too. Foolish Bear was one of them. (Foolish Bear still lives.) He had some Assiniboines too. I think that they were St. Louis fur traders. The Sioux did not burn the store then. The trader said the store was his, but I think it belonged to the people at the Yellowstone. (A.F. Co.)

Q — Did you see the place where your grandmother was buried?
A — Yes. She was put into the ground. The sticks broke. Tall grass grew in the hole. It looked like other graves in the ground. We could see the wrappings. I was nine years old when I saw it like that.

Q — Can you show me that place where she was buried in the ground?
A — If I did not get sick, I could. Foolish Bear could find it if I got sick. He was with the trader's scouts.

He knows the place where the store was. Maybe there are some stones there with fire markings.

I want you to find it before they put a stone on that Shoshone woman's grave. My grandmother did not die in Wyoming. That is another woman. (He means *Sacajawea,* the Shoshone woman.)

Q — Did *Sacacawea* speak French?
A — The old people say she talked a little French.
Q — Do you know where the son of *Sacacawea* died?
A — No.
Q — How many women did Sharbonneau have?
A — He was bad after women. He had many wives. He had some among the peoples, the Arikara — the Mandans — the Gros Ventres.

## Our Story of Eagle Woman, Sacagawea

No, I do not know if he had any Sioux women. They were our enemies. I want to say this: That trader's store was there five years after I saw it. People told me that.

### Regarding the Bulls Eye Story

### Interview of Joseph Packineau documented by A. B. Welch

Joseph Packineau, whose grandfather was a Frenchman who lived among the Mandans and Gros Ventre, is probably the best interpreter upon the Fort Berthold Reservation. The writer [A.B. Welch] called at his house in December, 1923, and while there the conversation turned to *Sakakawea*. His interview is given here, just as it was recorded then. He said: I am the son of Powder Horn and Plenty Sweet Grass, a Hidatsa woman. My father was the son of a Frenchman. My mother does not remember his French name, but his Indian name was Good Chaser. He could run buffalo good. My grandfather came from Canada and married a Gros Ventre woman by the name of Bug Woman. That was at the Knife River villages. His other wife was named Goes Along the Bank. My grandfather [father] was the son of Bug Woman.

My grandfather was killed by the Sioux. That story about this woman (*Sakakawea* being a Shoshoni) is wrong. We all know about it, what Captain Clark said. She was Gros Ventre and many people are still alive who knew her. I saw her right along when I was young. She was over eighty years old when she died. My mother knew her well and knew her father and mother too. They were all Gros Ventre. I am an interpreter and have gone to Washington several times in that capacity. I know all the stories of my people.

I know that interpreters get very tired and take short cuts in their talks. The man who told Lewis and Clark about her being a Shoshoni was tired, I think. He took a short cut to make easy talk for himself.

Since then, the story has been wrong. She was killed at last up in Montana some place by a war party. Bulls Eye is right. He is alive now. He is the grandson of *Sakakawea*.

## The Bulls Eye Story

*Henry Bad Gun, grandson of the 1830s' Mandan chief Four Bears (Mato Topa). (l-r) Sitting Crow, Spotted Horn, Henry Bad Gun, and Sam Jones, 1910. Henry Bad Gun was present when Bulls Eye told his story to Major Welch.*
— Fred Olson Collection, State Historical Society of North Dakota

The reason why she knew that country they went over and met people she knew, was because she had been there the year before that with her husband, Charbonneau. **They had seen the country and had made many friends with the Shoshoni.**

Name of *Sakakawea* —

At the special council at Shell Village, where the Gros Ventre gave me [A.B. Welch] the story of *Sakakawea*, they told me that the real meaning of the word was Eagle Woman. They pronounce it as though spelled with a T, *Tsakakaweaish*, with the ish at the end.

Corroboration of Chiefs —

Both **Chiefs Drags Wolf** and **Bears Arm** claimed that they knew exactly where *Sakakawea* was buried, that she was killed by enemies in Montana, that it was close to a trader's place on a creek in Montana and that the name of the trader was Culbertson.

## Our Story of Eagle Woman, Sacagawea

Grave of *Sakakawea* —

I [A.B. Welch] learned today from a Gros Ventre Indian, that the mother of Stanley Deane, who has often been my interpreter, but died in March 1928, knows where the grave of *Sakakawea* is located. She is very old and a Gros Ventre.

She says it is close to Culbertson, Montana. However distances do not mean much to the old Indians, and my idea is that she means out in that direction someplace.

### Major Welch stated:

The old woman of Stower [one who wrote about *Sacagawea*]; the wife of Charbonneau of Luttig [Ft. Manuel story], who died of a fever; the *Sacajawea* of Dr. Hebard [Wyoming story] — these stories may not be corroborated. But this story of Bulls Eye, the son of Otter Woman, who was the first daughter of Charbonneau and *Sakakawea*, the Bird Woman, can be for the old people of the Gros Ventre, the Minnitaree of Lewis and Clark, all know it and many of them were present when it was told to the writer, and will retell it to any white man they have confidence in.

*Sakakawea* was born in 1787; she was seventeen years of age when employed by Lewis and Clark in 1804; Bulls Eye, her grandson was four years old when she met her death in the fight upon the wagon train.

Bulls Eye was born in 1865, for his age is now fifty nine; consequently, *Sakakawea*, the Bird Woman, was killed when she was eighty two years of age, in 1869.

### Other Hidatsa tribal members told stories that helped corroborate the Bulls Eye story.

### *Sacagawea* Story told by tribal member Helen Wolf Wilkinson

for Aletha Jackson, direct descendant of *Sacagawea*
Maeshuwea [Eagle Woman—*Sacagawea*] and quite a few were gathering to go to the Crow Country; Bulls Eye was her grandson.

*Helen Wolf Wilkinson on horseback, 1935*
— Leo D. Harris/State Historical Society of North Dakota

He is the one, and then my mother's grandmother, Extra Corn Growth Woman. About that time Extra Corn Growth Woman's husband beat her up, so she ran away from her husband. So then she joined this group and traveled with them to the Crow Country. And right about the place they call Dancing Bear Creek, a place where the white people chopped wood and made log houses and stayed with them there. And their leader or spokesperson was a Sioux lady, and as they were getting close, the Chippewa surprised them and killed quite a few.

And then, Extra Corn Growth woman went and hid near the deep ravines, where the trees used to be. And as she was hid, she heard a lot of noise, and after it grew quiet she went to that house where the Sioux woman took her in and fed her.

The Sioux woman told her, "Those are Chippewas, they always come home here and they don't travel far." Saying that, she opened up a cellar and had her go down into that cellar. And while in the cellar, she had a really hard time keeping the [her] child quiet; she breast-fed him, did everything possible to keep him quiet.

Meanwhile, the Chippewa came back and were really noisy, eating and talking loud. After a long while, they must have left because it grew quiet.

## Our Story of Eagle Woman, Sacagawea

At which time, the Sioux woman opened the cellar and let her out. So that Sioux woman was also a helper of the white people. She said, "If they should come back, I will put you back into the cellar. They always hang around here, eat and go all the time."

And then she took her to where *Maeshuwea* was buried and showed her. As she was preparing to head to the Crow Country. **And over beyond where there was a grove of buckbrush, there were two graves, one a small one and one quite a bit larger. And third grave was *Maeshuweash*, and that was Bulls Eye's grandmother.**

And now days, the last born call her Bird Woman, so that name stuck. But her real name is Eagle Woman. *Maeshuwea*, her character, her demeanor, as a teenager was known to be tall, heavy-set and liked to fight. She was known to get involved when two women were fighting, she would help and she would take their blanket and walk away. It was known that her medicine was snake, and it was known that Cherry Necklace [*Sacagawea's* brother] would pick up a stick that was lying there and it would turn into a bullsnake, twisting and turning. And for that reason, they called them Shoshone. For these people were called the Snake people. So when she was a young girl, Lewis and Clark came to their village. And it was known that these people, it was known that it was their medicine. They were known to turn things around.

At which time Lewis and Clark said we wish to go towards the big water. She said I always go over there to the big water and I will take you there, and they were very happy so they took her along. She married a young man named Charbonneau. So she took them along the big water, which was their destination.

So on the way back, she said stop here, that's where my men folk are and I want to give them some stuff. So then they stopped near Crow Agency, a lot of Crow men came on horseback. So she seen one of her brothers, Cherry Necklace and another.

Her brother came to the edge of the village which was located by the river, and at this time she gave them alot of meat, salt pork and bacon that her husband Charbonneau had got for them.

*The Bulls Eye Story*

So then her brother said I would like to give something also; he took his saddle off of his horse. He took his horse onto the raft and put the reins into Charbonneau's hands, saying you can take it with you; it was a white horse. As they watched from the river bank, they saw the boat drift out of sight, and the only thing they saw in the distance was that white horse.

And so it has come to pass that there are many stories that are told; her name isn't Bird Woman, it is Eagle Woman. It was told that she was taken prisoner, but that's not true. That's the way it was when she was a teenager. That's all I know.

**Dancing Bear Creek was close to or at the place where Like-A-Fishhook Village was built, not near where it is believed that *Sacagawea* was killed and died. Perhaps Helen Wilkinson was referring to "Bear Sits," the location near where *Sacagawea* was killed and died as noted by Bulls Eye. Helen's story supports Bulls Eye's story that *Sacagawea* went with Lewis and Clark and that Cherry Necklace was her brother.**

**Bulls Eye Story, as told by Tribal Member Jim Driver on tape**
Translated by Carol Ann Fredericks Newman and Indrek Park

*The narrator, Jim Driver, briefly explains how he first heard part of the story as told by Bulls Eye, who was relaying his personal experience of the events that had occurred many years before.*

*The narrator then assumes Bulls Eye's perspective and proceeds to retell the story using Bulls Eye's own words.*

Long time ago, this Bulls Eye, he told a story when I was small. I only heard part of the story when he was almost finished with it. This is how he told it. At the time when Bulls Eye was five winters old, those were his relatives, [including] that Bird Woman. Her [grand] children were Bull-Facing-The-Wind, Bulls Eye, [and others]. According to his story, it happened somewhere towards the west.

[Bulls Eye said,] When I was small, when I was five years old. And then, there my grandmother said that the enemy were coming to confront us. "The enemy will meet us." And when I was five years old, she took me by my arm, at night in the moonlight. In the moonlight she took me to where there was a fire pit buried deep. And there, she said, "Sit here, my precious grandchild, sit here, don't come out, just sit like that. I'll come to get you in a little while." When she said that she sat down there.

I sat down and looked up at the stars and everything else there. I was looking at the stars. I just kept watching, and then the morning came. In the morning, when it was daylight, my grandmother arrived. My grandmother arrived and [said], "My precious grandchild, here you must have got no sleep." When she said that to me, I responded by saying, "Yes."

When she said, "Come this way! That's enough. Stand up!" I stood up. She grabbed me by my arm and she got me. She got me and she took me back to our wagon. When she got me and took me back [to the wagon], around it here were **white people who were all dressed in fringed buckskin and they were all lying there killed. I saw them.**

Then my grandmother took me and went on to the round front wheels of the wagon; that's where my mother was [sitting against the wagon]. She [my grandma] sat down and peeled it off [the scarf/blanket] from her [my mother's] face. "Oh, my daughter! I brought your son back."

"Where is he? Come here!" she said and so I went to her. My mother put her arms around my neck. She kissed me and she leaned her cheek against me. "My precious child, you are a man, you're a man. Our village, try to make it back there, you are a man," she told me. So I said "Alright." "As for me, that's the end of me," she said. But the tips of her hair, on these tips of her hair her blood was dripping. I saw my mother as her blood was spilling.

Then when my grandmother said, "Are you ready? You've seen your son, are you ready?" She responded, "Yes. It is good.

# The Bulls Eye Story

"I've seen my son now, so take your precious grandchild with you and try to make it back to our village," she said.

After I had seen her, my grandmother again covered her face. When my mother's face was covered with a blanket like that we stayed there, and after a while, when my grandmother [again] peeled the blanket off my mother's face, she was sitting there dead. She had died. Then my grandmother called, "Hey, my precious grandchild! Your mother has died." She covered her daughter's face. After she had covered her face, she said, "That's it, grandson. Let's go."

Here everybody had been massacred, all of them. They had been killed, and we had been left in utter despair/ruin.

When I saw my grandmother, she was all weak. She must have been wounded. Her face was bloody. Her eyelids around here were covered with blood. When I saw my grandmother she was all weak.

"Hey, my grandson! We will return home to our village. We will try to make it back home," she said. "Alright," I said.

Then they wrapped my mother up and after we left her that way and came back homewards, along the riverbank we were coming.

We slept, and the next morning when we were coming we got to a house; it was a white man's log house where we arrived. Then we stayed there, my grandmother died there. When she died, **the white men wrapped her up in canvas and they put her in a wagon and they took her to the back country,** that's what the white people did.

They signed to me [in the sign language] like that and had me sit down, and when they left, I stood up and looked through the window, and I saw them taking my grandmother away. My grandmother had died.

When we had been there at the creek, my grandmother had said that she was dying and [she had told me,] "My dearest grandson, I'm not going to live. Follow this river to the east. Keep going, sleep, and where the water beats on the bank you get back on the flats, you follow the flat ground. When there is a wooded area, keep going along the river bank, you get back on the flat, at night lie down further up."

"When you get up and keep going like that you will get back to our village. No matter what, you will get back to our village. You're a man, my dearest grandchild, try to get back to our village," she said.

So I said, "Yes." I was just five years old.

I was there for a while, for my meal box, since those white people had a lot of bread, they had quite a bit of bread, so I put a lot of bread in a paper bag. "Hey, I think I'll be on my way," I thought. "I wonder if the white people are at work in the morning," because there was no-one around, I prepared my meal.

I went to the river and I went along the river to the east from there. Because it was far, I just kept going and going and going. When the sun went down, I lay down for sleep. Whenever I got hungry, I ate my food and kept going, until there was a road along the river. I was going along and noticed some footprints, "There must be people here," I thought.

From there I followed the path upwards on the terrain and kept going. A little further from there was a log house. The dogs there barked at me, two huge dogs. As they were barking at me while I was standing there, a white man appeared.

He appeared and when he got after his dogs, the dogs turned around and went back. When he motioned with his hand to me, I went and this white man came. The white man looked at me and said, [in English] "Hi, hi, hi." He grabbed me by my arm and he just took me with him. As we went along, he took me right into his house. He let me in and then he fed me, so I ate.

I ate and filled myself up. I went around the house looking around for several nights.

Then [native] people came and camped at that house, camped beside the house. After they had set up a camp, the people came and saw me. They looked at me and took me to their camp.

They took me with them and called his name and it was that person. I think this was the person. Then like this they came and saw me and remembered me. They remembered me and a man whose name was Doesn't Run Away.

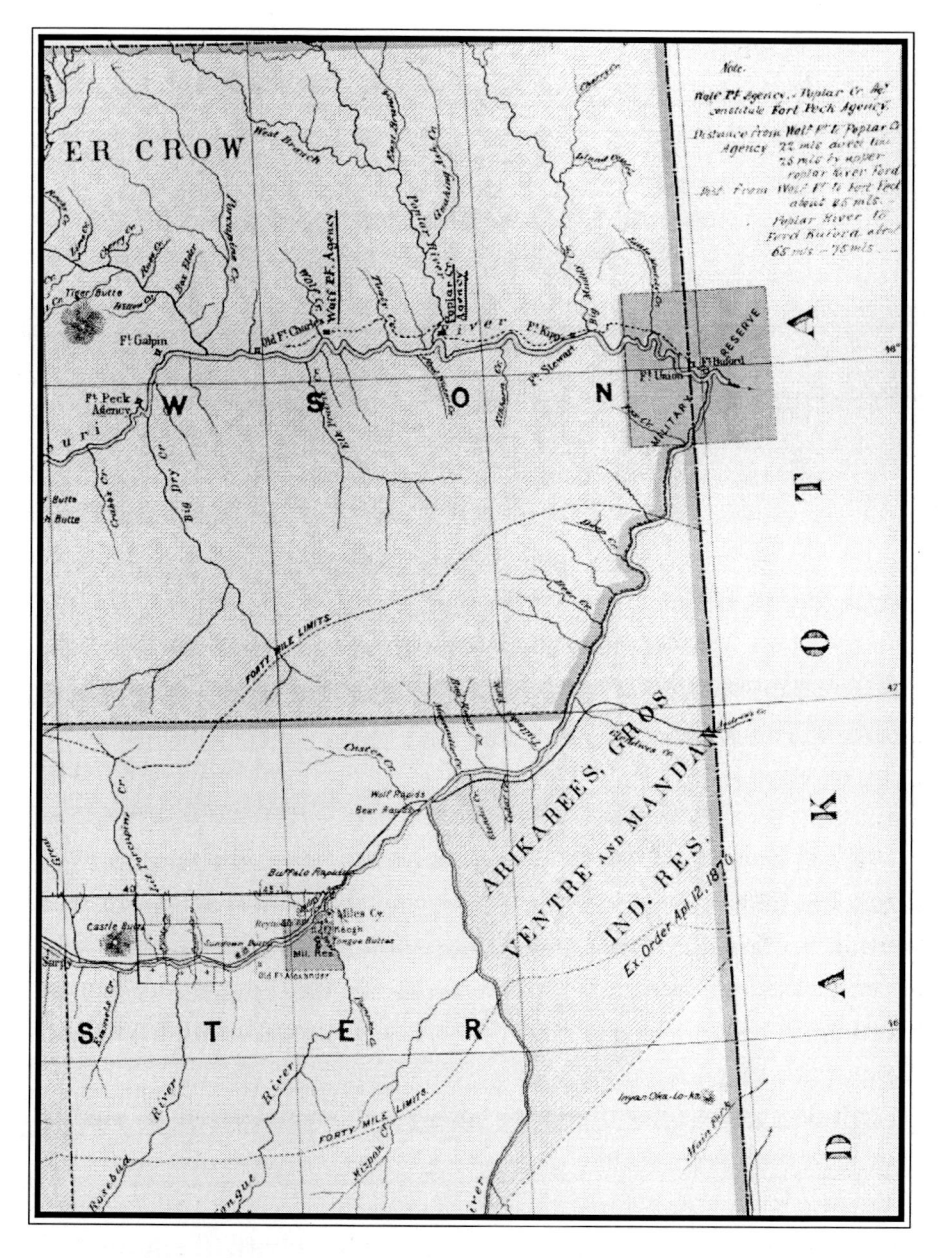

*Montana Territory, 1879. The Sand Creek area was around and south of the river from Wolf Point Agency. The group may have camped on the north side of the Missouri by Wolf Point. Note the locations of Sand Creek and Fort Buford. Sacagawea was buried in the Ft. Buford area. Ft. Buford, the military fort, was close to Ft. Union, the trading fort closed in 1867.*

*— State Historical Society of North Dakota/Library of Congress*

*Fort Buford, 1871* — State Historical Society of North Dakota

The one whose name was Doesn't Run Away took me. He took me and when he went with me back to their camp he asked me, "Why is it that you have come here and stay here?" So I told him. The grandmother was killed. "The enemy also killed my mother," I said and told them everything.

Then the people there got scared of me. They got afraid of me that I might infect you with my sore heart [smallpox? There was another outbreak in 1866]. And some of them wanted to leave. Here my elder Doesn't Run Away got angry. He got angry and got back on his horse, he took his gun and this one was afraid of that one and they found it again.

"It was sores, that's what y'all say. Are you afraid to die? If you dare to run away I'm going to shoot some of you. That's it, now get going, run away," he said. They didn't run away. So they didn't move, they just stayed. Then I stayed with them and so there they did take me. They took me and we moved camp and came back over here.

Like this then there my mother died. And when my grandmother also died, they are [buried] in the backcountry, I didn't see their burial. That's the way it was there.

## The Bulls Eye Story

That's all I heard that this Bulls Eye said [about] Bird Woman's story. And Bird Woman, she had a lot of siblings. suppose she had something like three siblings. She also must have had several elders. And so it goes/was.

Bulls Eye was Bird Woman's child [Bulls Eye was Bird Woman's grandchild.] Some of his children are Stands Up's wife. And White Raven [George Parshall] is one of his children. And those are his children. Otter shows her grandchildren, they are here now. They are still here. They are Bird Woman's descendants.

So this Bird Woman is from the Three Tribes here. But in the beginning when they talked, when the white people asked a question, their interpreter made a mistake and was saying that she was of the Snake People. He didn't know and was saying that she was an Arapaho woman. So he didn't know and kept saying that she was a Shoshone woman. But there is no truth to the Shoshone version. Here this Bird Woman is of the Hidatsa people. That's the way it is because what the elders told is all true.

### A Letter to Ken Burns, Film Maker

In January of 1997, Mike Cowdrey, an independent scholar/historian who has written several books on American Indians, wrote to Ken Burns, renowned documentary film maker, regarding Burns' plan to make a documentary on Lewis and Clark. Other documentaries/films claiming that *Sacagawea* was Shoshone and was buried in Wyoming, or at Ft. Manuel in North Dakota, had been produced, and Cowdrey wanted to make sure that Burns would tell the correct story — the Bulls Eye story.

Dear Mr. Burns:

I saw your address broadcast on C-SPAN, as well as that network's interview with you this morning. In the course of that discussion you mentioned that your current project is a documentary account of the Lewis and Clark expedition.

## Our Story of Eagle Woman, Sacagawea

While I regret that the enclosed material on *Sacajawea* may be reaching you at the eleventh hour (possibly 11:45), perhaps it can nonetheless save you from repeating to a new generation—or at least give you reason to annotate— some of the standardized myths of the past.

I refer to the interpretations some historians have given to John Luttig's journal (the assumption that the "wife of Charbonneau" who died at Ft. Manuel was *Sacajawea*), and the political campaign invented by Dr. Grace Hebard early in this century, to canonize a deceased (and unwitting!) Shoshone woman as the guide of Lewis and Clark, then to use her elaborated monument as a focus for growing the Women's Rights movement.

In May of 1923, a civic leader named Welch was invited by leaders of the Fort Berthold Indian Reservation to make a series of Memorial Day addresses at several communities on the reservation.

I do not recall Mr. Welch's full name, but he was an amateur historian, and may have been a clergyman as well. I do remember seeing several articles which he contributed to the State Historical Society of North Dakota *Collections*.

If you choose to pursue this story, you should be able to easily verify both his identity, and the existence of this statement, through the Historical Society at Bismarck. His report appears to have been prepared for the Historical Society, and is on file in their Paul Ewald Papers #10148.

Briefly, Mr. Welch was approached by a delegation of Hidatsas, who wanted his help in correcting what they considered a perversion of the historical record. They had been made aware that the published journals of Lewis and Clark identify *Sacajawea* as a "Shoshone captive."

The purpose of the Hidatsas was somehow to reach out to White historians — a very difficult task, from the wilds of North Dakota in 1923 — and convey the information that many Hidatsas *then living* had known *Sacajawea*, had known her parents, as well as her husband and children. They wanted Welch to understand that she was an *Hidatsa* woman, born of Hidatsa parents, whom they named.

Among the speakers who presented this evidence was one Bulls Eye, the grandson of *Sacajawea*, then 58 years old. As a four-year-old boy in 1869, he had been shielded by Bird Woman during the night attack of an enemy war party. His grandmother, courageous to the last, had been wounded in that effort, and died seven days later.

Later, Welch was able to confirm the details of this story with Joseph Packineau (or Packinaud), the government interpreter at Elbowoods, North Dakota (then the Agency), and himself half-Hidatsa.

Packineau told him:
That story about this woman (*Sakakawea* being a Shoshoni) is all wrong. We all know about it, what Captain Clark said. She was Gros Ventre (Hidatsa), and many people are still alive who knew her. I saw her right along when I was young. She was over eighty years old when she died. My mother knew her well, and knew her mother and father too. They were all Gros Ventre...

For your information, and to confirm that Joseph Packineau was a real person, I enclose a 1902 portrait of him and his family, made by the noted frontier photographer L.A. Huffman, from the Montana Historical Society collection (Neg. #Huffman 981-218). His father was one of the storied employees of the American Fur Company during the mid-19th century, who is mentioned often in the *Journal of Rudolph Friederich Kurz* (Bureau of American Ethnology, Bulletin 115), in the memoirs of Henry Boller *(Among the Indians)*, and of Gen. Philippe Regis de Trobriand *(Military Life in Dakota)*. The State Historical Society of North Dakota has much on both father and son.

*Our Story of Eagle Woman, Sacagawea*

I trust you have long since discovered that *"Sacajawea"* is a corruption of the Hidatsa name *Sakaka* (small bird) *Winyan* or *Wea* (woman). In pursuing the question of her nationality, another useful line of evidence is the indirect testimony of her son Jean Baptiste—the much-beloved little Pomp of Capt. Clark.

Enclosed for your information is an extract from Leroy R. Hafen, *The Mountain Men and the Fur Trade of the Far West*, which—as I expect you already know—performs the signal service of tracking Baptiste's movements after he led the Mormon Battalion to California in 1847.

Hafen gives the 1866 obituary of "J.B. Charbonneau," who had died of fever near the Owyhee River (present Jordan Valley, Oregon), while traveling to Montana. Although the writer of the obituary is unnamed (he was almost certainly the editor of the Auburn, California, Placer Herald), it is clear from the text that he had personally known Charbonneau for 14 years, and the details of his history were obtained from the man himself.

*Joseph Packineau and Family, 1902.* — L.A. Huffman, at Elbowoods, North Dakota

## The Bulls Eye Story

We learn thereby that Jean Baptiste Charbonneau did not consider himself to be a Shoshone, for he had told his friends that he was born in the country of the Crow Indians—his father being a Canadian Frenchman and his mother a half-breed of the Crow tribe.

At first glance this reference to the Crows might seem an anomaly, until one understands that the Crows and Hidatsa consider themselves to be the same people—the present-day Crows having separated from their Hidatsa brethren sometime in the late-17th century. For Jean Baptiste to say that his mother was "Crow," is merely to agree with the group interviewed by Mr. Welch, who insisted that she was Hidatsa.

In this light, the statement of Bulls Eye—who claimed to be the grandson of *Sakakawea*—becomes even more significant. Bulls Eye said that on the return journey of the Lewis and Clark expedition. "They passed through the country of our relatives, the Crows," where *Sakakawea* met with her brother Cherry Necklace, whose mother was a Crow...

I think there can be no question of any possible collusion between the editor of an 1866 California newspaper, and the Hidatsas who spoke to Mr. Welch in 1923; yet they separately agreed that two members of *Sakakawea's* own family—each unknown to the other—testified that she was an Hidatsa-Crow.

Although part of this evidence is indirect, I find it far stronger than anything compounded of Luttig's single sentence, or Dr. Hebard's romantic illusions. This is one hell of an important American story. I hope it finds you in time to contribute to your chronicle of the Lewis and Clark expedition.

*Our Story of Eagle Woman, Sacagawea*

In regard to Cowdrey's reporting the relationship between *Sacagawea* and Cherry Necklace, an individual history card from Ft. Berthold Agency documents Cherry Necklace's father as being Bad Lodge, Smoked Lodge, or Black Lodge (Hidatsa) and *Sacagawea*, Eagle Woman, as being Cherry Necklace's sister. Bulls Eye's account tells that Smoked Lodge was also *Sacagawea's* father. The mothers of *Sacagawea* and Cherry Necklace were Crow sisters.

Cowdrey also refers to the other stories of *Sacagawea*, the Wyoming story and the Ft. Manuel story. He strongly discounts them and supports the Bulls Eye story.

The Bulls Eye story explains how *Sacagawea* was Hidatsa, how misinterpretation or a lie made her out to be Shoshone, how she would have known the route to the West because she had been there before, and why she called the Shoshone chief "brother" because her father had adopted him as a brother (in a tribal way). These things defy the popular versions of the *Sacagawea* story. The fact that Jean Baptiste's obituary states that his mother, *Sacagawea*, was half Crow is highly significant. Statements about her by others, over the years, are included in the next chapters, "Our Voices."

**Sources Authored or Provided by MHA Tribal Members:**

Driver, Jim. Bulls Eye Story. Translated by Carol Fredericks Newman and Indrek Park.

Baker, Gerard. "The Corps of Discovery... One of Many" in *Lewis and Clark through Indian Eyes,* edited by Alvin Josephy Jr. New York: Alfred A. Knopf., 2006.

Wilkinson, Helen. Story of the attack on the group including *Sacagawea*, told for Aletha Jackson.

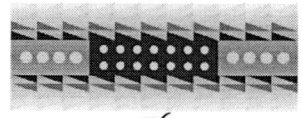

## The Bulls Eye Story

*Hidatsa Medicine Lodge at Like-A-Fishhook Village, D.T. 1872.*
*Sacagawea was living at Like-A-Fishhook Village when she traveled to Sand Creek.*
— Stanley J. Morrow

*Fort Berthold, D.T. This view, made from the blockhouse on the opposite corner of the fort, shows four traders and two dogs standing in the interior courtyard. The view is across the Missouri River; Fishhook Village was directly behind the photographer, 1872.*
— Stanley J. Morrow

## COLOR SECTION

In the section of color illustrations which follow, all but two of the 1832 paintings by George Catlin are in the collections of the Smithsonian American Art Museum, Washington, D.C. Catlin's portrait of The Man Who Leaps Ahead of All is at Virginia Museum of Fine Arts, Richmond. The Catlin painting of River Crow warriors bathing in the Yellowstone is at American Museum of Natural History, NYC. The 1833-34 paintings by Karl Bodmer are in the Joslyn Museum Collections, Omaha, Nebraska. Bodmer's lithographs are from Prince Maximilian of Wied, *Travels in the Interior of North America, 1832-1834.* Vol. 3, Bildatlas. London, 1843.

*Sacagawea with infant son Jean Baptiste by Dennis Fox, Jr., 2020.*

*Our Story of Eagle Woman, Sacagawea*

Big Hidatsa Village on Knife River by George Catlin, 1832. The artist showed himself and party being ferried across the river in a bullboat by a helpful Hidatsa woman.

Color Section

*Winter Village of the Hidatsas by Karl Bodmer, 1834.*

*Our Story of Eagle Woman, Sacagawea*

*Earthlodge Interior view (Mandan) by Karl Bodmer, 1834.*

## Color Section

*Toussaint Charbonneau, husband of Sacagawea, introducing the German Prince Maximilian of Wied to Hidatsa chiefs at Fort Clark in 1833. The artist Karl Bodmer, who accompanied the prince, is shown in a self-portrait at right.*

*Our Story of Eagle Woman, Sacagawea*

*Pehriska-Ruhpa (Two Ravens), Hidatsa chief, by Karl Bodmer, 1833.*

Color Section

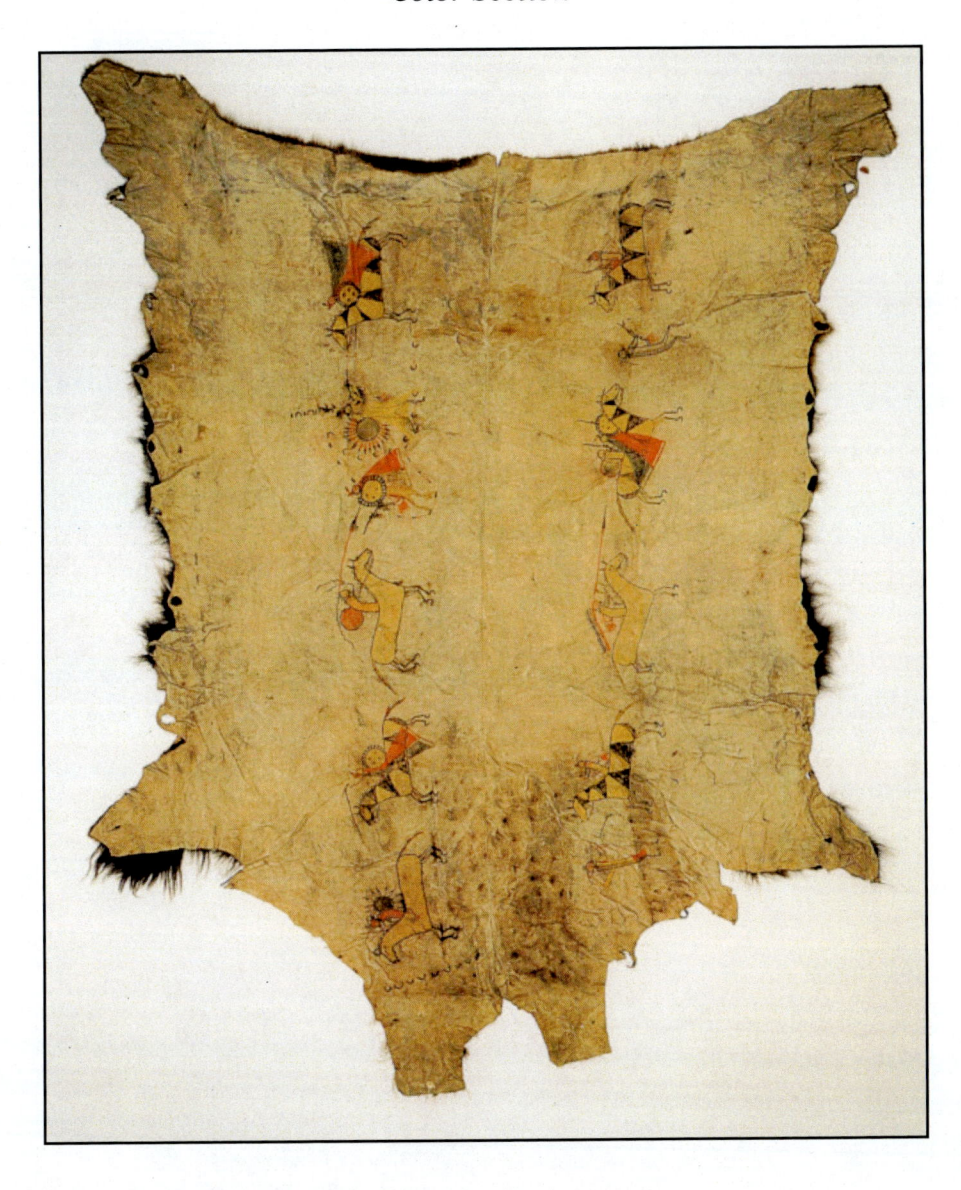

*Hidatsa buffalo robe painted by Two Ravens, showing some of his war exploits, collected by Prince Maximilian in 1833-34.*
*— Ethnology State Museum, Berlin, Germany.*

*Our Story of Eagle Woman, Sacagawea*

*Two Ravens, Hidatsa, dressed for the Dog Dance by Karl Bodmer, 1833.*

## Color Section

*E'e-a-chin-che-a (Red Thunder), son of Black Moccasin and a Chief at Big Hidatsa Village, by George Catlin, 1832.*

*Our Story of Eagle Woman, Sacagawea*

*River Crow Chiefs visiting at Knife River by Karl Bodmer, 1833.*

## Color Section

*Pa-ris-ka-roo-pa (Two Crows) [or Ravens], Hidatsa Chief, by George Catlin, 1832.*

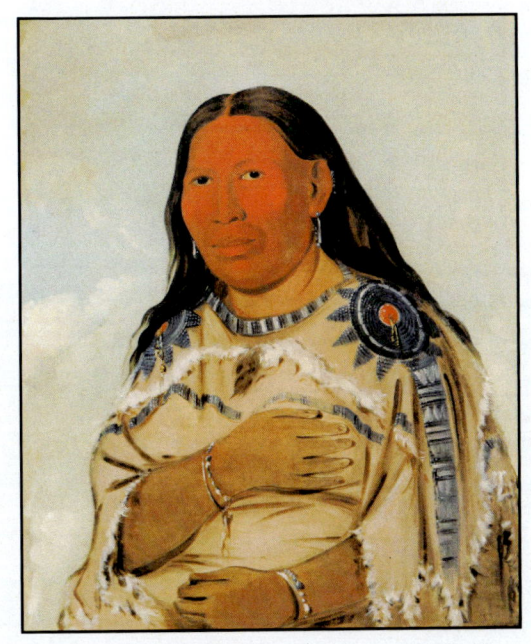

*Wife of Two Crows [or Ravens] by George Catlin, 1832.*

## Our Story of Eagle Woman, Sacagawea

*Four Wolves, River Crow Chief painted at Fort Union by George Catlin, 1832.*

*Woman Who Lives in a Bear Den, River Crow with hair cut short in mourning, by George Catlin, 1832.*

Color Section

*Seet-se-be-a (The Midday Sun), a Pretty Young Girl, Hidatsa,
by George Catlin, 1832.*

*Our Story of Eagle Woman, Sacagawea*

*Addih-Hiddisch (He Makes the Road to War), Hidatsa War Chief and uncle of Poor Wolf, by Karl Bodmer, 1833.*

Color Section

*Ba-da-ah-chon-du (The Man Who Jumps Ahead of All), River Crow Chief painted on a visit to Knife River by George Catlin, 1832. Many Hidatsa men, and their horses, would have been dressed in similar fashion.*

*Our Story of Eagle Woman, Sacagawea*

*Birohka (Beautifully-Furred Robe), Hidatsa Chief by Karl Bodmer, 1833.*

Color Section

*War Party of River Crows swimming in the Yellowstone by George Catlin, 1832.*

*Our Story of Eagle Woman, Sacagawea*

*Ahschupsa Masihichsi (Chief of the Pointed Horn), Hidatsa painted by Karl Bodmer at Fort Clark, 1833.*

*Hidatsa Scalp Dance by Karl Bodmer, 1833.*

*Our Story of Eagle Woman, Sacagawea*

*Buffalo Chase, a Surround by the Hidatsa in the hills south of Knife River, by George Catlin, 1832.*

## Color Section

*Teenage Hidatsa boys recovering drowned buffalo from the ice-choked Missouri River at Like-A-Fishhook Village, from the Lion Boy Ledger, ca. 1870. — Private Collection. Every spring, hundreds of frozen carcasses of animals that had fallen through the ice upriver on the Yellowstone and Missouri during the previous winter would float past Fishhook Village. It provided an opportunity for brave young men to help in feeding their families.*

*Indians Killing Buffalo in the Missouri River, engraving from Harper's Weekly by William de la Montagne Cary, 1874. These were certainly Hidatsa, Mandan and Arikara men near Like-A-Fishhook Village. Colorized for this edition.*

*Our Story of Eagle Woman, Sacagawea*

*Fort Berthold and Like-A-Fishhook Village by Count Philippe Regis de Trobriand, ca. 1870.* — State Historical Society of North Dakota

Color Section

*Hidatsa Burials in Cottonwood Trees near Fort Berthold* by Dr. Washington Mathews, ca. 1870. More than a century of such family graves were inundated by the creation of Lake Sakakawea, including most of the homes of their descendants.
— U.S. National Museum of Natural History

## Our Story of Eagle Woman, Sacagawea

The newly-rising Lake Sakakawea in 1954, as the waters began to drown all the forests and rich bottom lands of the Hidatsa, Mandan and Arikara People. The sites of Fort Berthold and Like-A-Fishhook Village are seen at middle right, only hours before they were forever destroyed.
— State Historical Society of North Dakota; *specially colorized for this edition.*

*Lake Sakakawea from Crow Flies High Butte west of New Town, ND, headquarters of the Fort Berthold Reservation.* — Trina Locke

# Chapter 4
## *OUR VOICES*
*Recent and Back to the 1940s*

**B**its and pieces of a story telling that Sacagawea was Hidatsa were and are included in conversations among the people of the MHA Nation: She was Hidatsa... Her name was changed from *Maeshuweash*, Eagle Woman, to *Sacagawea*, Bird Woman, because *Maeshuweash* was too hard for the white men to say, some say for Charbonneau to say... She liked the smell of coffee and would put it in her hair... Cherry Necklace gave Charbonneau a white horse when the party passed through Montana... She and her brother, Cherry Necklace, had snake medicine; the whites thought it meant that she was a Snake (Shoshone) Indian... The white men got it wrong...

Some tribal members gave statements and interviews especially around the time of the Lewis and Clark bicentennial which sparked a renewed interest in the story.

*Our Story of Eagle Woman, Sacagawea*

# From "Searching for *Sakakawea*," *Dickinson Press*, December 5, 1999

"Some descendants of *Sakakawea* on the Fort Berthold Reservation say that misunderstanding and misinterpretation of their language years ago resulted in historians and others saying *Sakakawea* was a Shoshone Indian and not Hidatsa, as many descendants say she truly is. They want to set the record straight."

**Delores Parshall Sand**

My father always referred to *Sakakawea* as Gramma. In here, (as she pointed to her heart) I know she was my Gramma. I don't care what the rest of the world says. We know she is ours...Sand's assertion...would mean that she is *Sakakawea*'s closest living relative on the Fort Berthold Indian Reservation. The uncle of Sand's father [George Parshall], Hidatsa chief Bulls Eye, claimed *Sakakawea* was his grandmother. Stories of the relationship have mostly been preserved through oral tradition.

**Calvin Grinnell** is a tribal member and historian for New Town's Three Tribes Museum, which represents the Mandan, Hidatsa and Arikara tribes. Based on his research, Calvin has written articles and created a presentation that promotes the Bulls Eye story and includes evidence that *Sacagawea*'s father, Smoked Lodge or Black Lodge, was in fact a signer of the 1825 Atkinson-O' Fallon Treaty, as Bulls Eye claimed.

"Charbonneau's statement that *Sakakawea* was a Snake (Shoshone) Indian could be a lie. Historians have determined that Charbonneau was a coward, a bungler and a wife beater. Meriwether Lewis called him 'a man of no particular merit.' Since Charbonneau wanted a job, he may have stretched the truth to improve his chances of being hired," said Grinnell.

**Marilyn Hudson,** tribal member and administrator of the Three Tribes Museum, said, "I don't think anyone has thoroughly researched the claim [that *Sacagawea* was Hidatsa]. During the past 200 years, [Three Affiliated] tribal members have been focusing on survival. We're at the point now where I think we will be able to do the research."

## Esley Fox Thorton from "Heritage in question," *Minot Daily News*, August 9, 2001

[Thorton said] that Charbonneau, *Sakakawea*'s husband who was a Frenchman, could not speak the Hidatsa language well or the English language, and Charbonneau told that *Sakakawea* was Snake Indian or Shoshone...

"But his story is how they tell it was," Thorton said, "That's law to them, because it was the first time they heard it. But Berry Necklace [Cherry Necklace, *Sacagawea*'s brother] and his brothers' and sisters' medicine was snake, and that's what he was trying to translate..."

Thorton said he obtained his information about *Sakakawea* from visits years ago when he lived with his grandparents, George and Ruby Parshall, of Shell Village, south of present-day Van Hook. He said his grandmother told him that there were eight children in *Sakakawea*'s family - Cherry Necklace was *Sakakawea*'s oldest sibling and her full brother. He said his grandmother described *Sakakawea* as being 'kind of hefty' who would get in fights to help the weak ones.

## Irene Fredericks in "Letter to the Editor," *MHA Times*, May 3, 2002

In the past two years I've listened and recorded the oral histories and stories of of our people as told by our elders. I've sat with elders who for the first time talked publicly about their own family's history. Our elders say they never spoke before, because of the misinterpretations...

They tell me the story of *Sakakawea* has never been right. Many of these individuals stated to me they never felt it was important to talk publicly about their relatives before, but they now believe it is time to set the record straight. These elders believe now, that our history needs to be respected and recognized for our youth and future generations, so that our people can once again take pride in our heritage... Throughout time, the history of our people has been written by those who never spoke our language nor understood us. Today, we write and speak the same language as mainstream society, yet our stories are still misconstrued and misinterpreted. *Sakakawea* is Hidatsa. That's what my elders tell me, that's what I believe, and that is what I will tell the world. Signed, *Kobodie Shibisha*, Black Medicine/Irene Fredericks.

## Wanda Fox Sheppard in "Correcting the story of *Sacagawea*," *Missoulian*, Sept. 3, 2006 by Jodi Rave.

Sheppard counts herself among the hundreds of *Sacagawea* descendants on the Fort Berthold Reservation, homeland of the Mandan, Hidatsa and Arikara Nation. *Sacagawea*'s Hidatsa descendants' voices, however, have mostly been unheard, unpublished. Her relatives have never been vocal, boastful, or pushy about their relationship because she was simply another relative.

Thousands of Natives and non-Natives heard the Hidatsa stories of *Sacagawea* during the Lewis and Clark bicentennial signature event, "Reunion at the Home of *Sakakawea*," in August on Fort Berthold. Several tribal citizens of Fort Berthold recounted stories about *Sacagawea*'s life among the Hidatsa and Mandan. The one many are becoming familiar with is told by Bulls Eye, which was published in the Van Hook Reporter in April, 1925.

The Hidatsa who claim *Sacagawea* as a relative say she had four children - [Jean] Baptiste, Otter Woman, Cedar Woman, and Different Breast. Bulls Eye was the son of Otter Woman. Cedar Woman had a daughter named Medicine Arm who married a white man named William Parshall.

The couple had three children, including George Parshall, a great-grandson of *Sacagawea* and Sheppard's grandfather. Sheppard knows all her relatives going back at least eight generations. *Sacagawea*'s real name was Eagle Woman, or *Maeshuwea*. But interpreters started calling her Bird Woman, or *Sacagawea*, and that has been wrong all these years, too.

Her [Sheppard's] grandmother Ruby White Bear Parshall and her aunt Pansy Parshall used to talk about how *Sacagawea* and her daughter Otter Woman were killed while traveling to Ft. Buford with five-year old Bulls Eye. "She [Ruby] kept telling me she [*Sacagawea*] was buried at Fort Buford," said Sheppard. Ruby and her husband George Parshall used to travel to Poplar, Montana, frequently. Ruby told Sheppard, "Your grandpa stopped at her gravesite, prayed, and made offerings to her and then we would go on." She [Sheppard] drove Ruby **to Fort Buford. "When we got to this place where she [Ruby] said she was buried; there were no fences.** But you could tell where the buildings were a long time ago. And there were burial mounds," said Sheppard.

**Pat Fredericks,** MHA tribal elder**,** from an interview by Calvin Grinnell, Tribal Historian:

My grandpa, Philip Snow, told me about *Sakakawea*, that Lewis and Clark, when they came up the Missouri River [on their return trip]. The Yellowstone and the Missouri were up here by the Montana line. That's where there was a village. When *Sakakawea* told that she knew the people there, [she] told them, 'Go call my brother, I got something for him.' So they went and called her brother, Berry Necklace (*Madzu-Awbaesh*), that was his name. And he came on a horse, a white horse with a "medicine hat," or red ears. Years ago they used them for buffalo; that's what he rode down and gave to his sister. So his sister in turn gave whatever she had, she had some stuff for him.

Grandpa told me and said that they were brother and sister. And the person that told this, I don't know where he got the Snake Indian that she was supposed to be, but what I know, Berry Necklace, her brother, was a medicine man. He fasted many days in a snake den.

And he could perform...he pulled one of his braids and one would be a rattlesnake and the other side would be a bull snake. He showed that to the people, and the person that was telling the story told the guys that wanted to know things; he turned it around and put it as a Snake Indian.

They called her *Maeshuweash*. It was *Maeshuweash*, it was her name. Then it went to Bird Woman, *Sakakaweash*, but her real name was *Ma-eshu-weash*, that means Eagle Woman. They fasted many days; they could do a lot of things and see things ahead. She Kills, that's how he's related. Berry Necklace was related to She Kills. That's how I am related to them. So that's one of the stories that I know about Berry Necklace that was one of our people here.

**Statements of MHA Tribal elders in 2018 and 2019 -**

**Edward Lone Fight (statement on November 5, 2018; New Town, ND),** former Tribal Chairman and tribal elder, stated what he learned from his mother, **Maybelle Goodbird Lone Fight** who was a descendant of Buffalo Bird Woman (*Waheenee*) and was a good friend with **Lula Four Dance** whose mother had been married to Bulls Eye. "The family of *Sacagawea* and Cherry Necklace was very holy. They had strong medicine. *Sacagawea* had been on a trip to the Shoshones the year before the expedition. She was an adopted sister of the Shoshone chief."

**Pete Fredericks (statement on June 14, 2018; New Town, ND),** tribal elder and rancher, stated, "She (*Sacagawea*) was on her way to get coffee when her group was attacked and she was killed."

**Marilyn Hudson (statement on February 18, 2018; Parshall, ND),** tribal elder and former director of the Three Tribes Museum, stated, "I recall **Naomi (Foolish Bear Black Hawk)** telling her story. It was at New Town High School during the Lewis and Clark [celebration] years.

Naomi corroborated Bulls Eye's story of *Sacagawea* and told of traveling that same **trail to Ft. Buford as a child, and the grave [of *Sacagawea*] was on a hillside where people would come to pay their respects." Marilyn** also stated that many years ago, when **Paige Baker, Sr**. was on the North Dakota Education Board, he told them that *Sacagawea* was Hidatsa and that the history books were in error.

An unnamed tribal elder came forward to tell that he had heard that the grave of *Sacagawea* had been moved from the Ft. Buford area to somewhere on the Fort Berthold Reservation in an undisclosed location.

**Cleo Stone Charging (statement on February 20, 2018; White Shield, ND)**, tribal elder and educator, stated, "My father **John Stone**, when he was on the tribal council in the 1960s, said, '*She [Sacagawea] is from right here*.' He did not say more because he was not related to her, and it would not be appropriate."

**Matthew Mason (statement on June 25, 2019; New Town, ND)**, tribal elder and rancher, stated, "We let the Shoshones get ahead of us. We should have told our story long ago."

### Voices Not Heard

*Sacagawea*, **and others who knew, did not speak of her experience for several reasons. They were taught not to brag, she was just their grandma, she was a woman, they were not related to her and didn't have a right to speak of her, the Lewis and Clark Expedition was not important to them, or they knew they would not be believed.**

**Sheheke**, friend of the Lewis and Clark party, when he returned from the east, his tribe did not believe his stories about life in the United States. Potter, T. *Sheheke, Mandan Indian Diplomat*.

*Our Story of Eagle Woman, Sacagawea*

# They have kept *Sacagawea's* story alive.

**Calvin Grinnell**
— Bernie Fox

**Marilyn Hudson**
— Chuck Hudson

**Pat Fredericks**
— Lovina Fox

**Wanda Fox Sheppard**
— Shyla Sheppard

## Recent and Back to the 1940s

## Documents

**Jefferson Bird Smith** (1888-1975), an MHA tribal member who had been educated at Carlisle Indian School in Pennsylvania, who served as a Tribal court judge and a Tribal Business Council Secretary and was often a spokesman for the tribe, wrote in his notes:

It is generally believed that *Tsa-ga-ga Wea* was captured or stolen from the Shoshone tribe, but the Hidatsa tribe refute the claim. The name, *Tsa-ga-ga Wea*, is Hidatsa for Bird Woman: *Tsa-ga-ga* is bird and *Wea* is woman. The late Bulls Eye, a respected member and leader of the tribe, claims that he is the grandson of Bird Woman. She was given in marriage in accordance with Indian custom to a Frenchman named Charboneau. Mr. Charboneau who had been living with the tribe was engaged as an interpreter and guide by Lewis and Clark. In the year 1804, Charboneau and his wife accompanied the Lewis and Clark expedition to the west coast. In 1805, *Tsa-ga-ga Wea* gave birth to a baby boy and named him Baptiste Charboneau. The baby was taken along on the westward journey. *Tsa-ga-ga Wea* has become famous by being the only woman in the Lewis and Clark expedition. It is the custom of the Indian that the women perform much hard labor around the home while the duties of the men are to provide food by hunting and protecting the village. Mr. Bulls Eye relates that his famous grandmother while visiting Montana became ill and died there. She was old. According to white man's report *Tsa-ga-ga Wea* died and is buried at Kenel, South Dakota on December 10, 1812, while another reported that she died at Fort Washakie, Wyoming, in April 8, 1884. Thus, the death of Bird Woman is a controversial matter. She was brave, determined, firm, steady and kindly.

**Carl Sylvester,** a tribal member who had also been educated at Carlisle Indian School and had been tribal chairman, wrote articles in the 1940s and 50s on tribal history and on events of the day to inform the people. In a letter to a Mr. Schultz of September 27, 1943, he wrote:

## Our Story of Eagle Woman, Sacagawea

*Sacajawea* (*Sacagawea*) was said to be of Shoshone extraction but such antecedents of *Sacagawea* is in dispute by these [Ft. Berthold] Indians. "*Sacajawea*" is an error in spelling. There should be no "j." The name is "*Sac'a ga wea*" meaning "Bird Woman." By the way, if you did not know already, the Hidatsa (Minnetaree), and the Crows of Montana, have been, comparatively recently, one nation, having had one language.

**In Sylvester's notes, he states:**

A challenging account says that [*Sacagawea*] was an Hidatsa, a younger sister to the famous sacred man, Berry [Cherry] Necklace. This medicine man was of the *Awatixa*... It is said that the reason for her willingness to join the explorers Lewis and Clark was that she was eager to see her other relatives who were Crow Indians roaming in the vicinity of the foot of the Rocky Mountains which lay in the explorers' path.

**Tribal Attempts to Correct the Story**

Three administrations of the Three Affiliated Tribes' tribal councils especially made attempts to set the record straight and inform the government that *Sacagawea* was Hidatsa. The **Martin Cross, Rose Crow Flies High** and **Tex Hall** administrations especially made such attempts.

The **Rose Crow Flies High** administration (1972-78) reported that the government officials said it would be too expensive and hard to change the story.

Under **Chairman Martin Cross**, during the Garrison Dam testimonies of the 1940s and 50s, information on *Sacagawea* was included. **Jefferson Smith** testified, "Because of the decree of our chief, Lewis and Clark were provided with corn, venison and other provisions through the winter."

*Recent and Back to the 1940s*

# All three of these tribal chairpersons are relatives of *Sacagawea*. They tried to correct the story.

*Chairman Martin Cross*
— State Historical Society of North Dakota

*Chairwoman Rose Crow Flies High*
— MHA Interpretive Center

*Chairman Tex G. Hall*
— Robin Blankenship

Smith went on: "Later on, *Tsa-ca-ca Wea* which means the Bird Woman, went with the expedition in the westward expansion. She was a member of the Three Affiliated Tribes." Mr. Case (attorney for the tribe) stated, "It is interesting to note that in 1804, the Lewis and Clark expedition came through North Dakota with the view of opening the west for colonization. They secured the services of a young lady by the name of *Sakakawea* who was a member of the Hidatsa tribe, I believe, of Mr. Cross' group." [Mr. Cross was a descendant of Cherry Necklace, brother of *Sacagawea*.]

The Three Affiliated Tribes also filed a claim with the Indian Claims Commission asking for monetary compensation for *Sacagawea*'s services. The claim was later dropped as claims were grouped by land claims according to **Marilyn Hudson,** daughter of Martin Cross and past administrator of the Three Tribes Museum.

Under **Chairman Tex Hall**, a proclamation was executed near the time of the Lewis and Clark bicentennial and, during his time, a statue of *Sakakawea* was also placed in Statuary Hall in Washington, DC. The proclamation states that the Hidatsa story of *Sakakawea*'s birthright, as told by Hidatsa chief Bulls Eye and published in the *Van Hook Reporter*, April 1925, is an excellent recording of the Hidatsa oral history, and one that the tribe has adopted.

In an article **in the *Mandan, Hidatsa, Arikara Times* of December 11, 2003, Chairman Hall** stated:

> The state of North Dakota has also accepted our version [of the *Sacagawea* story]. On October 16, 2003, our Congressional delegation led by Congressman Earl Pomeroy unveiled a statue of *Sacagawea* in the United States Capitol's Statutory Hall. She stands there as an Hidatsa woman and as one of North Dakota's notable citizens. We will not downgrade or dispute anyone else's versions, but we respect our own tribal histories. We are a federally-recognized treaty tribe and our business council has adopted this position. To do otherwise would be to disrespect our elders and ancestors.

The MHA Nation had a strong presence at the unveiling of the *Sacagawea* statue in Washington, DC.

*Recent and Back to the 1940s*

"Sakakawea," a re-casting of the Leonard Crunelle statue at Bismarck from a century earlier, installed at the Visitor Center of the U.S. Capitol Building, Washington, D.C., 2003 — Architect of the Capitol

## Other Tribal Actions

**Marilyn Hudson** also stated, "In 1956 the Tribal Council asked their Senators and Congressmen to sponsor a bill to name the new reservoir Lake *Sakakawea*. In accordance with their wishes, Senators Young and Langer introduced Senate Bill 1530 to name it Lake *Sakakawea*... It was not until 1967, 11 years later, that President Lyndon Johnson finally signed the document officially naming the reservoir "Lake *Sakakawea*."

### From "*Sacagawea* or *Sakakawea*?" *Indian Country Today*, August 22, 2002

"The American Indian tribe that claims the guide as its own may soon change its spelling of her name to *Sacagawea* [from *Sakakawea*]... **Amy Mossett**, the tribal tourism director [for the MHA Nation], said she proposed the spelling change to her business council because *Sacagawea* comes closest to the correct pronunciation for the guide's name, which means Bird Woman in the Hidatsa language."

**The fact that *Sacagawea* was Hidatsa and stories of her life were passed down from generation to generation. In 2001, the Mandan, Hidatsa and Arikara Nation (Three Affiliated Tribes) proclaimed that the Bulls Eye story of *Sacagawea* was the official position of the Nation.**

**In 2015, the Tribal Council began supporting a research project to gather and evaluate existing tribal information and identify and evaluate other research pertinent to the story of *Sacagawea* in order to finally examine and document the MHA Nation's story of Bird Woman. A *Sacagawea* Project Board of tribal elders was established to carry out this endeavor. The project was to develop this book built upon the previous work of Tribal Historian, Calvin Grinnell, to include primary sources and documentation gathered, to be accessible to young people, and to be written from a tribal perspective.**

## MANDAN, HIDATSA & ARIKARA NATION PROCLAIMS THE ORAL HISTORY STORY OF THE HIDATSA ORIGIN OF *SAKAKAWEA* TO BE THE OFFICIAL POSITION OF THE TRIBES

### A Proclamation

Approximately two hundred years ago in 1804-06, the people of the Mandan, Hidatsa & Arikara Nations provided invaluable assistance to the Lewis and Clark Expedition. Without their assistance it is doubtful the Expedition would have survived that first winter...

The contributions of our ancestors to the success of the Expedition have been largely overshadowed by the legend of *Sakakawea* as a Shoshone captive...

It is the duty and responsibility of the Tribal Business Council of the Mandan, Hidatsa & Arikara Nation to affirm and uphold the history, culture and traditions of their membership in order to strengthen the cultural identity of all members; and for the members of the Mandan, Hidatsa & Arikara Nation to accept the United States history widely-held belief that *Sakakawea* was a Shoshone is to deny the words and oral history of our ancestors.

**NOW, THEREFORE, WE THE MEMBERS OF THE TRIBAL BUSINESS COUNCIL** do hereby proclaim that the Hidatsa oral history story of the origins of *Sakakawea,* as told by Chief Bulls Eye, to be the official position of the Mandan, Hidatsa & Arikara Nation.

**IN WITNESS WHEREOF,** we set our hands this 31st day of August in the year of our Lord two thousand and one. Signed, **Tex G. Hall**, Chairman; **Randy Phelan**, Vice Chairman; **Austin H. Gillette**, Treasurer; **Marcus Wells, Jr.**, Secretary; **Mark N. Fox**, Member; **Malcolm Wolf,** Member; **Daylon Spotted Bear**, Member *MHA Interpretive Center.*

*Our Story of Eagle Woman, Sacagawea*

Resolution No. 02- -MWJR

**RESOLUTION OF THE GOVERNING BODY
OF THE
THREE AFFIIATED TRIBES
OF THE
FORT BERTHOLD INDIAN RESERVATION**

*A Resolution entitled, "The Hidatsa Spelling of Bird Woman"*

**WHEREAS,** This Nation having accepted the Indian Reorganization Act of June 18, 1934, and the authority under said Act; and

**WHEREAS,** The Three Affiliated Tribes Constitution authorizes and empowers the Mandan, Hidatsa & Arikara Tribal Business Council to engage in activity on behalf of an in the interest of the welfare and benefit of the Tribes and of the enrolled members thereof; and

**WHEREAS,** in the absence of standard alphabet for the Hidatsa language, the State of North Dakota used the English alphabet to spell the Hidatsa word for Bird Woman, and

**WHEREAS,** to ensure the most accurte Hidatsa pronunciation for Bird Woman, North Dakota consulted with linguists and adopted a linguistic and adopted a linguistic spelling whereby a 'k' followed by a vowel is pronounced as a hard 'g'; and

**WHEREAS,** the majority of English speaking people mispronounce SAKAKAWEA because unknown written words are pronounced phonetically rather than linguistically resulting in 'Sakakawea' being pronounced with an emphasis on 'K' rather than a hard 'G'; and

**WHEREAS,** the most correct English spelling for the Hidatsa word—Bird Woman—is not SKAKAWEA, and

**NOW THEREFORE BE IT RESOLVED,** the Tribal Business Council of the Three Afiliated Tribes hereby adopts *'SACAGAWEA'* as the spelling that most closely represents the Hidatsa pronounciation for the word Bird Woman.

**CERTIFICATION**

I, undersigned, as Secretary of the Tribal Business Council of the Three Affiliated Tribes of the Fort Berthold Indian Reservation hereby certify that the tribal Business Council is composed of seven (7) members of whom five (5) constitute a quorum, _5_ were present at a <u>Regular</u> Meeting thereof duly called, noticed, convened and held on the _8_ day of <u>August</u>, 2002, that the forgoing Resolution was duly adopted at such meeting by the affirmative vote of _4_ members, _0_ members opposed, _1_ members abstained, _1_ members not voting, and that said Resolution has not been rescinded or amended in any way.

— MHA Interpretive Center

*Recent and Back to the 1940s*

**The next section includes voices regarding *Sacagawea* from the early 1900s.**

**Sources Authored or Provided by MHA Tribal Members:**

Charging, Cleo. Personal Interview. February 20, 2018.

Fredericks, Irene. Letter. *MHA Times,* May 3, 2002.

Fredericks, Pat. Personal Interview by Calvin Grinnell, Tribal Historian.

Fredericks, Peter. Personal Interview. June 14, 2018.
Hall, Tex. Interview. *MHA Times.* December 11, 2003.

Hudson, Marilyn. Personal Interview. February 18, 2018.

Hudson, Marilyn. "A Brief History of the Three Affiliated Tribes." *Reunion at the home of Sakakawea: Lewis & Clark Signature Event.* New Town, ND: Mandan, Hidatsa & Arikara Nation, August 17-20, 2006.

Hudson, Marilyn, Director. "The Land I Am Standing On: A Theatrical Performance." *A Confluence of Cultures: Native Americans and the Expedition of Lewis and Clark.* Missoula: University of Montana, 2003.

Lone Fight, Edward. Personal Interview. November 5, 2018.

Mason, Matthew. Personal Interview. June 25, 2019.

Mossett, Amy. "*Sacagawea* or *Sakakawea*?" *Indian Country Today.* August 22, 2002.

Rave, Jodi. "Correcting the story of *Sacagawea*." *Missoulian*, September 3, 2006.

Sand, Delores, Grinnell, Calvin and Hudson, Marilyn. "Searching for *Sakakawea*." *Dickinson Press,* December 5, 1999.

Smith, Jefferson Bird. Personal Papers.

Sylvester, Carl. Personal Papers and letter to Mr. Schultz, 1943.

Thorton, Esley. "Heritage in Question." *Minot Daily News,* August 9, 2001.

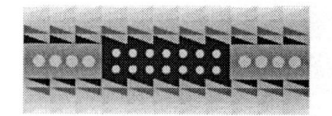

*River Crow young woman visiting Like-A-Fishhook Village, 1851, wearing a wool trade cloth dress decorated with elk teeth.*
— Pen & ink portrait by Rudolph F. Kurz. / Berne Historical Museum

## Chapter 5
### *OUR VOICES/SOME DISTORTED*
*Early 1900s*

With the centennial of the Lewis and Clark Expedition in 1904-1906, there was a focus on the event. Various individuals, organizations, states, and the federal government all sought to have influence regarding the story, and this included information about *Sacagawea*. There was also a general interest in Indian culture and history. Various tribal elders from Fort Berthold were queried regarding these matters. Following is information regarding *Sacagawea* and Cherry Necklace, her brother, gathered from informants in the early 1900s. It is important evidence for supporting our claim that she was Hidatsa/Crow.

**Bear's Arm** "was an Hidatsa born about 1864 to Old-Woman-Crawling at the *Awatixa* village. He was the owner of the Eagle-trapping rights.

## Our Story of Eagle Woman, Sacagawea

Bear's Arm was known to be knowledgeable of Hidatsa culture and his door was always open for visitors. Many late night sessions were spent with visitors and elders glad to find one of the younger generation willing to listen to stories of the old times." From *Biographical Dictionary of the Mandan, Hidatsa and Arikara* by Michael Stevens, online.

The famed ethnologist, Alfred Bowers, secured Bear's Arm as an informant while researching the Hidatsa. Bear's Arm gave Bowers a family tree for *Sacagawea* which included Otter, Bulls Eye's mother, and Cedar Woman, George Parshall's grandmother. Bear's Arm also said, "Charbonneau left and *Tsagagawia* was asked to go, but refused, and he never came back." From Bowers, Alfred, unpublished notes

Bear's Arm was also an informant for *Mandan-Hidatsa Myths and Ceremonies* collected by Martha Warren Beckwith, American Folk-Lore Society, New York, 1937. In a section of Beckwith's book, about Cherry Necklace, Bear's Arm states that "Bird-woman, who guided the famous Lewis and Clark expedition, was his [Cherry Necklace's] sister." Bear's Arm also stated that Cherry Necklace "must have died when he (Bear's Arm) was nine years old."

**It would have been about 1873 when Bear's Arm was nine years old and Cherry Necklace died. In an account by Naomi Black Hawk, she says that Cherry Necklace lived to be 95 years old. This would have had him being born in about 1778 and being about nine years older than *Sacagawea*. She was born about 1787 and died in 1869.**

**Calf Woman** was a Mandan bundle keeper who was custodian of the *Okipa* Lodge at Like-A-Fishhook Village. As an informant, she described Mandan ceremonies to Alfred Bowers, recorded in *Mandan Social and Ceremonial Organization*, 1950. One ceremony was held by Clam Necklace, a young man at the time. Calf Woman described the ceremony and stated that gifts were given to those in attendance. They included Eagle Woman, *Maeshuwea* (*Sacagawea*), and her daughters Otter Woman and Cedar Woman.

*Early 1900s*

**Buffalo Bird Woman,** "known in Hidatsa as *Maxidiwiac*, was born about 1839 in an earth lodge along the Knife River in present-day North Dakota. In 1845 her people moved upstream and built Like-A-Fishhook village, which they shared with the Mandan and Arikara. There Buffalo Bird Woman grew up to become an expert gardener of the Hidatsa tribe." She was an informant for Gilbert Wilson who published *Buffalo Bird Woman's Garden*, Minnesota Historical Press, 1987, first published in 1917 as *Agriculture of the Hidatsa Indians: An Indian Interpretation*.

*Buffalo Bird Woman, Waheenee, was an informant who provided a wealth of information on Hidatsa life.*
— State Historical Society of North Dakota

**Buffalo Bird Woman was about the same age as *Sacagawea*'s daughters, Otter Woman, Cedar Woman and Different Breast, and she knew their family.**

In *Buffalo Bird Woman's Garden*, Buffalo Bird Woman drew garden plots including two for Eagle Woman, *Maeshuwea* (*Sacagawea*), and Cedar Woman (*Sacagawea*'s daughter). In *Notes on the Social Organization and Customs of the Mandan, Hidatsa and Crow Indians*, 1917, Robert Lowie, recorded the kinship term Buffalo Bird Woman used for Cherry Necklace.

Buffalo Bird Woman was the sister of Wolf Chief, another prominent informant. In *The Way to Independence*, by Carolyn Gilman and Mary Jane Schneider, about the family of Buffalo Bird Woman and Wolf Chief and based upon the work of Gilbert Wilson, they included a picture of a bowl made by Cedar Woman (probably the daughter of *Maeshuwea, Sacagawea*).

## Our Story of Eagle Woman, Sacagawea

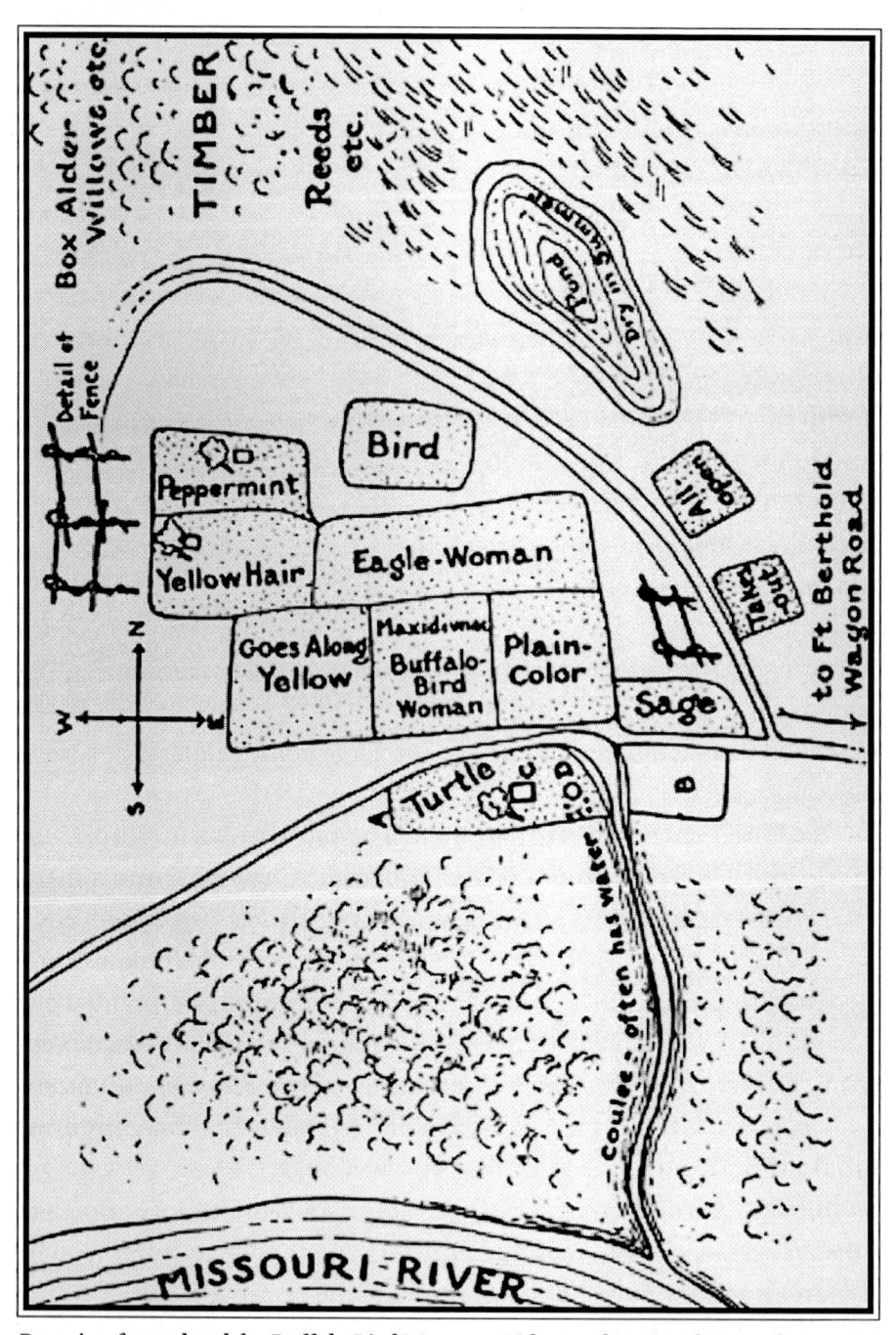

*Drawing from sketch by Buffalo Bird Woman, Hidatsa, showing that Eagle Woman (Sacagawea) was her neighbor and gardening partner in the fields near Like-A-Fishhook Village during the 1850s & 1860s.*
  — Gilbert L. Wilson / Minneapolis: University of Minnesota Press, 1917.

*Early 1900s*

**Wolf Chief**, "brother of Buffalo Bird Woman and son of Small Ankle, was a respected medicine man. He learned to read and write English and informed Washington about the unscrupulous ways of the government officials and traders. In 1889 he opened his own store in Independence District." From "Three Affiliated Tribes Cultural Page, Tribal Chiefs of the Mandan, Hidatsa and Arikara," *MHA Times*, January 14, 1997.

From 1923 to 1932, Wolf Chief worked with Alfred Bowers as a consultant doing an ethnological study of the Hidatsa people. He was also an informant for Gilbert Wilson.

*Wolf Chief at Fort Buford, D.T., 1874*
— Orlando Scott Goff/State Historical Society of North Dakota

Notes taken by Alfred Bowers from an interview with Wolf Chief in February-March of 1933, at Independence, included the following:

Time before smallpox [we] were instructed to move out and divide up -[we] did. Cherry Necklace (brother to Bird Woman) was the only one who went out to [the] Yellowstone when smallpox came. [I] tried to stop the Bismarck story of it (the published story of *Sacagawea*). Poor Wolf should know and say [they] were not captured as stories say. She was Gros Ventre [changed to Hidatsa] and belongs in Willow Village [Hidatsa]. My mother would tell me that Bird Woman's mother was a Chicken [an Hidatsa clan]. *[Sacagawea's mother was Crow and perhaps was adopted into this Hidatsa clan.]*

## Our Story of Eagle Woman, Sacagawea

She went up to [the] mountains and went up river to a falls, and a tribe [Shoshones] lived, [wanted] to kill off the party [Lewis and Clark] and [*Sacagawea*] begged them not to kill and they decided not to kill them and instead gave her blankets and beads and made friends. She used sign language. She made a sign, touched ground and motioned that our home was to [the] east and [made a] motion of shelling corn and they eat of it...

She gave all the gifts from [the] Snakes to [the] Crow, Cherry Necklace who was with the Crows up nearly to [the] mountains. (This may explain seeing her brother up there.) When smallpox [was] over, Gay Wood [what Hidatsas called Charbonneau] and Bird Woman went up river with whites to [Fort]Union. Cherry Necklace told these events and said she was his sister.

She died at [the] mouth of [the] Yellowstone near Ft. Buford (or Union). Seems Lewis and Clark mixed her ability to speak Snake with that of Crow, with her brother Cherry Necklace. Charbonneau [was] called Gay Wood.

*Tsagagawia* died when I was less than 20, about 16, for the news came back to our village [Like-A-Fishhook] and was before Crow Flies High went up [to Fort Buford, 1870]. While up there [in 1869], Otter [*Sacagawea's* oldest daughter] was killed by the enemy and Cedar Woman [also a daughter of *Sacagawea*] came back with Crow Flies High to Shell Creek [in 1894].

Before Crow Flies High went up, our people often [went] up on [a]hunt and when she died, they came up on [a] hunt and brought the two girls back, then the girls married and went back with Crow Flies High [upriver].

We never saw Charbonneau again. (Wolf Chief says he has seen *Tsagagawia* but not the Frenchman. She came down from Ft. Union). Her husband had left her by this time and gone and I do not think he lived with her in her old age. Daughters were with her when she died. I knew the two girls and Poor Bull [Lean Bull, Bulls Eye's Father]. Doesn't think any mistakes [made about her story] could have been true. Never heard of a scaffold or grave.

*Early 1900s*

*Goodbird and family. Goodbird was the son of Buffalo Bird Woman (Waheenee) and Son of the Star.* — State Historical Society of North Dakota

**Goodbird**, son of Buffalo Bird Woman, under the direction of **Wolf Chief** and with the assistance of **Butterfly**, drew a map of how Like-A-Fishhook Village was laid out when it was established about 1845. Cherry Necklace had two lodges, for two wives. Small Ankle, Buffalo Bird Woman and Wolf Chief's father, had the first lodge in the plan. From *The Hidatsa Earthlodge* by Gilbert Wilson, American Museum of Natural History, New York, 1934.

**Wolf Chief told that *Maeshuwea* (*Sacagawea*) went to the west among the Shoshone with a party. She used sign language to communicate with the Shoshones. She was Hidatsa/Crow and was a sister of Cherry Necklace.**

## Our Story of Eagle Woman, Sacagawea

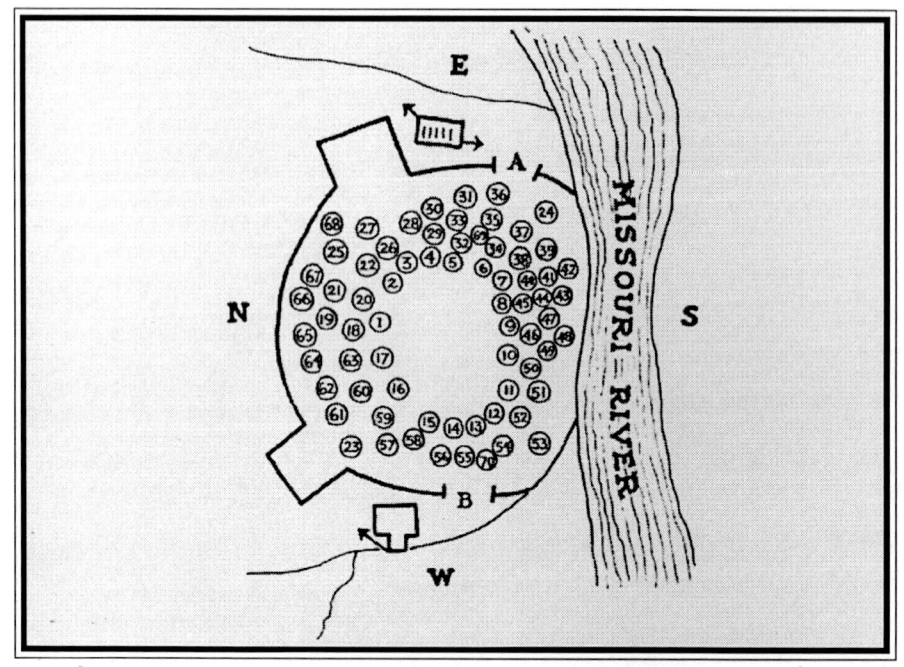

*Position of the Hidatsa Earthlodges in Like-A-Fishhook Village.*
— Goodbird (G.L. Wilson)

1. Small-ankle; 2. Has-a-game-stick, one wife; 3. Has-a-game-stick, a second wife; 4. Cherry-necklace; 5. Crow-paunch; 6. Mussel-necklace; 7. Kit-fox-fat; 8. Bear-heart; 9. Feather; 10. Other-kind-of-wolf; 11. End-rock; 12. Bear-nose; 13. Missouri-river; 14. Porcupine-pemmican; 15. His-red-stone; 16. Black-panther; 17. Dried-squash; 18. Dog's-urine; 19. Red-belly; 20. Poor-wolf (or Lean-wold); 21. Four-bear; 22. Wolf-walks-with-the-wind-at-his-back; 23. Blue-stone; 24. Reddening-a-knife; 25. Bowl; 26. White-dog; 27. Small-bull; 28. Rough-arm; 29. Hawk; 30. Wears-a-coat; 31. Crow-heart; 32. Cherry-necklace, a second wife; 33. Dog-cries; 34. Full-of-honor-marks; 35. Prairie-chicken-tells-lies; 36. Big-bull; 37. Prairie-chicken-cannot-swim, one wife; 38. Prairie-chicken-cannot-swim, another wife; 39, Goose; 40. Wolf-eye; 41. Eye-has-no-water; 42. Bad-horn; 43. Frost-mouth; 44. Magic-bird; 45. Flying-eagle; 46. Bloody-mouth; 47. Wooden-lodge; 48. He-raises-all-hearts; 49. Dry-of-milk; 50. Big-black; 51. Lone-buffalo; 52. Thrust-in; 53. Skin-worn-through; 54. Old-woman-crows; 55. Butterfly; 56. Nutadokie; 57. One-horn; 58. Paints-shoulder-yellow; 59. Man-has-long-hair; 60. Blacks-his-shield; 61. Intestines (or Guts); 62. Man-smells-bad; 63. Little-bear; 64. Wolf-head; 65. Bull-has-spirit; 66. Seven-bears; 67. Black-horn; 68. Paints-tail-red; 69. Red-thigh; 70. Has-a-game-stick, a third wife.

*Early 1900s*

*Sakakawea (Awatixa)* Village was destroyed and smallpox came in about 1837, so *Maeshuwea, (Sacagawea)* and Charbonneau left the Knife River villages and moved to or near Ft. Union. (A town was established and named Charbonneau near Ft. Union. It is now a ghost town.) Census records indicate that *Maeshuwea's* daughters were born around this time.

Charbonneau later became employed at Ft. Clark near present day Bismarck, ND.

Charbonneau died in 1840. *Maeshuwea (Sacagawea)* moved to Like-A-Fishhook Village after it was established in 1845. Evidence indicates that she lived with Otter Woman and Cherry Necklace at Like-A-Fishhook Village. *Maeshuwea (Sacagawea)* and her daughter, Otter Woman, were killed upriver near the Ft. Buford/Union area in 1869.

Tribal members brought *Maeshuwea's* daughter, Cedar Woman, back to Like-A-Fishhook Village, then she married and went back to live at the place where Crow Flies High had a camp near Ft. Buford, started in about 1870. She returned to Ft. Berthold, to Shell Creek, when Crow Flies High returned in 1894.

Census records show Cedar Woman living with Bulls Eye when he lived at Crow Flies High's camp at Ft. Buford and also at Shell Creek. She told stories of *Sacagawea* to Bulls Eye.

Following are the interviews of Charles Eastman that have been considered to add to the evidence that *Sacagawea* was Shoshone but are discounted herein.

## The Interviews of Charles Eastman

Dr. Charles Eastman, Santee Dakota, was commissioned by the United States government in December of 1924 to research Ft. Berthold and other accounts of *Sacajawea* (Shoshone) in order to determine her identity and her place of burial, as there was disagreement on these matters.

Eastman gathered information from Fort Berthold Agency and informants. He, however, believed beforehand that she was Shoshone and was buried in Wyoming, and his work attempted to prove that. He was stationed at Ft. Washakie, Wyoming. Eastman's work has been discounted by other researchers. Alfred Bowers, noted Hidatsa ethnologist, stated, "certainly the Wyoming studies are open to severe criticism." The following is an interpretation of the Bulls Eye story written by someone at Fort Berthold Agency and provided to Eastman.

### Sakakawea

Bulls Eye, the only living descendent of *Sakakawea*, is a member of the Gros Ventre tribe, residing at Shell Creek, a substation on this reservation. He is now some 60 years of age and was very much pleased to give such facts as he was possessed of with reference to this most interesting woman of historical fame.

He has also left a kodak picture of himself and his adopted son, in full dress regalia, to be forwarded thinking that this too might be of interest to you. A brief resume of the story as he told it follows.

*Early 1900s*

*Thomas Bulls Eye, Bulls Eye's adopted son.*
— MHA Interpretive Center.

At one time the Mandan and Gros Ventre Indians established villages on the banks of the Missouri river across from where the village of Stanton, N.Dak. is now located. The camp consisted of five villages; the three upper being occupied by the Gros Ventre or Hidatsa Indians and the two lower by the Mandan Indians.

When Lewis and Clarke started on their momentous trip to the west coast, they stopped enroute at the five villages and stayed for some time, approximately two years [actually, one winter]. Among other members of their party was a Frenchman by the name of Charbonneau, who became greatly attached and eventually married a bright young girl of the Gros Ventre village.

In fact all members of the party were attracted to her because of her aptness, her constant attempts to understand their language, and her general vivacity and endeavored to draw her into conversation. Among other things they asked her was her name and she told them. Their interpretation of her language was limited and they interpreted her name as Bird Woman which in Gros Ventre would be *Sa-ka-ka-wea*.

After months of weary travel they reached the Pacific coast and *Sakakawea* was overjoyed to find an Indian trader who not only had blankets and Indian trinkets but beads of every conceivable shape and color. She was particularly attracted to some beads known as moon beads and bought lavishly of the goods offered for sale to carry back with her to her own people as gifts and mementos of her adventure.

On the return trip they made a camp one evening, had eaten and were establishing themselves for the night when they heard the blood curdling war whoop of a band of Indians on the war path and, for a time, it seemed the entire party would be wiped out. *Sakakawea* fearlessly went out toward the warring braves and was recognized by one, a Blackfeet who had, in an encounter some years previous, killed her brother in an attack on the Gros Ventre villages.

The recognition was mutual and following a custom peculiar to these people, he immediately announced the fact that she was his sister, that being the Indian custom that when a young brave killed another it would virtually mean the adoption of the fallen hero's family in like relationship, and the Blackfeet brave hastened back to his camp to return in a short while with choice cuts of buffalo meat, blankets, beads and other offerings of friendship and good will.

Another incident is told where the party stopped near where the Crows were encamped and were visited by prominent members of the Crow tribe. One member of the party claimed *Sakakawea* as a distant relative and, who was very favorably impressed with her white husband, presented him with a saddle horse which was known for its power of endurance and its adaptability as a buffalo horse.

Charbonneau was greatly pleased and a flat boat was constructed to enable the party to take the horse with them and a goodly supply of hay was put up and the animal was taken with them.

From the story told by Bulls Eye, it was determined that he and his wife not only accompanied Lewis and Clarke on their trip to the west but made a trip independently at a later time; Charbonneau carrying a store of supplies and trading with the various Indians met along the way. Little or nothing can be learned as to his life, whether or not he had other wives or children, or his death.

*Sakakawea* had four children. Otter, the mother of Bulls Eye, the narrator, a second daughter by the name of Cedar Woman, who died early in life, Plain Track [Jean Baptiste], a boy who was born during the first trip westward and another daughter, Different Cherries[Breast]. After the death of Charbonneau, *Sakakawea* lived with her daughter, Otter Woman, who eventually married a Crow Indian. They resided at the five villages for some time but after the death of the husband of Otter Woman they went to visit the Crows. While there, they frequently visited a trader's camp operated by white men. Otter eventually married one of the white men who worked at the store and they, in company with *Sakakawea* and Otter's young son, Bulls Eye, started back across the country to the Gros Ventres villages.

They were following a dim wagon trail through a heavily wooded country and toward evening came to a stretch of land that had been swept by fire. Finding a stream nearby where they could get water, they camped for the night, cooked their evening meal and went to sleep enveloped by the silence of night, their only light being the light from the camp fire and from the starry firmament above them. They were awakened about the middle of the night by blood curdling yells of warring Sioux.

*Sakakawea* first thought of her young grandson and pressed him to her and hastened to a large stump which had been practically destroyed by fire and tucked him away inside the shell. Her son-in-law was killed, *Sakakawea* severely injured about the head and after the warriors went on, leaving their victims supposedly dead, she hastened to the stump to find that her little grandson had not been injured. She gathered him up in her arms and took him back to the wagon.

Finding that Otter Woman was still alive she propped her up against the wagon and watched her life blood slowly ooze from her mouth. With dying gasps her life swiftly ebbed away. The daughter, thoughtful only of her loved ones, admonished her mother to take the little son and go back to the village. Staying until death relieved her from her suffering, *Sakakawea* covered the body as best she could and started the long sad journey back to the trader's camp they had so recently left. The way was long and tedious and there was only a faint trail to mark the road but just as the sun was setting, they came to the brow of the hill from which they could look down on the peaceful camp, she with indomitable will that had characterized her through the long arduous trip to the west, struggled on until she reached the store, where she fell unconscious, completely exhausted from the strain that had been placed upon her.

Every possible care and attention was rendered her but she succumbed to the injury received about her head after seven days of weary struggle and was buried in a coffin constructed from rough lumber by the men at the post and was laid to rest as the sun was sinking at the foot of a hill near the trader's store near what the Indians call Sand Creek and now in the vicinity of Glasgow, Montana.

**The agency superintendent notes that the story was probably not totally accurate. Bulls Eye had probably told the story to someone at the agency who tried to retell it. It contains some things that are inconsistent with or in addition to Bulls Eye's rendering.**

**This account states that Bulls Eye was the only living descendent of *Sacagawea* although direct descendant, George Parshall, was still living also.**

*Early 1900s*

The account also says that Cedar Woman (*Sacagawea's* daughter, Bulls Eye's aunt and George Parshall's grandmother) died at an early age, but Cedar Woman, age 50, and George Parshall (Dog), age 16, lived in Bulls Eye's home in 1891 according to the Indian census.

The account indicates that Charbonneau was with the Lewis and Clark party before he married *Sacagawea*. The part about the Blackfeet man was not in line with Bulls Eye's story, although she did have an adopted brother at Shoshone.

The account also states that *Sacagawea* was buried at Sand Creek near Glasgow, Montana. Tribal members say she was buried at the foot or side of a hill at or near Ft. Buford.

The "distant relative" among the Crows was *Sacagawea's* brother, Cherry Necklace.

This account indicates that *Sacagawea* went on a trip west after the Lewis and Clark journey in addition to the actual expedition and a trip west the year before.

**A letter from Stephen Janus**, Superintendent of Fort Berthold Agency, dated December 30, 1924 to Charles Eastman stated:

Dear Mr. Eastman:-

In response to a request from the Superintendent at Ft. Washakie, I sent information from the files of this office about *Sakakawea*, the Indian woman who went with Lewis & Clark.

From this it appears that the Gros Ventre Indian Bulls Eye is the only living descendent of *Sakakawea*, and he is a regularly enrolled member of this tribe under this jurisdiction. If Bulls Eye tells the truth he is the grandson of *Sakakawea* and there is no reason to believe that this woman was a Shoshone. Nor would it appear that there is much likelihood that the grave at Ft. Washakie is really hers.

## Our Story of Eagle Woman, Sacagawea

For your own information I am sending you from the records the history previously sent to Supt. Haas [the account written by someone at Ft. Berthold Agency]. In going over this history I see much that appears to be given too much weight by the scribe, not by the narrator. And I think that a further interview with Bulls Eye, and other old Indians here associated with him, might discover further and important facts.

I should certainly be glad to see you again, and you may rest assured that I will gladly give you every assistance in looking up the true history of *Sakakawea*.

**Eastman visited Fort Berthold and took statements of individuals.**

STATEMENT OF BULL EYE'S

INTERPRETERS: Charles Hoffman and Eagle [a man] [tribal members].

My name is Bull Eye's. I am 66 years old. I am a member of the Shell Creek band of Gros Ventres. I am the son of Otter, a daughter of Eagle [Woman] and Tousant Charbonneau. My grandmother Eagle and my mother Otter were killed by a Sioux war party near the present town of Glasgow, Montana in 1869. My grandmother had the following children: Otter, Cedar Woman, Plain Track [Jean Baptiste] a boy, Different Cherries [Breast] a girl. I will tell you my grandmother Eagle's story of her trip across the mountains and to a big water. The story she tells is as follows:

When she was a very young girl she married Charbonneau a Frenchman. Soon after their marriage, the Frenchman, her husband, was employed by a large company of fur traders who were coming down the river from the north carrying their furs down to St. Louis. They went down with them towards St. Louis and took my grandmother along. My grandmother states that she and Charbonneau [were] again employed by some fur company and were southwest towards Mexico to some Spanish forts.

*Early 1900s*

There my grandmother saw some of the most beautiful blankets that she ever saw and she also saw beautiful shells and shell parts from the sea.

They worked with these fur people for two or three years in that country, when another big party of white men coming northwards into the mountains, as a guide and interpreter, and we went along to the Big Mountains into a big water (Salt Lake). They wintered thereby the big water.

(Speaking as *Sacagawea*) Next spring part of the company were sent down to St. Louis with the furs but the greater part were starting over the mountains in northwest with packed horses, buying furs from the Indians but we were moving on until we came to the Wind River and we followed the Wind River until we came to the Big Horn River, then I knew we were in our country again. When we came out on the Yellowstone they made boats and put our packs on the boats and were going down the Yellowstone River when we met some of the Crow Indians. Among them I met my brother. He gave a very fine white horse to my husband Charbonneau. Charbonneau had to make a flat boat to carry his horse down the river. After a while we reached the Missouri River and down that river until we reached home at the Gros Ventres village.

My grandmother by this trip had been to the Big Water and seen some of the sea shells etc., so that when some other white party came they took her as a guide across the mountains. At that time she carried my uncle, Plain Track, on her back on that trip. I received this information from my aunt, Different Cherries [Breast] who also was called Pretty Breast, who died 30 years ago (1896) for I was merely three or four years old when my mother was killed. My grandmother was also killed at that time.

We never have any Snake captives here. My uncle, Plain Track [Jean Baptiste], who was also called Cherry Necklace [probably after his uncle] was killed by the Sioux in warfare years ago. My aunt Cedar Woman died in childhood. We have never heard that our Indians have fought with the Snake or Shoshone Indians.

*Our Story of Eagle Woman, Sacagawea*

**Our friends the Crow Indians are the ones who have battled with them and it is my impression that if there is any Snake captives they must have been taken by the Crow Indians and not by the Gros Ventres. Our tribes were so surrounded by our Sioux enemies it was impossible for our people to go very far from our village, either in hunting or warfare.** My grandmother's name is Eagle, but her husband Charbonneau cannot talk Gros Ventres very well so they simply called her Bird Woman.

**Bulls Eye stated to Major Welch that the year that Charbonneau married *Sacagawea* they went to the West and had been to the Shoshones and to the Salmon River. The year after that was when the Lewis and Clark party came through and he and *Sacagawea* joined them. This time Bulls Eye said that they went to St. Louis and to the "Big Water" and near Mexico before the expedition.**

They did go to these places on a trip in 1815. He also said his aunt, Different Breast, was his informant, but he had named Cedar Woman as his informant before, and it was Cedar Woman who lived in his home, according to the 1891 census, and did not die in childhood. He also said that Plain Track, *Sacagawea's* son Jean Baptiste (Pomp), was killed by the Sioux long before. Jean Baptiste died in 1866 of illness and is buried in Oregon. Bulls Eye may not have known this information, however.

### STATEMENT OF CHIEF WOLF CHIEF

Judge of Indian Court and Chief of Gros Ventre
at Elbowoods; N. Dakota.
Fort Berthold Reservation.
Age 76 years

*Early 1900s*

I am hereditary chief of the Gros Ventre Indians. I lived here all my life. You asked me, Dr. Eastman, what I and my people know about *Sacajawea*, or Bird Woman, the guide of the Lewis and Clark expedition. We have absolutely nothing about her in our tradition and we never knew a woman by that name among our people, except once. A woman came among us sixty-five or seventy years ago, whose name was Bird Woman.

I do not remember where she came from and what tribe she belonged to. She remained here only a short period; then she went up the Missouri River on a steamer.

It does not appear as I think of it now, that she was any person of note, merely the fact that she stopped here for a while. This was the only Indian woman that my people know by that name, namely, Bird Woman.

The tradition of Lewis and Clark Expedition is clear in our minds but we have no Indian woman from this tribe or any other tribe who took an important part in that event. You said that this Bird Woman was one of a number of Shoshoni captives taken by our warriors, who were brought up here and she married a Frenchman by the name of Charbonneau. I don't want to dispute the records of Lewis and Clark, but they were undoubtedly misinformed.

**Our people never go to the Rocky Mountains for the purpose of warfare or hunting because we are absolutely surrounded by our enemies. Therefore we could never have taken any captives from the Shoshoni people.**

**It must have been taken by our friends, the Crow tribe, who made war with the Shoshonis** and that Charbonneau must have married these Shoshoni women up the river among the Crows and later came down to our tribe with them and remained with us here a little while when the Lewis and Clark Expedition came here and found them here. The fact that they were mere visitors here and then taken away by Lewis and Clark as mere employees, that they did not impress our people's minds as important people. **And when Lewis and Clark returned here, Charbonneau and his wife did not stay here very long, and then, as you say, went down to St. Louis Missouri.** [True]

*Our Story of Eagle Woman, Sacagawea*

It is true, some years afterward, from time to time, an old Frenchman by the name of Charbonneau came here and interpreted for the Mandans. I think I have told you the reason why my people did not know very much about *Sacajawea,* the Bird Woman. I repeat, that she was not a member of our tribe and she was not a captive of our tribe and she did not stay here long and our people did not realize that she had taken an important part in the expedition and therefore we did not include her in the milepost of our history. This is all I can tell you.

This statement was made to me by Chief Wolf Chief, in answer to my question.

(Two interpreters present.)      (Sgd.) ***Charles A. Eastman***
U.S. Inspector.

**Wolf Chief's interview by Eastman in 1925 contrasts with what he told Alfred Bowers in 1933 when he gave quite a bit of information regarding *Sacagawea*. There was also the story that those Eastman interviewed did not trust him because he was Sioux. Wolf Chief seemed to relay that he was only then hearing about her story from Eastman, reiterating the information and refuting any version of the story. Further, Eastman called her *Sacajawea*, which Wolf Chief may been protesting. Wolf Chief did say that the Crows had more to do with the Shoshones than the Hidatsas did.**

**Poor Wolf (Lean Wolf)** "was born in 1820 at Knife River. He died in 1899. His daughter, Rattling Medicine or White Duck, was an informant for Alfred Bowers." From "Three Affiliated Tribes Cultural Page, Tribal Chiefs of the Mandan, Hidatsa and Arikara," *MHA Times*, January 14, 1997. Poor Wolf gave accounts of the Hidatsa people trading in the Ft. Buford area. Following is a statement supposedly from a daughter of his regarding the Bulls Eye story.

*Early 1900s*

Statement of Mrs. Weidemann.
Elbowoods, N. D.
**The daughter of hereditary Chief Poor Wolf**
of the Hidatsas Indians, (She speaks Gros Ventre,
Sioux and English)
February 3, 1925.

I am 80 years old. I am a member of this Tribe and I lived here most of my life. My father is Poor Wolf, the Hereditary Chief of the Gros Ventres [Hidatsas]. He died 26 years ago at the age of 102. He was born about 1797. I am one of his younger daughters.

He is a Tribal Historian. I will repeat to you his account of Lewis and Clark Expedition, and the Indian woman who guided them, namely, *Sacajawea,* or the Bird Woman. I wish to say that my father was of very clear mind up to his death. "When I was about 8 or 9 years old Lewis and Clark with about 50 soldiers came to our village near the mouth of Knife River on the Missouri River They remained with us one winter. In the spring they went on North in boats and came back again at our village nearly a year afterwards. They stopped for a little while at our village and when they went away they took the Mandan Chief with them. The Chief's name was Sheheka [Sheheke].

While these white men stopped with us during that winter there was a Frenchman who had come down from North with two Shoshoni wives, was employed by them. These two Shoshoni women were very young, one being 16 years old and the other about 18. One was called the "Bird woman" or *Sacajawea,* the other was "Otter Woman." This Frenchman had married these two girls somewhere up North among the Crow Nation; who they were we knew very little about them.

When Lewis and Clark proceeded up North on their journey they took *Sacajawea* and her French husband with them, and left the other Shoshoni woman at our village, she being not well.

## Our Story of Eagle Woman, Sacagawea

When Lewis and Clark returned from their trip to our place this Frenchman and his wife, *Sacajawea,* came with them, but they did not go down the river with them when the white men went down. A year or so after this there were some fur traders who came down from up the river and stopped for a few days at our village, who took the Frenchman (Charbonneau) and his two Shoshoni wives, namely, *Sacajawea* and Otter Woman with them. We never knew what became of these Shoshoni women thereafter.

[Mrs. Weidemann said,] These were the words of my father, Poor Wolf.

My father further stated in his later days, that he heard one of these Shoshoni Women, namely, *Sacajawea,* "the Bird Woman" succeeded in returning to her tribe, the Shoshoni people in Wyoming and lived to be a great old age – died at Fort Washakie, Wyoming.

He further states, and I, too, heard when I was a little girl of somewhere about 13 or 14 years old, there was a woman among the wives of the Frenchmen and employees of the Missouri Fur company, came up from St. Louis and stopped at a Fort down below here and remained for a short period. Among these women one was called "Bird woman" or *(Sacajawea)*. She went up the river with the rest. It was told around here that she was the Shoshoni woman and wife of Charbonneau, guide of Lewis and Clark, but this woman was then gray-headed and that other woman was only a young girl, so that we are not sure it was the same woman.

Some of our people say she was the same woman, others say she was not. That's all we knew of the Shoshoni guide of Lewis and Clark.

You asked me also about the Tradition of Eagle, the mother of Bull-Eyes. I will first say that Eagle was a member of this tribe, also she has Crow blood. She has relatives among the Crow people. She and her daughter Otter were killed by a Sioux war party near Glasgow, Montana, in 1869. She was formerly the wife of the Frenchman (Charbonneau) who married the two Shoshoni girls and guided the Lewis and Clark expedition. She had three children from him, one boy and two girls and their names are, Cherry-Necklace [Jean Baptiste according to Bull's Eye],

Otter and Pretty-Breast. Cherry-Necklace was killed in war with the Sioux, and Otter, as I said before, was killed by the Sioux war party with her mother, and Pretty-Breast died here on this reservation 30 years ago. (1895).

Bull-Eyes claims now that his grandmother was the woman who guided Lewis and Clark, but it is not true. He has made a mistake or got confused with a wonderful trip that his mother had with Charbonneau, her husband. Charbonneau had married Eagle, who was to be a very pretty Gros Ventres girl.

My father said when he was about 21 or 22 (about 1820). Charbonneau married Eagle and a year or so after that he took her down the Missouri River with some fur traders and she was gone for quite a number of years, and she returned to her tribe, strange to say, from up the river. My father was then about 32 or 35 years old. What I am telling you now about Eagle is what my father has in his History of the Tribe. Now let me tell you the story that Eagle told herself of her trip, which she gave to my father when she came back, and my father had repeated so many times to our tribe and our family that I still remember the substance of it.

It is as follows: I will speak it as if Eagle is speaking. "When Charbonneau took me down the river among the white people we came to a great town called St. Louis.

We stayed there a year or so when Charbonneau found one of his Shoshoni wives, the "Bird Woman" *Sacajawea*, in a little town above St. Louis, called Portage (Portage des Sioux, Missouri). This woman had two sons with her one was about 16 and the other 15. The older one was called Bazile, the other Baptiste. They were bright young men and talked French quite well.

The Shoshoni woman, herself, talked French too. After a while Charbonneau wanted to take his wife back and I consented, then we lived together for a little while at St. Louis, when Charbonneau was employed by the Fur company and we were sent southwest on a big river, almost as big as the Missouri River.

## Our Story of Eagle Woman, Sacagawea

On this trip we came to a great many trading posts and we stayed at one place for a year, and we stopped another place two years. We came among many Indian tribes that I never heard of, some were called Wichita, some were called Comanchee, and Utes, and other tribes who came to trade at these posts where we were. After while Charbonneau, my husband, took another wife, a pretty Ute woman. I did not complain but Bird Woman made serious complaint and made it unpleasant for the Ute Woman. Finally Charbonneau punished her severely and in a day or so afterwards she disappeared.

At this time her two boys were away on a trip to other bands of Indians, as many of our men had to take these trips to various camps of Indians to get the furs. When the boys came back they made it very serious for Charbonneau and they were not friends after that.

The following summer the Fur Companies organized a large body of their employees with many packed mules to visit the mountain Indians towards the northwest and Charbonneau and I and the Ute woman joined the party. We traveled a long while until we reached a great Lake, the whites called it Salt Lake. Many of our men were trapping for beaver along the streams of the mountains and buying furs from the Indians. Some of the men were sent down a river to carry away the furs, but most of them remained with us and in the summer we moved Northeast, over the mountains, but before we moved, some Utes visited our winter quarters who were related to Charbonneau's Ute wife.

When we were moving Charbonneau's Ute wife wouldn't go, but she went home with her relatives. We never saw her again after that. We moved north and east slowly until we reached Wind River, and down the Big Horn until we came into the Yellowstone River; the men made boats and put all the furs in them and we floated down to the Missouri River; from there we reached home at the Gros Ventres village."

This was the story of Eagle's wonderful trip. Bull-Eye's mistaken this for the Lewis and Clark trip, therefore, he claims that his mother was the guide on the Lewis and Clark Expedition, which is not true. This is all I can remember.

*Early 1900s*

This statement was made to me in the Sioux language, although Mrs. Weidemann could have given it to me in Gros Ventres or English, just as well. It was given in presence Mr. H. and Mr. Eagle.

(Sgd.) Charles A. Eastman

The Weidemann account provides contradictory information to the Bulls Eye story in regard to when Eagle (Woman) married Charbonneau and states that she did not accompany the Lewis and Clark expedition.

The information was to have come from Mrs. Weidemann's father, Poor Wolf. However, the interview of Mrs. Weidemann gave the wrong dates for Poor Wolf's birth saying he was born in 1797 and was eight or nine when Lewis and Clark came. Poor Wolf was born in 1820. It also indicated that she was one of his younger daughters, yet it is known that Poor Wolf had daughters who were in their 50s at the time, and Mrs. Weidemann said she was 80 (She was 74). Further, records do not indicate that Mrs. Weidemann was Poor Wolf's daughter. They may have been related. Mrs. Weidemann stated that Charbonneau married Eagle Woman when Poor Wolf was about 21 years old in 1820. Again, Poor Wolf was born in 1820.

The trip she said she was retelling from Eagle Woman, however, actually did take place in 1815.

Because of many inconsistencies, Mrs. Weidemann's testimony is suspect. Mrs. Weidemann's statement included that her father had told her version of the story to many. Evidence of this was not found.

Some of Mrs. Weidemann's story was most likely contrived to support the Wyoming story. She, an Indian woman, was the wife of Henry Weidemann who was a blacksmith at Ft. Berthold and also had a trading post along Sand Creek near Fort Buford.

*Our Story of Eagle Woman, Sacagawea*

She was the sister of Bear's Arm who told researcher, Martha Beckwith, that *Sacagawea* was Cherry Necklace's sister and that she accompanied the Lewis and Clark expedition. Bear's Arm also gave Alfred Bowers a family tree for *Sacagawea* that included Bulls Eye's family.

Eastman's other interviews were also suspect. Wolf Chief's interview by Eastman differs from what he told Bowers about *Sacagawea*. The accounts taken by Eastman each contain some of the same information, even the very same wording which also makes them suspect.

Charles Eastman's work regarding the *Sacagawea (Sacajawea)* story has been widely discredited. The interviews gathered by Charles Eastman, however, were used to discount the Bull's Eye story and to strengthen the Wyoming story.

**Foolish Bear**, Hidatsa, was one of the respected tribal elders who retrieved the Water Buster Bundle in 1938 from a New York Museum. Foolish Bear accompanied Bulls Eye to see Major Welch in 1928 before Bulls Eye died and a couple of years after Charles' Eastman reported his support for the Wyoming story to the Commissioner of Indian Affairs.

In a continued effort to dissuade Grace Hebard, the author of the Wyoming story, Major Welch wrote to Hebard in a letter of April 21, 1928:

I have [had] other conversations with Bulls Eye relative to the subject. He says

*Foolish Bear*
— MHA Interpretive Center

*Early 1900s*

that the place of her death was at a 'one winter trader's store' (Temporary establishment where some trader came every spring or even wintered) on the north or left bank of the Missouri, some 'two or three days' west of old Fort Union. Bulls Eye came down last summer in company with Foolish Bear, a Hidatsa, and asked me to go with them to her grave, near that trading fort site. Foolish Bear remembers the place well he says, and when Bulls Eye was nine years of age [1873], took him to see her grave. She was buried in a shallow excavation, slim poles across it lengthwise, and a little earth over the poles. When he saw it, he could see some parts of a buffalo blanket, and 'tall grass grew there.'

Foolish Bear was an Hidatsa scout for the trader, and while at that post, the Sioux destroyed a pack train of goods from Ft. Union. Bulls Eye remembers that. Then the packers returned to Ft. Union and came again, but with a stronger guard and won through with the trade goods to this one winter trade store.

So it is probable that the place was operated by one of the AFC [American Fur Company] men from Union. Bulls Eye was at the place again when he was 17 years old, and 'stood there and sung a song.'

There is no doubt but that he believes the spot to be the grave of his grandmother. This was since the visit of Eastman to me here.

**Reports indicate disagreement about where *Sacagawea* was buried. Fort Union and Fort Buford were next to one another, one a trading fort and the other a military fort. Foolish Bear reported that a guard from Ft. Union helped to get goods to the trader at Wolf Point (where *Sacagawea* died), so that there was regular interaction between the two places, although this incident occurred after Ft. Union was closed in 1867.**

**Further, Poor Wolf, Lean Wolf, told an army lieutenant in early 1870 about how attacks would happen on the road west of Fort Buford along the Missouri River and how the army would recover bodies. *Sacagawea* family members, and others, believe her body was taken to Fort Buford and she was buried there.**

**Statements from Ft. Berthold informants provide evidence supporting the Bulls Eye *Sacagawea* story. The interviews of Charles Eastman, used to discredit the Ft. Berthold *Sacagawea* story and help promote the Wyoming story, are highly suspect.**

**Major Welch continued to promote the Bulls Eye story, but politics and people of higher authority prevailed. In the chapter following is information on the three competing stories of *Sacagawea*: the Wyoming story, the Ft. Manuel story, and the Bulls Eye story.**

*Poor Wolf or Lean Wolf*
— State Historical Society of North Dakota

### Sources Authored or Provided by MHA Tribal Members:

Lean Wolf, Poor Wolf. Account told to army lieutenant at Ft. Buford in early 1870.

MHA Nation. Individual History Card for Mrs. Weidemann.

*MHA Times.* "Three Affiliated Tribes Cultural Page, Tribal Chiefs of the Mandan, Hidatsa and Arikara," January 14, 1997.

Wilson, Gilbert. Buffalo Bird Woman. Buffalo Bird Woman's Garden: Agriculture of the Hidatsa Indians. With a new introduction by Jeffrey R. Hanson. St. Paul: Minnesota Historical Society Press, 1987.

Wolf Chief. Personal Interview conducted by Alfred W. Bowers in February-March, 1933, at Independence on the Ft. Berthold Indian Reservation.

*Fort Manuel, Dakota Territory, 1812.*     — W.O. Bassford

# Chapter 6
### *THREE STORIES*
*Wyoming, Ft. Manuel, Bulls Eye*

Sacagawea became a national heroine and symbol for the women's suffrage movement in the early 1900s. Women's groups and states who claimed her competed to show her honor. Conflicting stories of *Sacagawea,* based on parts and interpretations of the Lewis and Clark Journals, had emerged at the time Bulls Eye told his story.

    Dr. Charles Eastman, Santee Sioux and the physician at the Pine Ridge Reservation at the time of the Wounded Knee massacre, had become an investigator for the Commissioner of Indian Affairs Office in Washington, DC. Charles Burke, Commissioner, wrote to Eastman in December of 1924, in the Eastman, Shoshone files:

## Our Story of Eagle Woman, Sacagawea

The enclosed file indicates that Congress proposes honoring this woman [*Sacagawea*], but there is some controversy as to where the body is buried... We desire this investigation made and concluded at the earliest practicable date...if action is to be taken the report must be transmitted to the Senate Committee at an early date...it will be necessary... that your conclusions be substantiated by the facts.

Commissioner Burke listed burial sites as Wind River Agency in Wyoming, Fort Manuel in North Dakota, and an unspecified location in North Dakota from the Bulls Eye story.

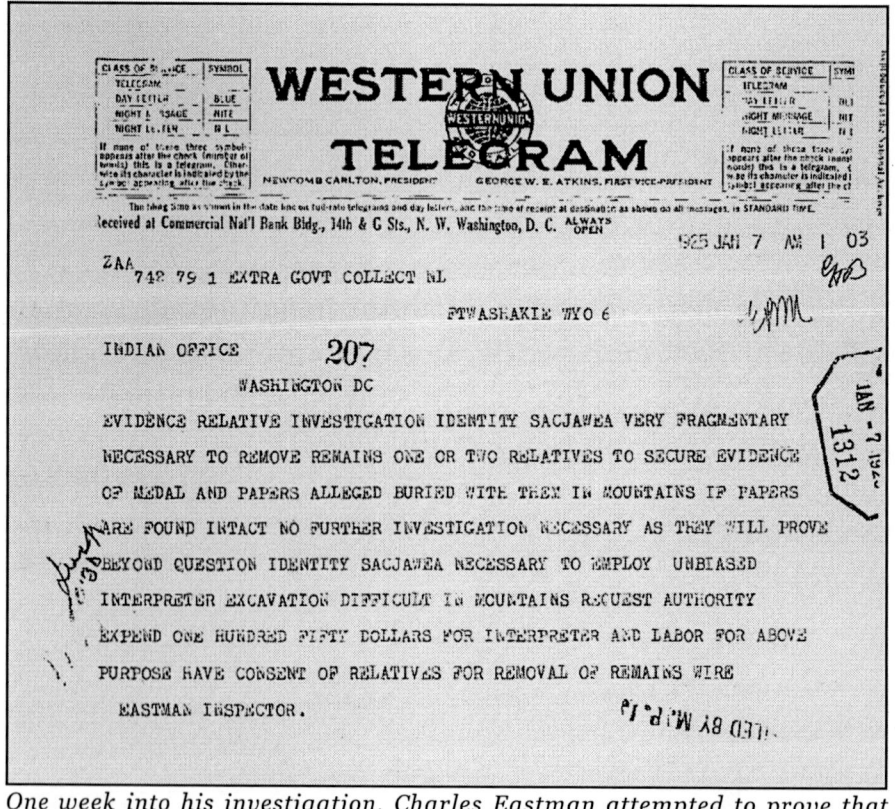

*One week into his investigation, Charles Eastman attempted to prove that Sacagawea was Shoshone from Wyoming by producing a Jefferson medal from a grave. The action was questionable and failed.* — National Archives.

## The Wyoming Story

Eastman submitted his report on March 2, 1925. The first and last statements follow:

> In pursuance of your instructions of December 13, 1924, relative to investigation and locating the final burial place of *Sacajawea* or Bird Woman, I entered upon the investigation by the first of January, 1925...I report that *Sacajawea* after sixty years of wandering from her own tribe returns to her people at Fort Bridger and lived the remainder of her life with her sons in peace until she died on April 9, 1884, at Fort Washakie, Wyoming. That is her final resting place.

Eastman, from a two-month investigation, embraced the story provided by Grace R. Hebard, a Wyoming historian and suffragist, according to R. K. Jager in *Malinche, Pocahontas, and Sacagawea*, 2015. Hebard's 30 years of research resulted in a book, *Sacajawea*, 1933. Critics questioned her research and story. She claimed *"Sacajawea"* was Shoshone and was a wanderer who had left Charbonneau and traveled around the country, getting free rides on stagecoaches because of her service to Lewis and Clark. Hebard had found a grave in a Shoshone cemetery belonging to a woman named Porivo whom she believed to be *Sacajawea*. Porivo was known to counsel her tribesmen to take on the ways of the white man, had been married to a Frenchman, and had a son named Baptiste just as the Journals stated. She also had a son named Bazile.

According to documents in the *Sacajawea* File, American Heritage Center at the University of Wyoming, several Shoshone tribal members told Eastman that they had never heard from Porivo that she had been a captive of the Gros Ventres (Hidatsa), that she had gone to the Big Water, that she guided any white people anywhere, or even that her name was *Sacajawea*.

*Cemetery at Fort Washakie, Wind River Reservation, Wyoming, with three graves attributed as those of "Sacajawea," center; her son Baptiste, left; and a second, purported son, "Bazil," at right, ca. 1933.* — MHA Interpretive Center.

Critics stated that Hebard relied upon unsubstantiated oral histories from Native Americans, and her assistant, Blanche Schroer, left papers indicating that she (Hebard) gave the Indian people bags of groceries in exchange for their signing affidavits stating that *Sacajawea (Sacagawea)* was Shoshone.

In Eastman's report to the Commissioner of Indian Affairs, he stated, "What evidence Dr. Hebard gathered came from very competent people, both intelligent and strong men." She had relied mainly upon statements made by prominent white men who had lived among the Shoshones and knew Porivo. Eastman was also heavily influenced by politicians who saw monetary benefits.

Eastman concluded that Charbonneau had two Snake (Shoshone) wives, Porivo *(Sacajawea)* and Otter Woman, and later, in 1820, married Eagle [Woman], Hidatsa. He stated that Otter Woman must have been Charbonneau's favorite wife because Eagle and Charbonneau named their first child after her. Eastman stated that this daughter, Otter Woman, was the mother of Bulls Eye [true]. He claimed that it was Otter Woman, wife of Charbonneau, who died at Ft. Manuel.

Evidence from Ft. Berthold indicates that **Charbonneau had two Hidatsa/Crow wives** whom he must have put forth as Shoshone in order to get the job with the Expedition.

The girls were **sisters, *Sacagawea* (Eagle Woman, Bird Woman) and Otter Woman**. They were familiar with the Shoshone people, language, and place because their father had an adopted brother among the Shoshones, their families interacted back and forth, and Charbonneau and *Sacagawea* had traveled through Shoshone country the year before the expedition.

According to those at Ft. Berthold, ***Sacagawea* and Charbonneau's daughter, Otter Woman, was named after Charbonneau's older wife who was *Sacagawea*'s sister. Otter Woman, the daughter, was the mother of Bulls Eye as Eastman stated.**

*A close view of the tombstone dedicated to Baptiste (NOT Jean Baptiste) Charbonneau, in the Fort Washakie cemetery, Wyoming. The year and place of this man's death, and his burial, are entirely wrong for the historical individual, Jean Baptiste Charbonneau, son of Sacagawea. Further, Sacagawea never had a son named "Bazil, or Bazile." Two wrong sons, proves their mother cannot have been the woman who accompanied Lewis and Clark.* — Phil Konstantin

**It was most likely Otter Woman (*Sacagawea*'s sister) and the older wife of Charbonneau who died at Ft. Manuel as Eastman believed.** There appears to be no mention of that Otter Woman after that time.

**Eastman based his conclusions on statements including those of Bulls Eye, Wolf Chief and Mrs. Weidemann of Ft. Berthold. It has already been noted that the statements of Bulls Eye and Wolf Chief for Eastman were suspect as they were different from statements they gave at other times, and misinformation about her and Poor Wolf was noted in Mrs. Weidemann's statement.**

Major Welch, in his papers, wrote that he had met with Eastman to personally tell him the Bulls Eye story when he visited Ft. Berthold during his investigation. Welch stated that he thought Eastman would recognize true Indian oral history, but instead it made Eastman doubt it. Welch had offered to accompany Eastman to interview people at Ft. Berthold, but he chose to go alone. Welch said, "Eastman being a Sioux, he got absolutely nothing from them." Their tribes were traditional enemies.

Will Robinson, of the South Dakota State Historical Society, wrote a letter dated January 18, 1955, to Blanche Schroer, assistant to Grace Hebard of the Wyoming story. It stated that Elaine Goodale Eastman, Charles' wife, had accepted the fact that the quality of the work he had performed in his investigation was "misinterpreted evidence."

**The "grave of *Sacajawea*" at Wind River is still visited by tourists. *Sacagawea*'s son, Jean Baptiste, is supposed to be buried there also, next to his mother, although it is well known that he is buried in Danner, Oregon. Many books, especially for children, have told the Wyoming story. It is generally believed, today, that Hebard promoted a case of mistaken identity.**

## The Fort Manuel Story

Critics of Grace Hebard and her Wyoming story, and the work of Charles Eastman, protested his conclusion.

These critics included Doane Robinson of the South Dakota State Historical Society, who shows in his papers, that they had become aware of an entry in the diary of Henry Breckenridge who was from Missouri. Breckenridge had traveled up the Missouri River in 1811 to Fort Manuel [Lisa] on the same boat as Charbonneau and *Sacagawea* who were returning from having been in St. Louis where they had left their son, Jean Baptiste, with William Clark. Charbonneau was headed to work at Ft. Manuel, a newly founded trading post on the west bank of the Missouri, 70 miles south of present Bismarck, North Dakota. The diary reads that on the boat were:

> A Frenchman named Charbonneau with his wife, an Indian woman of the Snake nation… Both of [them] accompanied Lewis and Clark to the Pacific and were of great service…The woman, a good creature of a mild and gentle disposition, [was] greatly attached to the whites, whose manners and dress she tries to imitate….[The woman] had become sickly and longed to revisit her native country.

In addition, in 1920, something written by the chief clerk at Fort Manuel Lisa was discovered. John Luttig had written for December 20, 1812: "This evening the wife of Charbonneau, a Snake [woman], died of a putrid fever. She was a good woman and the best of the fort."

Doane Robinson, of the South Dakota State Historical Society, stated that "the presumption is absolute that one and the same woman is mentioned in them (the two writings), and that woman is *Sakaka-wea*, the guide to Lewis and Clark."

Robinson, as well as other researchers, including those from other states that claimed *Sacagawea*, became involved in the quest to discredit the Wyoming story in favor of the Ft. Manuel story. Robinson especially criticized the information that Eastman had gathered from Fort Berthold.

Reviewing them now, it appears that there was much to be critical of in the Fort Berthold interviews that Eastman reported because they seem to have been doctored or misinterpreted to support the Wyoming story. Robinson, however, discounted all of the information from Fort Berthold, including Bulls Eye's story. Robinson stated:

> The material which Dr. Eastman gathered on the Missouri has not the least value of any sort....without written record...You might as well undertake to tell what your great-grandmother served for refreshments when she entertained the Guild in 1789...this matter has been entirely dormant among the Missouri river Indians for more than a century and not until 1920 has any question been raised about it...It goes to show how worthless and how contradictory traditions are...Judging from my own experiences, I believe I could go to the Mandan and Hidatsa and Gros Ventre and interviewing each adult separately get a different and contradictory 'tradition' of *Sakakawea* from each one of them.
>
> Indians are entirely human. Some are honest and some are dishonest, some are intelligent and others lack in intelligence; some have good memories and others are very deficient in that regard. They have their traditions, most of which have some foundation in fact, but in many years of almost constant trafficking in such things, I have never found one Indian tradition that was not disputed in its most material features by indisputable written records of the events.

Representatives from other states wrote to Charles M. Burke, the Commissioner of Indian Affairs, to support Robinson. Robinson's counterpart in North Dakota, Lewis Crawford, stated in regard to the Bulls Eye story, "The evidence.... is superficial and is based in part at least upon .... family pride rather than on historical data."

## Wyoming, Ft. Manuel, Bulls Eye

But not all were totally convinced. In a letter to a Mr. E. C. Jacobsen of Halliday, North Dakota, Russell Reid, of the State Historical Society of North Dakota and author of *Sakakawea, the Bird Woman,* 1933, states, "I have finished the book 'Sakakawea.' It is an interesting book and on the whole well done but I do not believe it has entirely disposed of the supposed burial place of *Sakakawea* at Fort Manuel."

In 1955, in a review of William Clark's personal papers covering 1825-1828, there was found a notation beside *Sacagawea*'s name on a list of members of the expedition. The notation read, "dead." This became further proof to those who supported Robinson and the story that she had died in 1812 at Ft. Manuel.

The proponents of the Wyoming story and of the Ft. Manuel story communicated back and forth, and with Washington, DC, in regard to who it was who died at Ft. Manuel. The Ft. Manuel camp, of course, believed it was *Sacagawea*. The Wyoming story people believed it was the "other Shoshone wife of Charbonneau, Otter Woman."

**Breckenridge had not named the woman on the boat with Charbonneau except to say she was Charbonneau's Snake wife. Luttig, also, had not named the woman who died in 1812 except to say that she was the wife of Charbonneau. This lack of specificity in naming the woman was also one of the arguments Eastman made against the Ft. Manuel story.**

In Major Welch's papers, he listed probable sightings of *Sacagawea* by non-Indians after 1812. One instance was that in the summer of 1825, General Henry Atkinson traveled up the Missouri River to negotiate treaties of trade with tribes along the way.

At the lower Mandan village, he signed a treaty with the Mandan and Hidatsa called the Atkinson-O'Fallon Treaty. One of the chiefs who signed for the Hidatsa was Smoked Lodge or Black Lodge, *Sacagawea*'s father. Atkinson noted in his diary, held at the Missouri Historical Society, that "Shabono" and his wife [*Sacagawea*] were there.

Toussaint Charbonneau is listed as the official interpreter at the treaty proceedings for the Mandan and Hidatsa tribes.

Also, on October 22, 1834, F.A. Chardon who was the Factor or manager in charge of Fort Clark, next to the large Mandan village of *Mih-tutta hang-kush* at the mouth of Knife River, wrote in *Chardon's Journal at Fort Clark, 1834-1839*. Pierre, S.D.: South Dakota Historical Society, 1932, "Charbonneau and his Lady started for the Gros Ventres for a visit (or to tell the truth) in quest of one of his runaway wives—for I must inform you he has two lovely ones —Poor old man." Toussaint Charbonneau was then 75 years of age.

One of the informants for Charles Eastman, as he performed an investigation for the government to determine where the real *Sacagawea* was buried, was Mrs. Weidemann at Ft. Berthold. The testimony she gave was suspect for several reasons and supported Eastman's claim that the Wyoming woman, Porivo, was *Sacagawea* or *Sacajawea,* Shoshone. There was, however, a part of Mrs. Weidemann's account that was very true according to fur trade history. It also matched [came from?] Bulls Eye's description of a two-year trip that *Sacagawea* and Charbonneau had made to the southwestern United States in 1816-17, although Bulls Eye mistakenly thought it had occurred the year before the expedition.

Mrs. Weidemann stated that Eagle Woman *(Sacagawea)* told that she and Charbonneau had gone down river to St. Louis, probably to check on their son, Jean Baptiste. While there, Charbonneau was hired by a fur-trading company, and they were sent with a large group of traders and trappers far into the Southwest, along a river nearly as big as the Missouri (Arkansas River). While there, she saw many tribes of strange Indians, some named "Wichita" and "Comanchee." She saw very beautiful woven blankets and collected beautiful seashells.

They wintered in that country, and the next year the trappers moved northwest along the Rocky Mountains until some of them were sent back to the east along another river with some of their horses.

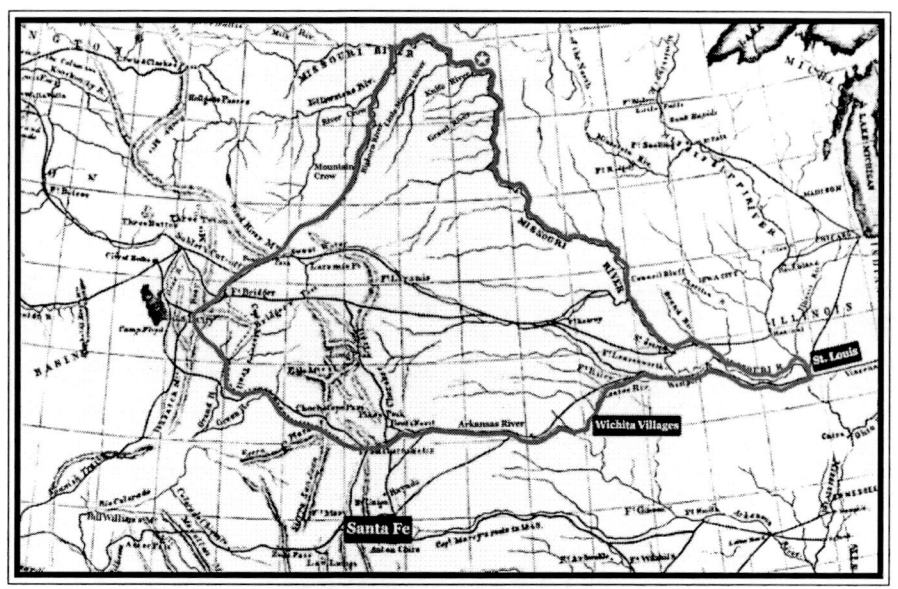

*The Travels of Charbonneau and Sacagawea, 1815-1817.*
*The "star" marks the beginning and end point of their journey.*

**Sacagawea**, with Charbonneau and some of the other trappers, continued north across Wyoming until they struck the Bighorn River, which they followed down to the Yellowstone, thence to the Missouri and back "from Upriver" to the Hidatsa villages on Knife River.

Compare all of that to a completely separate account based only on documents of the fur trade on file at Saint Louis and Washington, D.C.:

"In 1815, A.P. Chouteau and Jules DeMun led a party of traders to the then American-Mexican border area along the upper Arkansas River. In February 1816, DeMun went back to Saint Louis for supplies and men. [Toussaint] Charbonneau was one of the engagees hired at $200 for the year. DeMun's new party left Saint Louis on 15 June and reached the Kansas River on 11 July, where they were to rendezvous with Chouteau. Delayed by a fight with Pawnees, Chouteau did not arrive until 10 August, when the partners put together their outfit of forty-five men and set out again for the upper Arkansas.

## Our Story of Eagle Woman, Sacagawea

There, they traded with the Indian [tribes], trapped beaver, and got into trouble with Spanish officials in Santa Fe. In the spring of 1817, shortly after seventeen men had been sent down the Platte River with the worst of the party's horses, the rest of the traders were arrested, taken to Santa Fe, and imprisoned. After their goods were confiscated, the men were released and ordered never to return. They arrived at Saint Louis on 7 September. While Charbonneau could have been one of those arrested, it is more likely that he was one of the seventeen who went down the Platte. His disposition of the case [when he was paid $400 for two years' work], signed with an X, mentions nothing of the arrest and was taken in December, while the dispositions of those mentioning the arrest were taken in September. Whichever party he was with, he was definitely in Saint Louis in December [1817]." From Dennis R. Ottoson, "Toussaint Charbonneau, A Most Durable Man," South Dakota History 6, Spring, 1976.

Note that the geography described by Eagle Woman coincides exactly with the route of the Chouteau-DeMun trading party: from Saint Louis, west along the Arkansas River to the vicinity of Santa Fe, thence north along the Rocky Mountain front to the Platte River. The North Platte River heads in southern Wyoming, and it was there that *Sacagawea* said the party separated, with some going east with horses, while she continued with others north across Wyoming to the Bighorn River, thence home.

It is not possible that Bulls Eye or Mrs Weidemann could have concocted a tale of events that **actually happened** in 1816-1817. Only Eagle Woman could have been the source of this information. Historians have not recognized the importance of this information. Anyone who might have searched the fur trade records for references to *"Sacagawea"* would have been disappointed. August Chouteau and Jules DeMun weren't paying her. So there was no "contract" with her name on it and no need to mention her at all.

This provides irrefutable proof that the wife of Charbonneau who died at Fort Manuel in December, 1812, could NOT have been *Sacagawea*, who was still alive, and with the Chouteau party in 1816-1817.

**It was Otter Woman who died at Ft. Manuel. She was the first wife of Charbonneau and *Sacagawea's* older sister. The people at Ft. Berthold knew it was not *Sacagawea* who died there, for they knew she lived to be 82 years old.** Captain Clark took formal custody of Otter Woman's children, Lisette (1) and Toussaint (10 in 1813), along with *Sacagawea's* son, Jean Baptiste, according to an account by Charles Russell found in Major Welch's notes. *Sacagawea* and Charbonneau had allowed Clark to keep Jean Baptiste so he could attend school in St. Louis. *Sacagawea* probably felt that it would be good for her niece and nephew to also be raised in St. Louis.

**Alfred Bowers, who did extensive research on the people of the Ft. Berthold Reservation, stated in a letter dated October 13, 1975, "One thing we can be sure of, Bird Woman was not the one reported as dying at Fort Manuel Lisa near the North/South Dakota border."**

**In terms of the historical record in America, however, it appears that the Ft. Manuel story won. There is a monument to *Sacagawea* near Mobridge, South Dakota, in that regard. But the full story of *Sacagawea* of the MHA Nation was not yet totally revealed.**

### The Bulls Eye Story
**There are many reasons why the Bulls Eye story was never given credibility by outsiders.**

### Misinterpretation
Misinterpretation of people, places and events because of language or ignorance resulted in misinformation. The use of so many different languages among those involved in the expedition absolutely resulted in misinformation being recorded in the journals.

It was also a fact that Toussaint Charbonneau was neither a reliable nor understandable interpreter. Washington Matthews reported in *Ethnography and Philology of the Hidatsa Indians*, 1877, that although Charbonneau had been living among the Hidatsas for 37 years, at the time being described, he could still not pronounce their language correctly. Hidatsa is a difficult language, like Japanese, that relies on tone for meaning. Rene Jessaume, the other French speaker who interpreted from Charbonneau to Lewis and Clark in English, was not a reliable interpreter, either.

The journals were edited by different people. These editors approached this task with their own world views. After the expedition, Nicholas Biddle of Philadelphia was hired by William Clark to compile and edit his and Lewis' notes.

Biddle did not know the West or Indian people. For example, the interpretation that *Sacagawea* found her Shoshone brother when the party reached their camp is used to further establish her heritage as being of that tribe. Biddle had no knowledge of tribal ways such as the adoption of *Cameahwait*, the Shoshone chief, by *Sacagawea's* father, thus making *Cameahwait* a "brother." Alfred Bowers, in *Hidatsa Social and Ceremonial Organization*, explains in detail that Hidatsa men of distinction adopted sons and brothers from other tribes for intergroup visiting and trading. Bulls Eye told of this relationship and that *Sacagawea* had visited her Shoshone brother and relatives a year before the expedition.

**Biddle spelled her name "*Sacajawea*," adding the "j," which gave her a Shoshone name, supported the Shoshone story, and then set off a whole story line of its own. Using the j enabled researchers to state that her name in Shoshone meant Boat Launcher. Researchers have dwelled heavily on trying to figure out the correct spelling of her name and its basis.**

## Lies

Charbonneau was known to be "of no particular merit." His actions on the expedition were often noted as not acceptable, and he has been described as being of questionable character and lazy.

It is no surprise that he would have lied and said that *Sacagawea* was Shoshone or at least let a half-truth (to white people) stand in order to get a job. (*Sacagawea* was considered a family member of the Shoshone family whose father had been adopted as a brother by her father, Smoked Lodge. She may not have seen this as a lie.) It appears that Charbonneau continued his lies throughout the trip and beyond. Because of the inconsistencies between what the informants whom Charles Eastman interviewed at Ft. Berthold stated and what they had told others, chances are that the statements taken by Eastman were adapted by him and/or the informants intentionally gave false information, another example of untruths.

## Speculation

When the journals were edited and authors took over, there came a barrage of speculation to make the story better or to make it suit a certain group. For example, James Hosmer, in *History of the Expedition Under Captains Lewis and Clark, 1804-1806*, added to the journals that *Sacagawea* gestured with her fingers in her mouth when meeting with the Shoshones, using the language sign to show they were relatives. He added that she threw a blanket over the heads of herself and *Cameahwait* when they first met, so they could speak in private. Hosmer also added that the Shoshone family of *Sacagawea* had nearly all died. This was used to explain why she did not stay with them but rather returned to the Mandan and Hidatsa villages. *Sacagawea*'s story is full of such speculation.

## Politics

When Charles Eastman did his investigation and report regarding the identity and place of burial of *Sacagawea*, it was influenced by political pressure from formal women's groups and politicians—local, state and national.

These groups were using *Sacagawea*'s story to win politically. Charles Eastman listened to those who had the most influence.

When Eastman submitted his report, the powerful among the historians and the politicians in various states attacked, again in the quest to "win," not because they had so much respect for *Sacagawea* or the Indian people. The powerful in North Dakota, at the time, did not provide the necessary support for the Ft. Berthold story.

Further, and most important, Indian people have never had political clout in this country. It remains to be seen if this document sways any thinking. It will, however, preserve our story for future generations.

### Perpetuation of Myths

The experiences of *Sacagawea* as a member of the Lewis and Clark expedition have been remembered with more statues of her than of any other woman in American history, and there have been movies, television shows, and works of art that attempted to dramatize her as a symbol of women's achievements. The popular stories of *Sacagawea* fill the needs of many in this country, socially, emotionally and economically. It is hard to stop myths that have become so ingrained and believed because of their being told over and over and also because they have been so *useful* to many.

When Chairwoman, Rose Crow Flies High of the Three Affiliated Tribes, requested that the story of *Sacagawea* be revised to tell the Ft. Berthold version, she was told by "Washington" that it would be too costly to change the story.

### Discounting Oral History

The academic establishment in this country has been slow to recognize the value of oral history.

Doane Robinson, of the South Dakota Historical Society at the time of the Eastman report, emphatically stated, "I do protest against the Indian Bureau arbitrarily going upon record in support of a theory sustained only by tradition and in opposition to [written] records of the highest authenticity."

Only recently have Native people started to assert themselves in requiring that their oral history be recognized. The family of Crazy Horse has told his story in *Crazy Horse, the Lakota Warrior's Life and Legacy*, 2016. An article on Lakota storytelling in *Indian Country Today*, August 4, 2004, stated, "A lot of people assume that the only information about Indians that is reliable is the documented information, and they say that memory is unreliable, but that's not true. In any Native culture, anywhere, there are stories that white historians have never heard…"

The Pueblo people stated in the *Albuquerque Journal*, December 28, 2018: "Today we honor our elders. We are deeply indebted for much that is known today, for the elders preserve the oral history of the People. As Pueblo people, we must secure our inherent rights to speak the truth, without fear of intimidation and retaliation. It is time to speak the truth, and de-colonize our Pueblo minds."

A group of young academics meet each year at Salish-Kootenai College, a tribal college in Montana, to discuss the need for Native ways of telling our stories. They protest the requirements for academic research and writing at colleges and universities.

## A Complex Story

The Bulls Eye story is complex. Even Major Welch, who strongly promoted the story, got it wrong at times. For example, when providing more evidence that he had gathered from Sweet Grass Woman, mother of interpreter Packineau, he stated on March 7, 1930, "No, Otter Woman did not die in S. D. in 1812, I am positive of that… [Sweet Grass Woman] remembers Otter Woman well and said that she died, killed rather, by the Assiniboines from Canada."

Welch did not realize or remember that there were three women named Otter Woman, *Sacagawea*'s mother, her sister, and her daughter who was killed with *Sacagawea* in 1869. Sweet Grass Woman was speaking of *Sacagawea*'s daughter. The Otter Woman who died in South Dakota was *Sacagawea*'s sister. Detractors have looked for any inconsistency they could find to discredit information, in order to support their versions of the story.

## Lack of Documentation

Although the story of *Sacagawea* was prevalent among the MHA people during the 20th Century, their stories and other pertinent documents were not gathered, compiled and fully analyzed. There was the Bulls Eye story, but tribal leaders knew there had to be more. Major Welch did have more than the story itself.

Following is the story of how the Bulls Eye story was acquired and how additional documentation came years later.

### THE STORY OF BIRDS BILL, BULLS EYE, AND MAJOR A.B. WELCH

by Jerry Birdsbill Ford (Bird Ford)

My father, Lawrence Birdsbill, *Gidipi E Gigshish* (Dressed Buffalo), was born in 1913 in an earth lodge at Shell Creek Village, on the Ft. Berthold Reservation in N.D. I attribute most of the information in this story to him. His father, my grandfather (*Tsakakapi*), Birds Bill, a Mandan and Hidatsa Indian, was born in 1873, at Fishhook Village on the Missouri River. Grandpa was given the Christian name Anthony later, when he was baptized into the Catholic faith.

He had 10 children by his first wife, Plain House Black Hawk, who died in childbirth in 1924. He later married Emma Grady and had three more children.

## Wyoming, Ft. Manuel, Bulls Eye

My father, Lawrence Birdsbill, was the third youngest of the first set of children. Grandpa Birds Bill was a war veteran, and so instilled the love of Indian culture, as well as American culture in his children. My Dad, also a veteran, was proud to tell us that Grandpa Birds Bill was Chief of the Old Scouts Society.

Grandpa Birds Bill was also a member of the *Xoshgas*, a group of primarily Hidatsa and some Mandans that we called Renegades. They had left the reservation for 25 years in the latter part of the 19th Century to seek freedom from Government restrictions.

*Birds Bill of the Gros Ventre (Hidatsas)*
— *Everett R Cox/Welch Dakota Papers*

They moved to Ft. Buford in Montana under the leadership of Crow Flies High. Here they flourished by continuing to live as they had done before, hunting, and following their traditions such as dancing, praying, and singing, for a generation. The U.S. Army returned these Hidatsa to Ft. Berthold by force in the 1880s; the Birds Bill family then settled in Shell Creek with other *Xoshga* relatives.

My father told me that one of Birds Bill's duties in the early days was to survey and inventory the reservation in order to provide individual allotments to each tribal member. His partner and friend in this endeavor was Major A.B. Welch, a U.S. Army Corps of Engineers veteran of the Spanish-American War (1898), and World War I. Major Welch not only liked to survey the reservation; he enjoyed visiting with the residents, and writing their stories in pencil on long yellow legal pads that he carried everywhere with him.

These stories included tribal stories, histories, cultural and genealogical data. Welch visited both Ft. Berthold and the Standing Rock reservations with the same style of interviews. At Ft. Berthold, he attended both family and tribal celebrations (pow wows) as well as special events, where he always took notes.

My Grandpa Birds Bill shared a lot of information while performing surveys with Major Welch not only about his own family but also about other Shell Creek citizens. One of them was regarding a Hidatsa Indian named Bulls Eye. It seemed that everyone in Shell Creek knew that Bulls Eye's grandmother was *Sacagawea*, but no one knew about this outside the reservation, and Bulls Eye was now ready to share his story with the outside. He asked Grandpa Birds Bill to call a Council to do this properly.

Major Welch was invited to Dead Grass Hall at Shell Creek Village on Memorial Day, May 29, 1923, to speak at the ceremony and, later, to hear testimony from Bulls Eye regarding the long-suppressed story of his grandmother, *Sacagawea*. From Welch's own story about that day, he provided the following.

From the hall they proceeded to the cemetery in a procession of horses and riders, led by the Old Scouts who fought with Custer at the Battle of the Little Big Horn. They were followed by the Legion boys, and then by the Church Societies carrying their banners. The women decorated the graves with Buddy Poppies and flags, and the old men placed a war bonnet there.

After the ceremony the volleys were fired and taps were sounded by Birds Bill, the German War veteran. Everyone was then dismissed except those invited to attend the Council.

Bulls Eye was in his 50s at the time that Major Welch interviewed him. The Tribe was quite concerned that Bulls Eye's story regarding his Grandmother *Sacagawea* would not be preserved, and so Grandpa Birds Bill convened a Council meeting to discuss this matter by his authority as the Chief of the Old Scouts Society. He gave instructions to the Crier, who went out and called around the camping circle of tipis and tents for the old men to come.

Old Scout Chief Birds Bill then blew his bugle to ensure that everyone concerned came to the meeting. Only when everyone was assembled, did Bulls Eye's testimony begin. At this point, Bulls Eye was finally able to provide the outside world with the true story of his Grandmother, *Sacagawea*. The interesting thing about this Council was that the Tribal elders were there to not only to listen but also to correct Bulls Eye should he get any dates or facts wrong, because many there also knew the story and the players. Each elder signed his name as a formal Witness to this testimony. Major Welch was convinced that this was the true story of *Sacagawea's* ancestry and homeland.

In 1924 Bulls Eye was interviewed for his story by the Bismarck Tribune, but the story received minimal distribution. In addition, all this information from Major Welch was essentially lost from 1924 until the year 2000. That is when I, Bird Ford, received a frantic phone call from my cousin Eddie Hall. This fascinating story began with an early version of eBay. One day a gun was put up for sale, and the description said that the gun had been owned by Sitting Bull. A tribal member from Standing Rock took exception to this ad, and called to berate the person who had it for sale. He was assured by the seller that yes, indeed, the gun had belonged to Sitting Bull, as it had a tag on it stating this fact and signed by his Great Uncle Major A.B. Welch who had worked on that reservation. The concerned tribal member then called LaDonna Brave Bull Allard, the Standing Rock Tribal Curator, for advice.

She decided to get involved and so she also called the seller. LaDonna did this because she knew that a certain Major A.B. Welch had surveyed that Tribe back in the 1920s and realized that at long last, he may have surfaced.

Major Welch had no children of his own, but instead had five nieces and nephews who inherited his documents. Apparently, this data, including photographs, stories, histories, cultural artifacts, etc. was divided among these descendants. La Donna then set up a meeting with the descendants at Standing Rock.

Since many of the items were also related to Ft. Berthold, she called our Tribe to ask for a representative to come to the meeting, but got no results. So, then she called Eddie Hall, my nephew, whom she had known for years, and who worked at BIA in Washington D.C. Eddie could not get anyone at the Tribal Office to call him back either.

Eddie then called me and I immediately called Marilyn Hudson, curator of the Ft Berthold Tribal Museum, and who I had also known for years through the BIA. Marilyn told me that she had continually searched the internet in vain for Welch's name and data. Ever since the internet got started, she would enter Major A.B. Welch's name in the browser, hoping to find anything at all about him, but repeatedly got nothing. She literally cried when I told her that after all this time he had been found and that Ft. Berthold was invited to Standing Rock to attend a meeting with his descendants, who were bringing Welch's data with them. I understand that they brought a trainload of data with them to the meeting, and that this was only a part of the documentation.

It was an emotional gathering. I was told that the meeting was full of tears when tribal members saw pictures of their long-deceased ancestors and read through their interviews. For the Welch family, however, there was continued awe and amazement. One said that since childhood they had looked at and played with this material in their attic, but never once believed it represented real people.

They did not realize that there were Indians or Indian Tribes still in existence or that there would be anyone alive associated with this material. When they saw all the tribal members crying over their relative's documents, history came alive for them.

LaDonna thanked me for calling our Tribal Museum, and she sent me what she initially found on the Birds Bill family. She said that she had more and asked us to drop by her office and look through her files for further documentation. She later provided the Tribal Museum with information relative to the Ft. Berthold Indians.

During our Tribe's Lewis and Clark Bicentennial in 2006, I visited our Tribal Museum and attended a slide show by Calvin Grinnell on the Welch data, which by then was substantial. It was quite a find, to say the least.

The Welch family has since put some of this data on the Internet, which is entitled "Oral History of the Dakota Tribes, 1800s-1945." It includes 145 interviews and/or pictures of both reservations' tribal members by name, including Birds Bill and Bulls Eye. It was gratifying to me that the Birds Bill family's oral history story regarding Bulls Eye and *Sacagawea* was confirmed by Welch's documentation.

It has also been rewarding to me to serve years later on the Ft. Berthold *Sacagawea* Committee, a Tribally-sponsored project established to provide Bulls Eye's story to the world. We are even gathering DNA evidence. Finally, it is still amazing to me that this information would never have come to light if that one Welch descendant had not decided to sell Sitting Bull's gun on eBay.

### Conflicting Information

Naysayers, and even some Tribal members, have pointed to the interviews of Charles Eastman as evidence that *Sacagawea* was Shoshone. They also utilize a statement by Bowers, the renowned ethnologist who studied the people of Ft. Berthold extensively.

He stated in his work, *Hidatsa Social and Ceremonial Organization*, 1963, *Sacagawea* was Shoshone, but adopted by the Hidatsas. Adoption among tribes was common at the time of *Sacagawea*.

In a letter to James Connolly in 1975, Bowers gave several reasons why he was not convinced of the Bulls Eye story. He stated that he believed Cedar Woman could not have been Bulls Eye's informant because she was married to a Crow and lived among them. Census records, though, have Cedar Woman living in Bulls Eye's home.

Bowers also noted that information gathered did not have Cherry Necklace and *Sacagawea* being of the same clan. They would have been of the same Crow clan since their mothers were Crow sisters but may have each been adopted by a different clan when they went to live among the Hidatsas. Bowers also mentioned that Bulls Eye was very young to have remembered what had occurred in 1869 and would have had to rely on second parties to the actual events, of which there were none. Bowers also spent a good portion of his letter discrediting Major Welch as not understanding the Indian people. Toward the end of his letter, he did say that he knew that at the point of her separation from Gay Wood [Charbonneau], that *Sacagawea* "lived in close association with the Cherry Necklace family." He went on to say that this information should be further pursued since he did not believe that *Sacagawea* died near Cannonball, North Dakota.

Another reason to explain the acceptance of many that *Sacagawea* was Shoshone is that they were told this by white society or taught that in school.

**We have gathered a great deal of evidence to support our claim that *Sacagawea (Maeshuwea)* was Hidatsa/Crow, but there are further pieces of evidence:**

Major Welch, in his notes, states that Dakotah (Sioux) women whom he questioned about the heritage of *Sacagawea* stated that she was not a captive but was of the Missouri River villages.

Accounts of Jean Baptiste Charbonneau, including his obituary, state that he was part Crow Indian or give evidence of such. Those accounts may be found in written works of George B. Sanderson, T.D. Bonner, and Susan M. Colby. An unpublished quote, in the diary of Dr. George B. Sanderson about Jean Baptiste when he was with the Mormon Battalion in 1847, states, "a very enterprising daring fellow. He is half Crow Indian, his father a Frenchman." T. D. Bonner, in writing the autobiography of James Beckwourth, stated that Beckwourth spoke of Jean Baptiste's mother, whom he called "Mary,"

[It was common to give Indian women this white name] and said she was "a Crow, very pleasing and intelligent, and may have been, for aught I know, connected with some of my many relatives in that tribe." [Beckwourth had several Crow wives, 1826-1835.]

In regard to *Sacagawea* and her daughter, Otter Woman — Bulls Eye's mother, being on their way to Sand Creek to secure coffee and visit their Crow relatives, Sand Creek was an area occupied by Crows, other tribes, and traders at the time.

A report by the Indian Agent for Fort Berthold in the mid 1870s states that one-half of the Indian population was away as military scouts, were hunting for game, were visiting friends [and probably relatives] among other tribes, or were establishing winter homes located between Fort Buford and [Fort] Peck.

This was an area that was more conducive to providing for the people than at Ft. Berthold at the time, from *100 Years at Ft. Berthold* compiled by Rev. and Mrs. Harold W. Case, 1977. Although this was after the death of *Sacagawea* in 1869, it is likely that the same conditions existed at that time.

According to *Montana Place Names* by the Montana Historical Society, the town of Wolf Point, Montana, began as a trading post in the 1860s at the confluence of Wolf Creek and the Missouri River.

In *Fort Union and the Upper Missouri Fur Trade*, Barton H. Barbour quotes Charles W. Hoffman who was a cook at Fort Buford, the military fort near the site of Fort Union, the fur trading fort.

Hoffman stated that in 1868 "there was scarcely a day the Indians did not show themselves," and that as many as three thousand Sioux were in the area attacking soldiers and others.

A book authored by George Washington Webb, *Chronological List of Engagements Between the Regular Army of the United States and Various Tribes of Hostile Indians Which Occurred During the Years 1790 to 1898, Inclusive*, 2018, states that, in 1869, on August 9, a skirmish occurred and four citizens were killed at or near Ft. Buford by a Sioux war party.

*Our Story of Eagle Woman, Sacagawea*

*James P. Beckwourth, ca. 1850. He and Jean Baptiste Charbonneau were trapping partners. He spoke of Jean Baptiste's mother.* — T. D. Bonner

*Wyoming, Ft. Manuel, Bulls Eye*

*A Chronological Record of Events at the Missouri-Yellowstone Confluence Area from 1805 to 1896, and A Record of Internments at the Fort Buford Dakota Territory Post Cemetery 1866 to 1895*, published by the Fort Buford 6th Infantry Regiment Association, Inc., 1971, also states that on August 9 in 1869 four citizens were killed by a Sioux war party. They were taken to and were buried in the Ft. Buford cemetery. This account may or may not have been the one in *Sacagawea*'s story but is an example of incidents that occurred in 1869.

**When *Sacagawea* passed, she was buried in the Ft. Buford area according to living tribal members.** She may not have been buried in the Ft. Buford cemetery because she was an Indian woman. It is noted that Indians listed as buried in the Ft. Buford cemetery were not noted as "citizens" as others were. The Indians buried in the cemetery appear to all be men.

The old Post Trader's store at Fort Buford, D.T., ca. 1870-71. Sacagawea was buried in the Fort Buford area. — photographer unknown.

*The Xoshga Hidatsa village of Chief Crow Flies High, near Fort Buford, D.T. 1874 Although the Hidatsa were known as the "earthlodge people," they used tipis when they traveled or camped and often camped near Fort Buford.*
— A.C. Leighton

Included in reams of rampant speculation by those who did not know the background or circumstances, some have stated that *Sacagawe*a was prostituted on the expedition. Rebecca K. Jager in *Malinche, Pocahontas, and Sacagawea,* 2015, with much research to draw from, states that there is no evidence of such. If anything, Lewis and Clark protected *Sacagawea* from this, and such relationships would have compromised her important role in the expedition.

**Many tribal members from Ft. Berthold were and are related to *Sacagawea (Maeshuwea)*. The next chapters will examine those family relationships.**

### Sources Authored or Provided by MHA Tribal Members

Ford, Jerry Birdsbill "Bird." The Story of Birds Bill, Bulls Eye and Major A. B. Welch, Unpublished.

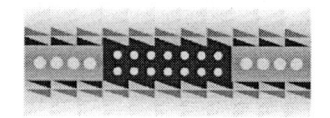

*Bulls Eye, Grandson of Sacagawea, 1927.* — Welch Dakota Papers

# Chapter 7
## *OUR FAMILY CONNECTIONS*
*Sacagawea and Cherry Necklace*

**M***any people of the MHA Nation know they are related to Sacagawea.* **These claims were made and reported especially during the time of the Lewis and Clark Bicentennial.**

From "Welcome Lewis and Clark's Bicentennial Celebration" in *Mandan, Hidatsa, Arikara Times*, **Aug. 2006:**

> The bicentennial of Lewis and Clark's journey through the west has signified more than the celebration of just that; it has brought together the descendants of those people who greeted and welcomed the travelers mapping terrain in an age-old territory. Twenty miles east of Mandaree [North Dakota], a celebration was held that honored the past and welcomed new changes for the future.

Mandaree community members organized a celebration that offered many people a chance to view the Bicentennial from an often unheard perspective.

The descendants of *Sakakawea* and Cherry Necklace [*Sacagawea*'s brother] came together to voice the tale of the encounters that the Mandan and Hidatsa people had with Lewis and Clark as they made their way through the Northern Plains. The tales spoken of tell of how *Sakakawea* was originally from the land of the Mandan and Hidatsa people.

"We are the sixth generation, it's about time they're telling it the right way," said **Wanda Sheppard**. "It's a time for us to bring our story... to have an opportunity to do that...the history books say that she (*Sakakawea*) was Shoshone. The history books embrace this mythical figure of *Sakakawea*, but to us she was real." "We know who her relatives are," said **Tex Fox**, a *Sakakawea* descendant who attended the Mandaree celebration."

From **"Heritage in question,"** *Minot Daily News*, **August 9, 2001:**

**Marilyn Hudson,** a tribal member and administrator of the Three Tribes Museum near New Town said, "I would say (she was) definitely raised at Knife River and definitely was Hidatsa, and that you really have to examine the journals and question the accuracy of the journals."

Hudson said her family is related to *Sakakawea* through her father, the late Martin Cross. Her paternal grandfather was Old Dog, whose father was Many Bears; Many Bears' father was *Sakakawea*'s brother Cherry Necklace. "Not only did my father tell us that we were related to *Sakakawea* but he made a stand in Washington that *Sakakawea* was Hidatsa and not Shoshone," she said. Hudson said her father made that stand at a Congressional hearing in the 1950s when he was chairman of the Three Affiliated Tribes.

**Calvin Grinnell,** with the Three Affiliated Tribes Cultural Preservation Office, said he believes that *Sakakawea* probably was born and raised in the Knife River area. He said he remembers his great aunt, Cora Snow Bird Bear, telling him and his siblings that they were related to *Sakakawea*. From his research and oral histories, he believes that *Sakakawea* was part Crow and part Hidatsa, but not Shoshone. He said the Crow were part of the Hidatsa Tribe at one time. "Because of her Crow relatives who lived in the mountains, she got to know that part of the country, which is why people think she's Shoshone," he said.

Following is information on *Sacagawea* and her family members.

### *Sacagawea*

*Sacagawea* (Bird Woman in Hidatsa and changed from *Maeshuweash*, Eagle Woman) was born about 1787 at an Hidatsa village, according to oral history. She was half Hidatsa and half Crow. Her father was Smoked Lodge (Black Lodge, Bad Lodge) and was Hidatsa. He signed the 1825 Atkinson-O'Fallon Treaty for the Hidatsas. Her mother was Comes Out of the Water or Otter Woman (1) and was Crow. Bulls Eye said *Sacagawea*'s mother was Hidatsa. The Hidatsas and Crows were one tribe at one time and often intermarried and went back and forth between the two tribes. Several sources indicate that *Sacagawea* was half Crow.

*Sacagawea* was most well known for going on the expedition with the Lewis and Clark Corps of Discovery. Although she was a valuable member of the group, her role on that trip is still debated. Many accounts of *Sacagawea*'s life and time on the trip, especially, have been based on speculation and attempts to romanticize her story. Who she was and where she is buried are also still questioned by historians.

The story goes that Charbonneau either lied about her background and said she was Shoshone in order to get the jobs for both as interpreters on the journey, or that someone relayed that she had snake medicine (the medicine one had was an important marker for Indian people), and that it was interpreted as her being a Snake Indian. There is also evidence that *Sacagawea* had ties to a Shoshone family through a tribal adoption, and Charbonneau could have used this as qualifying her as being from that tribe.

As a young girl, she was tall, heavy set and athletic according to oral history. It has been reported by Crow and Hidatsa informants that young *Sacagawea* was probably living at Crow when Charbonneau got her there from her father and took her to live with him [Charbonneau] back among the Hidatsa and Mandan.

It was the practice at the time for a man to marry sisters. Charbonneau had married *Sacagawea's* sister, **Otter Woman (2)**, at least two years before. Otter Woman was named after their mother, Otter Woman (1), and is mentioned in various accounts as another wife of Charbonneau.

*Sacagawea* had four children. Jean Baptiste or Pomp, as he was called by Captain William Clark, was the child that she took along on the expedition. She also had three daughters: Otter Woman (3) (the same name as her sister and mother), Cedar Woman, and Different Breast. *Sacagawea* had a brother, Cherry Necklace – Crow and Hidatsa, who was a highly regarded medicine man. *Sacagawea* was killed in 1869 along with her daughter, Otter Woman (3), as reported by Bulls Eye.

### Toussaint Charbonneau

According to *French and Native North American Marriages, 1600-1800* by Paul Bunnell, 2007, frontier guide Toussaint Charbonneau was born about 1758. His wife was *Sacajawea* [Sacagawea], about 30 years younger than he. He was engaged with the Northwest Fur Company in 1793 at age 35, and became a trader at Fort Pine on the Assiniboine River.

In 1795, he left from the Lake of the Woods area and moved down to Red River and west to Upper Missouri where he stayed. He went on the Lewis and Clark Expedition to the Pacific Ocean. The record states that Toussaint was from Quebec.

According to *Early Fur Trade on the Northern Plains, Canadian Traders Among the Mandan and Hidatsa Indians, 1738-1818*, by Wood and Thiessen, Toussaint Charbonneau was born in or near Montreal in 1759. He is believed to have settled among the Hidatsa and Mandan in the period between 1796 and 1799. He is mentioned in many of the accounts of the Upper Missouri from the time of the Lewis and Clark Expedition through the late-1830s.

He was married to *Sacagawea* but had other wives as well over his lifetime. He lived in the Knife River villages. In 1833, Prince Maximilian noted that Charbonneau lived in the middle village of the Hidatsa, now known as the *Sakakawea* site. He resided elsewhere because of temporary employment with various trading companies and the U.S. government. Charbonneau's last assignment was as an employee at Ft. Clark. He died in 1840 at the age of 81 or 82.

One of Charbonneau's main assignments was as interpreter on the Lewis and Clark Expedition. "Neither Lewis nor Clark spoke any language but English, which none of the Indians they met spoke. A question or statement from Lewis or Clark meant first translating it from English into French through a French-speaking Corps member, then from French to the Native language. Responses from various tribes often meant further translation, and every response meant the same steps in reverse" in *An American Journey, Lewis and Clark* by Daniel Thorp, 1998. In *The Village Indians of the Upper Missouri* by Meyer, 1977, it states that there was disagreement regarding Charbonneau's linguistic abilities.

*Pencil drawing by Duke Paul of Wurttemberg at a trading post near the mouth of the Kansas River, July 3, 1823. The young duke, traveling for adventure in his first visit to the United States, was so impressed with Jean Baptiste he invited the young man to accompany him home to Germany as a companion, where he remained until 1829, learning German and Spanish while traveling with the Duke around Europe and North Africa.*

*Although the original drawing was destroyed during World War II, it had been photographed in 1935 by Dr.Charles L.Camp, an American geologist.*

*Jean Baptiste Charbonneau, son of Sacagawea and Toussaint, at age 18.*

## Jean Baptiste Charbonneau

*Sacagawea's* son, Jean Baptiste, was born February 11, 1805. His father was Toussaint Charbonneau, a French Canadian trapper living with the Hidatsa. Sacagawea took Jean Baptiste along on the Lewis and Clark Expedition. He was called Pomp. As a young boy, he lived in St. Louis with William Clark and attended school.

Jean Baptiste earned fame as an explorer, guide, fur trapper, trader, military scout during the Mexican War, mayor (alcalde) of Mission San Luis Rey de Francia, and a gold prospector and hotel operator in Northern California.

When he was the mayor at Mission San Luis Rey, he did not approve of the way the Indians were treated at the missions and by the ranchers. He spoke French, English and learned German and Spanish during six years in Europe from 1823 to 1829 when he was there to further his education. He also spoke western American Indian languages. Jean Baptiste died May 16, 1866. He is buried at Danner, Oregon. The Wyoming story of *Sacajawea* says that Jean Baptiste is buried in Wyoming. This, of course, is disputed.

## Sacagawea and Cherry Necklace

*Mergentheim Castle, Wurttemberg, southwest Germany, where Jean Baptiste Charbonneau was a guest of Duke Paul of Wurttemberg during 1823-1829.*

**Obituary of Jean Baptiste Charbonneau,** son of *Sacagawea*, from *Lewis and Clark Through Indian Eyes*, edited by Alvin M. Josephy, 2006.

Death of a California Pioneer – We are informed by...a letter announcing the death of J.B. Charbonneau, who left this country some weeks ago, with two companions, for Montana Territory. The letter is from one of the party who says Mr. C. was taken sick with mountain fever, on the Owyhee [in Oregon], and died after a short illness.

> **THE PLACER HERALD.**
>
> AUBURN, JULY 7, 1866.
>
> DEATH OF A CALIFORNIA PIONEER. — We are informed by Mr. Dana Perkins, that he has received a letter announcing the death of J. B. Charbonneau, who left this county some weeks ago, with two companions, for Montana Territory. The letter is from one of the party, who says Mr. C., was taken sick with mountain fever, on the Owyhee, and died after a short illness.

Obituary, Placer Herald, Auburn, July 7, 1866

Mr. Charbonneau was known to most of the pioneer citizens of this region of the country, being himself one of the first adventurers (into the territory now known as Placer county) upon the discovery of gold; where he has remained with little intermission until his recent departure for the new gold field, Montana, which, strangely enough was the land of his birth, whither he was returning in the evening of life, to spend a few remaining days that he felt was in store for him.

Mr. Charbonneau was born in the western wilds, and grew up a hunter, trapper, and pioneer, among that class of men of which Bridger, Beckwourth and other noted trappers of the woods were the representatives.

*Sacagawea and Cherry Necklace*

> **OREGON HISTORY**
>
> **JEAN BAPTISTE CHARBONNEAU**
> 1805-1866
>
> THIS SITE MARKS THE FINAL RESTING PLACE OF THE YOUNGEST MEMBER OF THE LEWIS AND CLARK EXPEDITION. BORN TO SACAGAWEA AND TOUSSAINT CHARBONNEAU AT FORT MANDAN (NORTH DAKOTA) ON FEBRUARY 11, 1805. BAPTISTE AND HIS MOTHER SYMBOLIZED THE PEACEFUL NATURE OF THE "CORPS OF DISCOVERY". EDUCATED BY CAPTAIN WILLIAM CLARK AT ST. LOUIS. BAPTISTE AT AGE 18, TRAVELED TO EUROPE WHERE HE SPENT SIX YEARS, BECOMING FLUENT IN ENGLISH, GERMAN, FRENCH AND SPANISH. RETURNING TO AMERICA IN 1829, HE RANGED THE FAR WEST FOR NEARLY FOUR DECADES, AS MOUNTAIN MAN GUIDE, INTERPRETER, MAGISTRATE AND FORTY NINER. IN 1866, HE LEFT THE CALIFORNIA GOLD FIELDS FOR A NEW STRIKE IN MONTANA. CONTRACTED PNEUMONIA ENROUTE. REACHED "INSKIP'S RANCHE", HERE, AND DIED ON MAY 16, 1866.

*Signboard erected by Oregon State Park Dept., about 50 feet from the grave site of Jean Baptiste Charbonneau.*

He was born in the country of the Crow Indians – **his father being a Canadian Frenchman, and his mother a half breed of the Crow tribe.** He had, however, better opportunities than most of the rough spirits, who followed the calling of trapper, as when a young man he went to Europe and spent several years, where he learned to speak, as well as write several languages. At the breaking out of the Mexican War he was on the frontiers, and upon the organization of the Mormon Battalion he was engaged as a guide and came with them to California.

Subsequently upon the discovery of gold, he, in company with Jim Beckwourth, came upon the North Fork of the American River, and for a time it is said were mining partners. The reported discoveries of gold in Montana, and the rapid peopling of the Territory, excited the imagination of the old trapper determined to return to the scenes of his youth. [Placer Herald, Auburn, California, July 7, 1866].

## The Daughters of *Sacagawea*

*Sacagawea* may have had other children after Pomp in the years following, but, if she did, they probably died in childhood as many others did. Further, although she was with Charbonneau, he preferred young women. After the smallpox epidemic of 1837, however, the Hidatsa made an effort to repopulate their tribe. That is when *Sacagawea* gave birth to three daughters when in her early 50s, Otter Woman (3), Cedar Woman, and Different Breast.

**Otter Woman** (3), the mother of Bulls Eye, was born about 1838. Her husband was Lean Bull. Bulls Eye stated that Otter Woman (3) later married a white man who worked at a trading post along the way to the Crow reservation. Later in her life, *Sacagawea* lived with Otter Woman (3). Otter Woman (3) was killed along with *Sacagawea* in 1869.

**Cedar Woman** was the mother of Medicine Arm who was the mother of George Parshall. Cedar Woman's husband was Pan or Head (according to Aletha Jackson, George Parshall's daughter). Wolf Chief reported that Cedar Woman later married Brave, a Crow Indian. Cedar Woman and her grandson, George Parshall (Dog), lived with Bulls Eye according to the Ft. Berthold census of 1889-1893. Cedar Woman was reported to be 50 in 1891. Elsewhere, she was reported to have been born in 1839. According to Bulls Eye, Cedar Woman told him the stories of *Sacagawea*.

**Different Breast** or Different Chest, Pretty Breast, was the youngest of *Sacagawea*'s daughters. Not much is known of her. She may have been the daughter who died at a young age.

## The Grandchildren of *Sacagawea*

Jean Baptiste had several children. During his European tour at Wurttemberg in Germany, he fathered a child with Anastasia Katharina Fries, a soldier's daughter. The baby, **Anton Fries**, died about three months after his birth.

On May 4, 1848, **Maria Catarina Charguana (Charbonneau)** was born to Margarita Sobin, a Luisieno Indian woman from Mission San Luis Rey in California. The infant girl's baptism was performed by Father Blas Ordaz of the Mission San Fernando Rey de Espana near Los Angeles. Margarita Sobin later married Gregory Trujillo who may have raised Maria. Charbonneau's daughter and Margarita's other children were registered as members of the La Jolla band of Mission Indians. Jean Baptiste is also reported to have had a daughter, **Louise** with a woman named Rufine when at Bent's Fort in 1846. A census report from New Mexico lists a **Maria Luisa Shahuano**, born in 1837, believed by some to be the daughter.

**Bulls Eye** was born in 1864 and died in 1928. He was the son of Lean Bull and Otter Woman (3), daughter of *Sacagawea* (Eagle Woman). He had two wives, Blue Blanket (sometimes translated Green) and Brings the Pipe. According to Bulls Eye's records at Ft. Berthold Agency, he had at least twelve children, all of whom died at a young age. Two of his children were George and Lucy who were given the white last name of "Evans." Lucy was born in 1893 and died in 1909, at age 16. George was born in 1895 and died in 1912, at age 17. They were *Sacagawea's* great-grandchildren.

Bulls Eye raised his nephew, George Parshall (His cousin Medicine Arm's son), and also George's oldest son, Thomas, who became Thomas Bulls Eye. Bulls Eye was a member of the *Xoshga* band. The *Xoshgas*, under Chiefs Crow Flies High and Bobtail Bull, left the Fort Berthold area and moved near Fort Buford in 1869 or 70. Bulls Eye told the story of his grandmother, *Sacagawea*, to Major Welch in 1923.

## Our Story of Eagle Woman, Sacagawea

*Bulls Eye's children, George and Lucy Evans, great-grandchildren of Sacagawea, ca 1902. For the photograph, Lucy's mother has draped her in an heirloom, mid-19th century painted buffalo robe.* — State Historical Society of North Dakota.

**Medicine Arm** was the daughter of Cedar Woman (*Sacagawea*'s daughter) and was George Parshall's mother. She lived part of the time in or near Montana with her husband, William Parshall, and George's brother and sister, Charles and Nettie (Berries). William Parshall was a soldier at Ft. Buford, was a surveyor, and later had a business in Williston, North Dakota. Medicine Arm was born in 1856. She and her children were living with Bulls Eye and Cedar Woman in 1890 according to the census report.

## Other Descendants of *Sacagawea*

**George Parshall** was the great-grandson of *Sacagawea*. His parents were Medicine Arm and William Dennis Parshall who was a scout stationed at Ft. Buford. George had a brother, Charles, and a sister, Nettie or Berries. When his siblings lived with their father and mother in Montana, George and his grandmother, Cedar Woman, lived with Bulls Eye, Cedar Woman's nephew (considered her son). Bulls Eye was considered to be George's uncle and actually raised him. With Bulls Eye, George was a member of the *Xoshga* band. His Indian names were Plenty Dogs (referred to as Dog) and White Raven. George was born in 1875 and died on July 29, 1950, at age 75.

George knew very little English because he was hidden when the government came to round up the kids to go to school. George made tobacco from the inner bark of red willows. He liked to fish for bullheads. He swam/bathed in Shell Creek early in the mornings, even in the coldest weather. He participated in ceremonies and went out of his way to learn and keep alive the old teachings.

George Parshall was a surveyor and surveyed the towns of Parshall, Van Hook and Sanish. The city of Parshall was named after him. Following is what was written about him during the City of Parshall's 50th Anniversary Celebration in 1954:

> In, or about, the year of 1910, the northern portion of the Fort Berthold Reservation became a part of the public domain. Appraisal of the land had to be made. Mr. George Parshall was a member of the group who evaluated the land. Being the son of a surveyor who had surveyed for the government in years prior to this may have been one of the reasons why George Parshall was always intensely interested in work of this type. It became the custom to apply the name of a member [of those who evaluated the land] to a probable townsite, so when this group came upon the townsite on the land described as SE 1/4 Sec. 25, Twp. 152, Range 90, to it was given the name of Parshall.

This city was established in the year of 1914 and the name, Parshall, was officially adopted.

In an address given by Jefferson B. Smith at the 1954 dedication of the monument commemorative to George Parshall, in the city of Parshall, he says: "he was a fine, calm undaunted, appreciative man. He loved life. He valued the friendship of everyone, helped many, hurt few. His devotion to his family was very noticeable. He was sincere and dependable. He had a strong mind and a resolute will. He loved his country; he was an outstanding citizen. None ever met him and left without being impressed with his goodness."

George left Ft. Berthold for seven years and lived with relatives at Crow. His daughter, Grace Fox, told the story of why he left. She said that George was rough on horses and killed a few. Bulls Eye, his uncle, was raising George. Bulls Eye was a medicine man and was called on to doctor people. On one occasion, he received a nice saddle horse for his work doctoring someone. Bulls Eye told George he could not ride the horse because of the way he treated horses. George got upset and told Bulls Eye to take the horse as his son [instead of him], because he was leaving. He went to the Crow reservation. After seven years, Bulls Eye and his wife, Brings the Pipe, went after him. When they saw George, he had three long braids like the Crows. He agreed to go home. George Parshall inherited land in Crow from Cold Wind, Mrs. Thomas LaForge Wind, Iron Necklace, Catches Enemy, Woman Now, and Big Magpie.

George and his wife, Ruby (White Bear), gave their oldest son, Thomas, to Bulls Eye to raise because Bulls Eye's children died. It was a practice for older grandchildren to live with and help their grandparents, and Bulls Eye was considered their grandfather. The son was named Thomas Bulls Eye. George and Ruby's other children were: Grace Parshall Fox, Aletha Parshall Jackson, Rose Parshall Crow Flies High, Pansy Parshall, Delores Parshall Sand, Charles Parshall and Paul Parshall. George has many, many descendants at and from Ft. Berthold.

*George Parshall at Shell Creek, N.D., ca.1902.*
— State Historical Society of North Dakota.

    At one viewing of DNA evidence from Ancestry.com there were 70 DNA matches between Parshall descendants and people who had ancestors on their trees with Charbonneau surnames. Ancestry.com DNA evidence also ties Parshall descendants to some Charbonneau descendants as fourth cousins or closer, all descendants of Olivier Charbonneau and Marie Marguerite Garnier Charbonneau, great-great grandparents of Toussaint Charbonneau.

    George Parshall was present when Bulls Eye told the story claiming that *Sacagawea* was Hidatsa to Major Welch in 1923. In George's household, they spoke regularly of their grandmother, *Sacagawea*. George is buried at Parshall, North Dakota.

# Our Story of Eagle Woman, Sacagawea

*Delores Parshall Sand, daughter of George Parshall and oldest living direct descendant of Sacagawea.*

— James Ford

## Sacagawea and Cherry Necklace

**INDIVIDUAL HISTORY CARD.**
(Formerly Abstine Family History Card.)

Tribe: Grosventres    Sex: M    Census or Allotment No.: 80
English name: Bulls Eyes    Born: 1864    Died: 3-12-28
Indian name: Ki-ra-pis-tas    English translation of Indian name: Bulls Eyes

| | | DIED | CENSUS OR ALLOTMENT No. |
|---|---|---|---|
| Father: Lean Bull | Gros | date unknown | unallotted |
| Father's father: I-ti-in-pu-i-tas | Gros | " | unallotted |
| Father's mother: Goes towards other Woods | Gros | " | unallotted |
| Mother: Otter | White 1/2 Gros 1/2 | " | unallotted |
| Mother's father: Unknown - *Charbonneau!* White | | " | unallotted |
| Mother's mother: Eagle Woman - *Sacagawea* | | " | unallotted |

| BROTHERS AND HALF-BROTHERS | | CENSUS OR ALLOT. No. | UNCLES, FATHER'S SIDE | CENSUS OR ALLOT. No. |
|---|---|---|---|---|
| Big Head   Died 6/26/21 | 1/2 | 390 | Don't Know | |
| Two Wolves   Died 7/25/1898 | 1/2 | 10 | | |
| Died | | | **UNCLES, MOTHER'S SIDE** | |
| Died | | | Don't Know | |
| Died | | | | |
| **SISTERS AND HALF-SISTERS** | | | **AUNTS, FATHER'S SIDE** | |
| None   Died | | | Plain Blossom   died 9/8/1897 | 254 |
| Died | | | **AUNTS, MOTHER'S SIDE** | |
| Died | | | *Grandmother of Mrs. Marshall* Cedar Woman   died date unknown | unallotted |
| Died | | | Different Breast   died date unknown | unallotted |
| Died | | | | |

*Bulls Eye, Individual History Card, 1928.*
— MHA Interpretive Center

## Our Story of Eagle Woman, Sacagawea

Census in 1891, Bulls Eye's aunt, Cedar Woman, and her grandson, Dog (George Parshall) lived with Bulls Eye. She is listed as Bulls Eye's mother in the Indian way.
— MHA Interpretive Center

*Sacagawea and Cherry Necklace*

*Delores Sand, Pansy Parshall, Rose Crow Flies High*
— MHA Interpretive Center

# Parshalls,
# Direct Descendants of *Sacagawea*

## Our Story of Eagle Woman, Sacagawea

*Grace Parshall Fox* — MHA Interpretive Center

*Aletha Jackson* — Ziggy Jackson

*Charles Parshall* — MHA Interpretive Center

*Paul Parshall* — MHA Interpretive Center

## Cherry Necklace, *Sacagawea's* Brother

Cherry Necklace was a highly-respected medicine man among both the Hidatsa and Crow. He was the son of Smoked Lodge, Hidatsa, and Girl Woman, Crow. Bulls Eye had stated that Cherry Necklace lived with parents, First and Looks Down, but notes indicate that this was in the Indian way. They were relatives but not his parents. Cherry Necklace was born in about 1778 and died in 1873 at 95 years of age.

*Sacagawea* was Cherry Necklace's sister. Of course there has been controversy over whether she was Hidatsa or Shoshone. Bowers, in *Hidatsa Social and Ceremonial Organization*, states that *Sacagawea* was Shoshone, adopted by the Hidatsas, and was therefore considered to be Hidatsa. This is puzzling, since Bowers had interviewed Wolf Chief about this, and Wolf Chief told Bowers that she was Hidatsa and was Cherry Necklace's sister. (Their father was Smoked Lodge, Hidatsa.) Bowers was not pursuing the *Sacagawea* story, however, and was more interested in the general culture of the Hidatsa. Further, he was receiving federal funds from the government and was likely to state the party line.

In *Coyote Warrior* by Paul Van Develder, 2004, the author states that the Cross family members are descendants of Cherry Necklace and that Cherry Necklace adopted *Sacagawea* as his sister. DNA evidence from descendants of Cherry Necklace and *Sacagawea*, however, supports the fact that they are blood related, and their descendants have always claimed their blood relationship.

It was the general practice of the time for Indian men to marry sisters. Because Cherry Necklace and *Sacagawea's* mothers were Crow sisters, both Cherry Necklace and *Sacagawea* would have had to be adopted into an Hidatsa clan. The Hidatsa are a matrilineal society. Perhaps an adoption took place into a clan for *Sacagawea*. This also suggests that *Sacagawea* may have been viewed as somewhat of an outsider because her mother was Crow, thus the interpretation that she was Shoshone would not have been questioned as much.

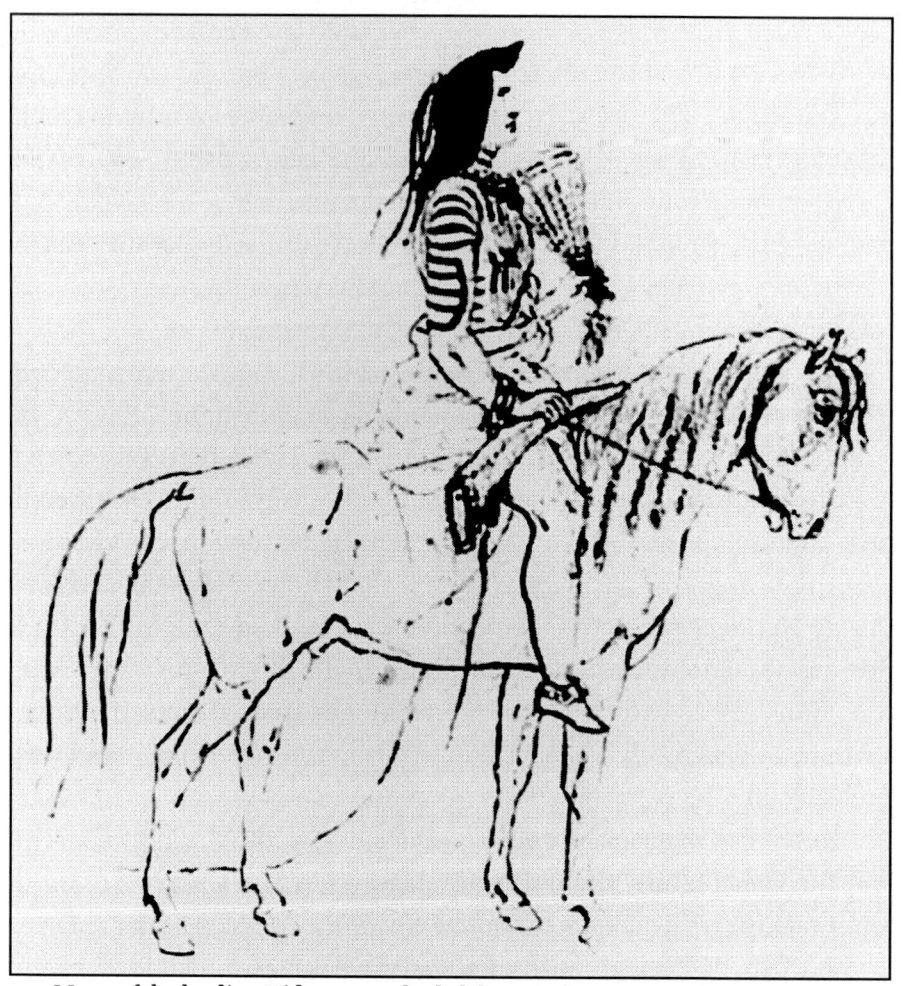

Many of the leading Hidatsa men had elaborate chest, arm and neck tattoos. One description of Sacagawea's brother Cherry Necklace mentioned "His neck was tattooed all over." Ink drawing by Rudolf Friedrich Kurz, at Like-A-Fishhook Village, 1851.   — Berne Historical Museum.

Cherry Necklace is included in books about the Crows and about the Hidatsas. He had snake medicine, as did *Sacagawea*. He is listed as a survivor of the smallpox epidemic among the Hidatsas and had two lodges in Like-A-Fishhook Village. Records indicate that he had three different wives. His children are listed as Long Bear, High Rump, Raises His Arm, White Face, Brown Bear, Pink, Many Comes Up, In the Water, Plenty Medicine and Many Bears.

He has many descendants at Ft. Berthold, including Conklin, Lone Bear, Gunn, Foolish Bear, Good Bear, Cross, White Owl, Bolman, Finley, Newman families. (These provided family tree information, and there are others.) Following are stories about Cherry Necklace.

**From "Medicine Men and Medicine Ceremonies, Cherry-Necklace" in *Mandan-Hidatsa Myths and Ceremonies* collected by Martha Warren Beckwith, 1937. Story by Bears Arm.**

My mother when she was young saw a famous medicine-man named Cherry-Necklace. **Bird-woman, who guided the famous Lewis and Clark expedition, was his sister.** A young Gros Ventre named Four Bears was wounded in the side and had little chance to live. Cherry-Necklace took the young warrior into his tent and doctored him. The tent was pitched along the bluff beside the river. He allowed not even dogs inside. His mystery was a male otter. He used to place a skin of a male otter about the young man's head and take him down to the river.

People were allowed to watch from the bluff and many came to see. He let the boy walk ahead to the river and into the stream until the water came almost up to the wound. The people watched him closely. He took the [otter] skin and sang a mystery song, sprinkled it and prayed saying, "They are depending upon you, not upon me. It is not I who am holy but you, and I pray you to doctor this young warrior." He dunked the skin under water and it disappeared. He stepped back and the otter came out alive from the water, swam about the man, then turned downstream and came up to the warrior swiftly, put its head up to the man's wound, touched it and swam back. Streams of blood ran out and colored the water red. Three times the otter did this. The fourth time, as it humped its back, the medicine man took it up in his two hands, put it again under water, and when he took it out it was nothing but a skin. Everyone in the camp turned out to see and all were amazed.

He led the warrior back up the bank to the camp. The healed man became a mighty warrior and chief of the Gros Ventres. He represented them at Fort Laramie in 1851, and it is through him that the government is today paying the Indians for their lands. This happened in 1837, right after the smallpox epidemic that destroyed the Gros Ventres nation. The place where it happened was near old Cold Harbor [Coleharbor, North Dakota].

The spirits conferred upon Cherry-Necklace the power to doctor, but not to take part in battle. There are other miracle stories told about this old man. He used to take dried willow leaves, put them under his robe, rub his hands over them and take out wild tobacco leaves of the kind that grows in high places. Then he would take a piece of bark shaped like a plug of tobacco, rub this and pull out tobacco. Out of these two he would make the mixture which he was especially fond of smoking. *Bears Arm himself has seen this medicine man. He must have died when Bears Arm was nine years old.*

Another incident. Cherry-Necklace was once out in the breaks in a place where there was timber below. He heard voices and sneaking up to the point where they could be heard, he listened. They said, "If he smokes with seven (persons including himself) all will go well, if with two or three he must place sticks about (to represent the balance of the seven). If one comes in through the door too quickly, the smoke from his pipe will go down the person's throat in the form of a worm, but the medicine man will have the power to take out the worm, which must be thrown into the fire." He [Cherry Necklace] peeped over the bank and saw seven black-tail deer, who all ran away.

During the night he [Cherry Necklace] dreamed how to handle the smoking. Hence no one ever goes into the lodge of Cherry-Necklace hastily while he is smoking. Should some careless person do this, he will feel a little worm going down his throat. The medicine-man can take out the worm by dipping his fingers in ashes and making a rubbing motion of the skin, but without cutting the skin, then he shows the worm and throws it in the fire. A man named Good Bear told of coming in where the old man was smoking and having two worms removed from his throat.

## Sacagawea and Cherry Necklace

This medicine-man [Cherry Necklace] was adopted into a rattlesnake's den and was hence able to poison anybody indirectly. He had power both for good and for bad. When he used the rattlesnake medicine, a fellow had to look out.

### From *Hidatsa Social & Ceremonial Organization* by Alfred W. Bowers, 1963.

Alfred Bowers gathered the information for his book starting in the 1930s. The book tells that Cherry Necklace was the singer for the Holy Women Society. It states that Cherry Necklace was an hereditary bundle holder for the Hidatsa and sold rites in it to his son, High Hump [Rump]. It contains the story of Cherry Necklace healing Four Bears and tells that it was Cherry Necklace's brother, One Buffalo, who arranged for Cherry Necklace to treat Four Bears.

### From: "Religion of the Crow Indians," by Robert Lowie, *Anthropological Papers American Museum of Natural History*, Vol. XXV, 1922.

The owner of the lodge, according to him [Little-Rump], was named Cherry-Necklace of the *xuxkaraxise* [Crow] clan; he had married an Hidatsa woman and lived among her people. His neck was tattooed all over. 'Cherry-Necklace would not permit anyone to expectorate in his lodge, because if they did they would feel a worm in their neck. Once a man who had expectorated had a worm sucked out of his neck.'

### From "Biographical sketches of Chief Sitting Crow's Life," unpublished paper

One of his [Sitting Crow's] closest chums was a grandson of an old Indian named Fruit (Cherry or Berry) Necklace. Fruit Necklace had once been a very poor man, but was now a very rich old man.

In his youth he had once gone up to a rattlesnake den, where he prayed and cried for 3 days and nights, absolutely not eating a thing, nor drinking a drink of liquid. Finally he had to lay down from fatigue, and he went to sleep. When the snakes returned that evening, they found Fruit Necklace barring the way into the back of the den, and in order not to disturb him, the snakes all jumped across his body.

The last snake, a little fellow, did not get all the way across, and fell with his tail against the sleeping Indian. For this indignity, the chief of the snakes invited him into the back part of the den where he told him that since this snake had flicked him with its tail, he would now have to promise good luck to Fruit Necklace, and that from now on, if Fruit Necklace wanted anything all he had to do was to come to the den and pray for it, and the snake god would see that it transpired.

Thru this power, Fruit Necklace rose to great power and gained many horses and scalps. He had the power to heal all illnesses, and there never was a more powerful medicine. His habit was to sit in a corner with his face to the wall, smoking his pipe, whether visitors were there or not. Young Sitting Crow was in the same room many times, and whenever they got too close, Fruit Necklace would caution them to stay away, as his powers seemed so strong at times, he did not want to take a chance on his friends getting harmed by it.

## Cherry Necklace by Mr. Rufus Stevenson, Sanish, ND. Interpreted by Paige Baker, Sr.

After a few years, the Hidatsa moved west to the Knife River. And when they settled and made their village, the Mandans came over to visit them in their new home. After they had gone back to their own village, they decided to move in with the Hidatsa. They set up their village at the end of the Hidatsa village and theirs was called the End of the Village Dwelling.

After they had lived together for a few years, the whole village was called the Five Villages.

After living there for many years, some white settlers came to the village and started a trading post. The Indians, not knowing quite what the white men were doing, accused them of being thieves, and these white people put poison in the river to get even.

But there was one white man who thought a lot of the Indians and warned them to move from the village, back to the hills until everything was purified of the poison, then they could return. But after the white man warned them of the disease that may be called by the poisoning, they still did not believe him. They said that they had lived there by the water for a long time and it was theirs. Instead of moving back from the river, they moved west along it. And as they settled in new places, they had sickness in their villages, known as smallpox to the white men. Each time they camped, people would die, until they hit the Little Missouri and went along it, as far west as it goes.

It turns south and where it turns south, they left it and continued on west to the Yellowstone River. Finally they came to a place called Cherry Necklace fasting grounds. When they moved onto this place, after Cherry Necklace fasting, they decided to make their village there. Cherry Necklace built a sweat house there and when he had finished, he let every member of the tribe go clear through, in one door and out the other and he tapped them on the back as they went through. When they went through, each one was washed clean of smallpox. When this was done they counted the male warriors, from little boys on up, that could carry weapons. The total was only fifty.

*Our Story of Eagle Woman, Sacagawea*

## From interview of Pat Fredericks by Calvin Grinnell, both relatives of *Sacagawea*

My grandpa Phillip Snow's dad was Takes the Gun (Miduxha-Nootzhis), and he got sick and kept going down and going down. He went to Berry Necklace [Cherry Necklace] and asked him if he could heal him. So he said O.K. He said, "You come tomorrow." He said, "There will be some juneberry trees." He said, "They're going to be moving when you come, when you come there." He said, "If you see me sitting like I am now, I'll never be able to help you. But," he said, "if you see a bear laying there, then I can help you."

So the next day he [Takes the Gun] went over there like he [Cherry Necklace] said, and he seen a bear laying there. He told him when you see this, don't be afraid, come right up. He seen the bear and he came up to him and then he was sitting there. He said, then I can help you.

Grandpa said he [Cherry Necklace] took him [Takes the Gun] in a sweat tent and he start singing, and in his [Takes the Gun's] back he pulled one of these cockleburs that was wrapped with horsetail, he pulled that out. "Now we'll wait," he said. "I won't send it back to the guy that did this to you. But if he does [something else] then I'll send it back." He [Takes the Gun] said he never did [anything else]. Grandpa said then his dad got better.

**Marilyn Young Bird**, another relative of *Sacagawea*, also interviewed **Pat Fredericks** at the time of the Lewis and Clark Bicentennial. Pat gave additional information about Cherry Necklace:

"Cherry Necklace, a well known medicine man [and *Sacagawea*'s brother] with traveling route knowledge, told *Sakakawea* where to cross the Rocky Mountains, the location of and how to navigate the big waters and falls they were certain to encounter over the course of their journey. Cherry Necklace provided instructional information that helped *Sakakawea* excel."

*Sacagawea and Cherry Necklace*

## INDIVIDUAL HISTORY CARD.
(Formerly Allottee Family History Card.)

Tribe: Grosventres    Sex: M    Census or Allotment No.: 201
English name: Long Bear    Born: 1834    Died: Feb. 4, 191?
Indian name: Wah-pi-tsi-ha-tski    English translation of Indian name: Long Bear

|  | DIED. | Census or Allotment No. |
|---|---|---|
| Father: Cherry Necklace — 1/2 Crow 1/2 Gros | date unknown | unallotted |
| Father's father: Bad Lodge or Smoked Lodge — Gros | " " | unallotted |
| Father's mother: Girl Woman — Crow | " " | unallotted |
| Mother: Bug Woman — Gros | " " | unallotted |
| Mother's father: Tangled Woods — Gros | " " | unallotted |
| Mother's mother: | | |

| BROTHERS AND HALF-BROTHERS | Census or Allotment No. | UNCLES, FATHER'S SIDE | Census or Allotment No. |
|---|---|---|---|
| High Rump — Died date unknown | unallotted | Pan — died date unknown | unallotted |
| Raises His Arm — Died date unknown | unallotted | One Buffalo — died date unknown | unallotted |
| White Face 1/2 — Died 11-29-23 | 355 | Raises The Heart — died date unknown | |
| Brown Bear 1/2 — Died date unknown | unallotted | UNCLES, MOTHER'S SIDE | |
| Died | | | |
| SISTERS AND HALF-SISTERS | | AUNTS, FATHER'S SIDE | |
| Pink — Died date unknown | unallotted | Eagle Woman *Sacagawea* — died date unknown | unallotted |
| Many Comes Up — Died date unknown | unallotted | Bear Woman — died date unknown | unallotted |
| In The Water 1/2 — Died date unknown | unallotted | Otter — died date unknown | |
| Plenty Medicine 1/2 — Died 4-7-28 | 1469 | AUNTS, MOTHER'S SIDE | |
| Died | | Red Head — died date unknown | unallotted |

Individual History Card, son of Cherry Necklace. Note Aunts.

— MHA Interpretive Center

## Our Story of Eagle Woman, Sacagawea

*George Parshall and Fred Gunn, relatives. Fred Gunn, a descendant of Cherry Necklace and George Parshall, a descendant of Sacagawea.*
— MHA Interpretive Center

## Sacagawea and Cherry Necklace

*White Face, son of Cherry Necklace, and his wife He lived to be 106 years old.*
— State Historical Society of North Dakota

*Many Bears, son of Cherry Necklace and his family, August 24, 1898.*
— Photo from Rev. Harold Case, State Historical Society of North Dakota

**Many people from Ft. Berthold were and are related to *Sacagawea*. Evidence is from family acknowledgements, Ft. Berthold Agency records and DNA studies. The next section will tell of more relatives of *Sacagawea* and the Crow connection.**

**Sources Authored or Provided by MHA Tribal Members:**

Fredericks, Pat. Personal Interview by Calvin Grinnell, Tribal Historian.

Fredericks, Pat. Personal Interview by Marilyn Young Bird at the time of the Lewis and Clark Bicentennial.

Hudson, Marilyn and Grinnell, Calvin. "Heritage in question." *Minot Daily News*, August 9, 2001.

*Mandan, Hidatsa, Arikara Times*. "Welcome Lewis and Clark's Bicentennial Celebration." August 17, 2006.

*Sacagawea* Project Board Members. 2015-2020.

Stevenson, Rufus. "Cherry Necklace." Interpreted by Paige Baker. Sanish, ND.

Unpublished paper. "Biographical sketches of Chief Sitting Crow's Life."

Wolf Chief. Personal Interview conducted by Alfred W. Bowers in February-March, 1933, at Independence, on the Ft. Berthold Indian Reservation.

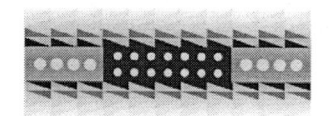

*Otter Woman, the mother of Sacagawea, and two female relatives came from Crow to Hidatsa country in about 1864 partly to find a suitable husband for a young granddaughter. Photo of Crow women camping in the Wolf Mountains, by W.A. Petzoldt, ca 1906. — McCracken Research Library, Cody, Wyo.*

# Chapter 8
## *OUR FAMILY CONNECTIONS*
### *More Relatives of Sacagawea*

**Sacagawea and Cherry Necklace came from an Hidatsa/Crow family. Other members of their family were ancestors of the Fredericks, Young Birds and Peases. These people have been among those to emphasize that *Sacagawea* was Hidatsa and Crow, not Shoshone, and have always recognized their relationship to the descendants of *Sacagawea* and Cherry Necklace. DNA evidence and Ft. Berthold and Crow agency records confirm this.**

Sacagawea's mother was **Otter Woman** (1) (Comes Out of the Water) and Cherry Necklace's mother was **Girl Woman**. They were Crow sisters who were both married to **Smoked Lodge**, Hidatsa. **A third sister**, unnamed, was the ancestor of the Fredericks, Young Bird, and Pease families. **This sister married Medicine Bull**, probably Hidatsa.

209

This sister and Medicine Bull had a **daughter, All Moves** (Moves Along), who married **Walks with Wolves**, also probably Hidatsa. All Moves and Walks with Wolves had a **daughter, She Kills**, who was enrolled as Hidatsa.

She Kills married Four Times, Crow. She Kills and Four Times **had a daughter, Goes Between** (Travels in the Middle). Goes Between married James Walker and was the **mother of Susie Walker Young Bird and Mary (Whitman, Nagle) Fredericks** of Ft. Berthold and **Sarah Pease** who lived at Crow.

Goes Between had a brother, Black Shield. In Bowers, *Hidatsa Social and Ceremonial Organization*, it states that Black Shield's father was a Crow Indian, Came Four Times. It states that Black Shield got the Bear Ceremony from Cherry Necklace who was his maternal grandmother's brother. Black Shield's maternal grandmother was All Moves. She would have been Cherry Necklace's cousin but sister in their kinship system.

One story, told by Naomi Foolish Bear — descendant of Cherry Necklace, is about Otter Woman (1), the mother of *Sacagawea,* and other female relatives of *Sacagawea* coming from Crow to Hidatsa country in about 1864 with a young granddaughter.

## Story told by Naomi Foolish Bear, Black Hawk

What I have heard from the old people that raised me who were living then; I was told by my elders that our old people came from the Crow country, a man by the name of Cherry Necklace and his sisters.

This man by the name of Cherry Necklace and his sisters, they had been lost. His sisters, three of them, for many days they were lost, along with riding horses. For that reason, their brother Cherry Necklace, saying that his sisters may have been killed by the enemy, searched for many days for his sisters and did not find them. And he searched, he tracked them, and their tracks were coming this way, towards Fishhook Village.

## More Relatives of Sacagawea

*Relatives - Naomi Foolish Bear Black Hawk, Cora Young Bird Baker, Fred Gunn, Naomi and Fred, descendants of Cherry Necklace. All related to Sacagawea or Maeshuwea.* — MHA Times, MHA Interpretive Center

So, at which time Cherry Necklace, seeing which way the footprints led, went back to the Crow village. Having gone back to the village, he told the people that they had not been killed by the enemy, for he said, "I have seen their footprints headed in the direction of Fishhook Village." Upon telling the people, immediately he started fixing his food supply and other supplies he needed and his horses. He immediately proceeded to come this way, following the Yellowstone River.

As he continued to come this way, he traveled until he came to *Mide-shaw-ashish*. Stopping at Hidatsa camps from place to place, he would stop and rest, continuing on this way. At most times he traveled by night, finding a coulee or washout, he would hide his horse and rest. But there were times when he could travel by day; then he would again find a ravine and hide his horse and rest.

He traveled until he came to *Hidatsa Adish*, the place known as Running, at the head [mouth] of the Yellowstone River.

Some Hidatsas were still there, and seeing them there, he asked them, "Did you see any travelers coming by way of the water?" These Hidatsas were there hunting. Then he came a little further, following the Yellowstone and he rested. When he asked them, they said they did not see anybody.

He continued traveling and resting until he came to the place called Hanging Gun. He must have traveled a long time until he came to two Hidatsa villages, one on each side of the river and he stayed at one of them. And he asked them people at the village, "Did you see any riders?" And the villagers said, "Yes, three ladies and they went east with the hunters who were headed in that direction." They traveled along the river and didn't stop until they came to Fishhook Village. When Cherry Necklace saw that, he didn't worry about them, knowing they were in safe company.

And they came along the edge of the river, they came upon a home that was lit, and at that time, Cherry Necklace saw that most of the homes were earth lodges. He was with others, as they were talking, as he looked around, he saw a lot of activity in the village, but he said we will go to that one, where the smoke hole was lit. So they [the ladies] went to the furthest earth lodge; they saw that the people were still awake and they got off their horses with their blankets and things. They got off their horses and entered the lodge, "These are a different tribe." And so some of the men took their horses and put them out to pasture. They said, "These are people from a different lodge."

These people, the home they arrived at, were the people of the present-day John Brave; that was his family. That was John Brave's mother and grandmother, a long time ago. That's whose home the Crow ladies arrived at. And it had been some time, a few nights, they stayed there that the family took them in and made relatives with them. A while later, a man by the name of Cherry Necklace showed up. At that point, I forgot who is older, the ladies or Cherry Necklace.

So I don't know how many days he was looking for his sisters, when he came to Fishhook Village, and asking around, he went over there and found them.

Upon going over there, he went and joined them and stayed a short time. There were a lot of men and a lot of women; there were about four homes and they lived here and there. So they stayed with them.

Their brother Cherry Necklace asked them, "Why did you come over here?" He said, "Over there, there used to be men who came, asking for them, and they were fearless warriors. And the reason they came was because they wanted to marry them." "And I don't know why our family members didn't want these men to be with us. Since they didn't like them, we figured these men must be bad. And that is the reason why we left and came to the Hidatsa people."

After that, their brother Cherry Necklace and the sisters continued to live among the Hidatsa people and after that, they all got married to Hidatsa men. And even their brother Cherry Necklace married a Hidatsa woman.

For that reason, as they continued to stay there among John Brave's family, it was known that John Brave's [family] belonged to the Low Cap clan. They said it is good that we live with a Low Cap family. Saying that, they were adopted by John Brave's family, which was Low Cap. That is the way it was told to me by my mother...

As time went on, I found out those three Crow ladies' names. One's name was Moves Along, another's name Travels in the Middle or Travels a Long Distance, and Comes Out of the Water. And now the one known as Comes Out of the Water [Otter Woman (1)—the mother of *Sacagawea*], her descendant is George Parshall. Travels in the Middle's [Goes Between] descendants are Young Birds. And the last one, Moves Along's [All Moves] descendants, are Fredericks. [Young Birds and Fredericks are both descendants of Travels in the Middle (Goes Between) and Moves Along (All Moves). All Moves is Goes Between's grandmother.]

Our [Naomi's] grandmother, Has Many Medicine [Plenty Medicine], Cherry Necklace's daughter, when she died, there was no one to send her off with a proper burial, cause her dad [Cherry Necklace] was a Crow [because his mother was Crow, not in the Hidatsa matrilineal line].

## Our Story of Eagle Woman, Sacagawea

So the people said, what about a Low Cap? But others said, she's not a Low Cap. Her dad is a Crow. George Parshall said it would be best if a Three-Clan bury her. So then, a woman by the name of Hurt buried her. [Bowers' book states that Cherry Necklace was adopted into the *Maxoxati*, Alkali Lodge, Three Clan.]

Comes out of the Water's [Otter Woman's (1)] daughter is *Ma-shu-weash*; in Hidatsa, it is *Ma-ish-shu-weash*, Eagle Woman. Later they changed it to Bird Woman. That's George Parshall's grandmother. That's what I was told a long time ago, that these people were not Hidatsa, but were Crow. Their elders are Crows. And today, it is told they are Hidatsa because they lived here so long. I have been told two women went back to the Crow country. Travels in the Middle's [Goes Between] grandmother [Moves Along] went back. Comes Out of the Water [Otter Woman (1)] went back. Cherry Necklace was 95 when he died. And my grandmother [in the Hidatsa kinship system because Naomi was a descendant of Cherry Necklace], *Mida-bow-gay*, she was Otter Woman (3) [Bulls Eye's mother]. And that's what my grandmother, Has the Otter, told me.

And then it was known that Cherry Necklace went with a lot of Hidatsas towards Singing Butte. That's where he fasted, he had a spring, Big Frog Spring. He took all the relatives and he put them all at that spring and they all got well. At that time, the Hidatsas residing at Fishhook Village were all getting weak. Only then did they come back. And that is the history of it all, there's alot more to it, and should I recall, if I remember it I will tell you.

**The women were called "sisters" because they were Cherry Necklace's close female relatives through his mother. Comes Out of the Water (Otter Woman (1))** was the mother of *Sacagawea* and Cherry Necklace's aunt. **Moves Along (All Moves)** was Cherry Necklace and *Sacagawea*'s cousin (sister). **Travels in the Middle (Goes Between)** was the granddaughter of Moves Along (All Moves).

*More Relatives of Sacagawea*

The "sisters" came in about 1864 probably partly to find a husband for Goes Between who would have been in her early teens at the time. She did marry James Walker at Ft. Berthold in about 1865 (Her oldest daughter was 10 years old in 1876 — See story by Helen Pease Wolf.) Crow/Hidatsa relatives went back and forth between the two tribes. Naomi's story says that Moves Along (All Moves, ancestor of the Pease, Young Bird and Fredericks families) and Comes Out of the Water (Otter Woman (1), *Sacagawea's* mother) went back to Crow.

Cherry Necklace would have been about 86 when the women came to the Hidatsas. Comes Out of the Water (Otter Woman (1), *Sacagawea's* mother) would have been about 92. Moves Along (All Moves), Cherry Necklace and *Sacagawea's* cousin (sister), would have been about 50. *Sacagawea* would have been about 77 when they came.

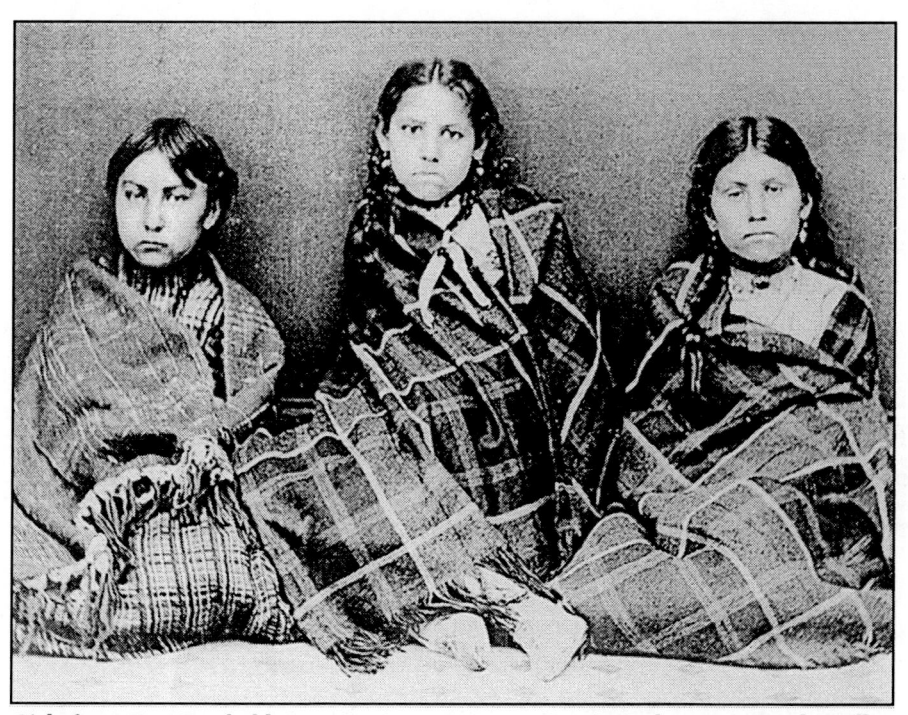

*Girls from Fort Berthold, L. to R.: Anna Dawson, Carrie Anderson & Sarah Walker upon arrival at the Hampton Normal & Agricultural Institute, Hampton, VA, 1878.*
— Hampton University Archives

*Our Story of Eagle Woman, Sacagawea*

*The same three girls again, 14 months later, with Sarah Walker at center.*
— Hampton University Archives

**Those who came to live with the Hidatsas, even if they were part Hidatsa, were adopted into an Hidatsa clan if they followed a matrilineal line from another tribe. This was the case with the women who came from Crow.**

*More Relatives of Sacagawea*

**Following is a story about Sarah Walker Pease, descendant of All Moves (Moves Along), She Kills, and Goes Between.**

## My Mother, Sarah Walker Pease

from *Reaching Both Ways* by Helen Pease Wolf, half Crow and half Anglo

My mother, Sarah Walker (Pease) brought with her a varied and intriguing story of two cultures.

Sarah's father, James Walker, was of Scotch-Irish descent. He left his home in New York in 1850 to travel west intrigued by the prospect of finding gold.

He entered the Fort Berthold Indian Reservation along the Missouri River in the Dakota territory at the Hitatsis (Hidatsas) Grosventre (misnamed) Indian village, and he decided to stay a short time in order to study Indian village life. His red wavy hair, which he wore to his shoulders, caused a stir among the Indians, but they liked his friendly disposition.

One day he made friends with a young Indian lady named Walks Amongst (Goes Between). This friendship developed and they became engaged and later were married by a Jesuit priest.

James Walker built a family home on the edge of the Indian village, and he furnished the house with needed furnishing that he made. He and Walks Amongst (Goes Between) were happy, even though sign language was their only way to communicate.

The following spring, Sarah, my mother, was born. Later, the Walkers had two more daughters, Mary (Whitman, Nagle, Fredericks) and Susie (Young Bird). The girls learned to speak and understand both languages (English and Crow) and this drew the family together. They had a cow and chickens and shared the eggs and milk with the village Indians. Sarah and her two younger sisters made friends with the many children in the village.

One April morning, Sarah went to the village to play with the children. She carried her Christmas doll on her back and wore one of her mother's shawls.

## Our Story of Eagle Woman, Sacagawea

Looking east, the children saw soldiers approaching, with a loaded wagon following in the background. All the children ran and hid, except Sarah. She stood watching the soldiers approach. An attractive man with shoulder length hair got off his horse and talked to Sarah. She noticed that the soldier was a General. She had no fear because her daddy was a white man. The soldier admired her pretty doll and her long braids and she smiled.

Before leaving, the soldier gave her a pack containing stick candy, hardtack, and dried fruit. She thanked him, then watched as the soldiers rode on, traveling west. Sarah stood quietly by, waving and smiling until all had passed. When the soldiers left, the children came out of their hiding places, and their mothers scolded Sarah for speaking to the soldiers. Later, when she told her parents about this experience, they were puzzled too. She shared her bag of goodies with her two younger sisters. Sarah was ten years old when this happened on an April morning in 1876.

Two months later, news spread quickly about General George Custer's [death]. This shocking news grieved little Sarah, as she realized that General Custer was the man she had talked with on that April morning. Years later, when retelling this story to her grandchildren, her pretty brown eyes would fill with tears.

Sarah had never attended school. Her sisters were growing up and her parents were mastering both English and Crow. To attend school meant leaving the reservation. While she didn't want to leave the reservation, she was curious when Colonel Pratt, a distinguished officer of the United States Army, visited the reservation to enroll interested Indian children in Hampton Institute in Virginia. This was a private Christian school for Blacks, but the government was willing to pay the tuition for Indian children on a trial basis. Sarah was one of the first enrolled with five other girls and three boys from the Hitatsis (Hidatsa) reservation.

Sarah began to get ready by sewing calico school dresses. Her mother was somewhat reluctant to let her go so far away, but her dad encouraged her. With much preparation through the summer months, she was now ready to leave the reservation. Many friends lined the Missouri banks to see them off, and Colonel Pratt was on hand to supervise the trip.

It wouldn't have taken much for Sarah to change her mind as she looked at her beloved family before boarding the steamboat which took the children down the Missouri river on the way to Virginia. Tenderhearted Sarah found herself alone and sobbing but the Colonel soon had her in his arms and wiped her tears with his handkerchief. At St. Louis, they continued their trip by rail, arriving safely at Hampton where they were warmly welcomed by the student body and teachers.

Everything appeared different, but Sarah decided she was going to like the school. Children from many other reservations were there, and Sarah made friends easily. She especially liked the devoted Christian teachers and felt fortunate Booker T. Washington was one of her supervisors. Before long Sarah had mastered the Sioux language.

At the end of the first school term, the five girls returned to the reservation, and that left Sarah alone. The three boys died of climatic change and loneliness. While attending Hampton for eight years, Sarah went up in the New England states during the summer months and worked for families doing general housework and back in the fall for school. This continued until she finished school.

After finishing school, Sarah left for Montana to accept a position at Bonds Unitarian Mission. On her way, she stopped at the Fort Berthold Reservation to make a short visit with her relatives. Her parents had died while she was away at school, but she enjoyed the company of her two sisters.

She later arrived at the Bonds Unitarian Christian Industrial School for Crow Indian children located in the lower Big Horn Valley overlooking the beautiful Big Horn River. Here she served as school seamstress, matron, and interpreter.

There were very few English speaking Indians at that time. Sarah's tender understanding helped the students deal with life away from home. She held the school and teachers in high esteem.

## Our Story of Eagle Woman, Sacagawea

She told of hearing the children weeping when they first arrived, and she would begin to speak to them in their language, and then they wouldn't feel so lonely. Sarah spent two years at the Bonds School. While at the Bonds School, Sarah met George Pease, a half blood Crow who was employed at the Catholic Indian Mission at St. Xavier, Montana. This mission was located along the Big Horn River sixty miles south of Bonds School. George visited Sarah when he could. They were married by Rev. Bond in the small school chapel.

Crow Relative, Mary Young Bird Lone Fight, She Kills, relatives of Sacagawea.
— MHA Interpretive Center

## More Relatives of Sacagawea

Sarah Walker Pease and her sisters, Mary and Susie, were the daughters of Goes Between (Walks Amongst or Travels in the Middle), granddaughters of She Kills and great granddaughters of Moves Along or All Moves. Susie Walker Young Bird's individual history card states that Goes Between died in about 1880.

| Indian name A-ru-ma-tsub *Mary Fredericks* | | English translation of Indian name, Berries | | |
|---|---|---|---|---|
| | | | DIED | CENSUS OR ALLOTMENT No. |
| Father James Walker | | White | date unknown | unallotted |
| Father's father | | White | " | unallotted |
| Father's mother | | White | " | unallotted |
| Mother Goes Between | | Gros | " | unallotted |
| Mother's father Four Times | | Crow | " | unallotted |
| Mother's mother She Kills | | Gros | 10-18-20 | 281 |
| BROTHERS AND HALF-BROTHERS | CENSUS OR ALLOTMENT No. | UNCLES, FATHER'S SIDE | | CENSUS OR ALLOTMENT No. |
| None | | | | |
| Died | | | | |
| Died | | | | |
| Died | | UNCLES, MOTHER'S SIDE | | |
| | | Strikes the Drum died date unknown | | unallotted |
| Died | | Black Shield died date unknown | | unallotted |
| Died | | AUNTS, FATHER'S SIDE | | |
| SISTERS AND HALF-SISTERS | | | | |
| Susie Walker Died 8-5-44 | 262 Crow Agency Montana | | | |
| Sarah W. Pease Died | | AUNTS, MOTHER'S SIDE | | |
| Died | | Bear Woman died date unknown | 1/2 | unallotted |
| Died | | | | |
| Died | | | | |

*Individual History Card for Mary Fredericks, Ft. Berthold Agency*

She Kills died in 1920 at the age of 85; she lived at Ft. Berthold and is buried at the Mandaree Catholic Cemetery. Her grave was moved there with the coming of the Garrison Dam. Gerard Baker, grandson of Susie Young Bird, remembers his mother, Cora, telling about She Kills raising some of her grandchildren and that she had Bear Medicine and would go into a trance while using it.

*Mary Walker Fredericks and Susie Nagle on right.*
— MHA Interpretive Center

### The Hidatsa — Crow Connection

In early March, 2004, leaders of the Crow Nation and leaders of the Mandan, Hidatsa, Arikara Nation met in a historic gathering at the MHA Nation.

## More Relatives of Sacagawea

According to the histories of both tribes and their oral teachings, the Crow people and the Hidatsa people were at one time one unified tribe. An article in the *MHA Times* of March 18, 2004, provided details of the meeting. Crow Tribal Council Chairman Carl Venne explained his visit was to reinvigorate the culture and the heritage of the tribes.

*Sarah Walker Pease, Mary Walker Fredericks and Susie Walker Young Bird. The Sisters were daughters of Goes Between.* — MHA Interpretive Center

## Our Story of Eagle Woman, Sacagawea

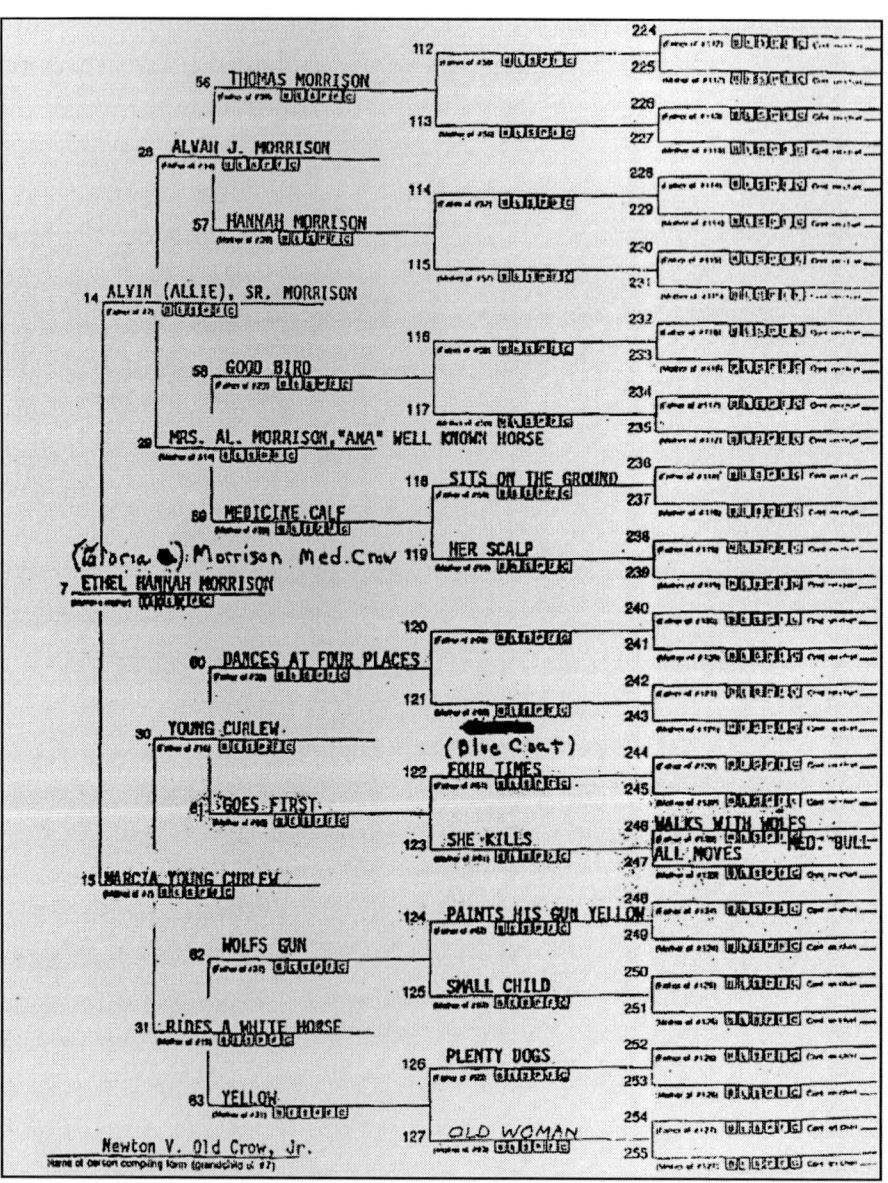

*Family tree from Crow Agency that contains relatives of Sacagawea and ancestors of the Fredericks, Young Bird and Pease families.*
— Morrison Family

*More Relatives of Sacagawea*

## SACAGAWEA (MAESHUWEA) FAMILY TREE

Girl Woman — sisters — Otter Woman (Comes Out of the Water) — sisters — Unnamed Crow woman
+Smoked Lodge                                    +Smoked Lodge                                +Medicine Bull
→                                                →                                            →

Cherry Necklace                  Sacagawea (*Maeshuwea*, Eagle Woman)                 All Moves (Moves Along)
+Bug Woman — sisters — Red Head  +Toussaint Charbonneau                               +Walks with Wolves
+Different Woman                 →                                                    →
→
                                 Jean Baptiste Charbonneau (Pomp)                     She Kills
Children -                                    and                                     +Four Times
Long Bear                        Otter Woman   Cedar Woman   Different Breast         →
High Rump                        +Lean Bull    +Head or Pan
Raises His Arm                   →             →                                      Goes Between
Pink - Female                                                                         +James Walker
Many Comes Up - Female           Bulls Eye     Medicine Arm                           →
White Face                                     +William Parshall
Brown Bear                                     →                                      Mary Walker Whitman
In the Water - Female                                                                 Nagle, Fredericks
Plenty Medicine or Has Many                    George Parshall                        and
Medicine - Female                              →                                      Sarah Walker Pease
Many Bears                                                                            and
→                                              Delores Parshall Sand and siblings    Susie Walker Young Bird
                                                                                      →
Their descendants -                            Their descendants -                    Their descendants -

*Sacagawea (Maeshuwea) Family Tree*

225

"Our younger people might forget this history, but at one time we were one tribe," stated the Crow chairman.

Chairman Venne mentioned that some of the oral stories say the tribes separated because maybe one family got [upset] over some food.

Venne noted, so many of the stories at Crow are Hidatsa stories, and most of the Hidatsa stories run parallel with the Crow tribe. "Everything we do is just about the same and come from this real powerful medicine way back in our ancestry. There's so many common things. There's alot of relatives at Crow that are Hidatsa."

Dr. Barney Old Coyote, a member of the Crow Nation and tribal elder, also accompanied the delegation to the MHA Nation. "We had a pipe ceremony where our tribal leader smoked the pipe with the leader of the Three Affiliated Tribes and the council. I felt very humbled to realize this was my heritage as a Crow Indian, and that I am descended from this tribe. We're back in the country where we began. We look forward to continuing this relationship and maybe we can have changes in our way of lives, but we will always be one people."

"I think there's a great future and I'm thinking of all the bad things that have been done in the past, more particularly the bad representation that has been written and published about these two people, the Three Affiliated Tribes and the Crow people by non-Indians. **I see a great opportunity to correct those things through this cultural exchange and relationship so that in the future, not only Lewis and Clark [stories], but we correct all the other books that have been published."**

**Marilyn Young Bird,** a relative of *Sacagawea* from Fort Berthold, provided information from an interview at the time of the Lewis and Clark Bicentennial with Pat Fredericks, another relative known to be very knowledgeable of *Sacagawea*'s story.

Pat said:

At one time, the Hidatsa and Crow people were one Nation and lived together in the northern plains of Turtle Island [North America]. They lived together in the vicinity of Knife River, located in the state of North Dakota. As a consequence of differences in leadership styles, a portion of the Nation left the Knife River area and settled near the mouth of a river now called the Yellowstone River. Today, we and other tribes recognize these relatives as the Crow Nation.

Many families traveled back and forth between the two locations for the purpose of visiting relatives. *Sakakawea*'s family did the same. Led by her father, Smoked Lodge, and accompanied by her brother Cherry Necklace and her sister She Kills, *Sakakawea* traveled to and from the Yellowstone country many times.

**Meriwether Lewis** wrote *The Travels of Lewis and Clark*. "These people (Crow Indians) regularly visit the Mandans, Menetares (Gros Ventres) [Hidatsas] with whom they barter horses, mules, leather goods, and many articles of Indian apparel, for which they receive in return, guns, ammunition, axes, kettles, awls, and other European manufactures.

When they return to their country, they are in turn visited by the Snake Indians, with whom they barter most of the articles they have obtained from the nations down the Missouri, for horses and mules, of which those nations have a greater abundance than themselves."

**Following are stories from the Crow people indicating that *Sacagawea* lived there as a young girl.**

### Story by Joe Medicine Crow, Crow Tribal Historian

There is a Crow Indian story about the Indian woman who had become famous as the only woman in the Lewis and Clark expedition.

## Our Story of Eagle Woman, Sacagawea

Douglas Rides the Bear, an elder, related the following story to Crow Tribal historian, Joe Medicine Crow, in the early 1960s: Long, long time ago, before there were a group of white men coming into the Crow country, a tribe of Indians (Shoshone) came to visit the Crows somewhere in the headwaters of the Missouri or Yellowstone rivers. These people came from the west on the other side of the big mountains (Rockies).

In the Crow camp was a sick child. Healers could not help the little girl. It was reported that a woman of the visitors was very good in taking care of sick children and bringing them back to health. The woman was summoned and she agreed to take care of the child. Soon the little Crow girl was doing well.

Then the time came for the visitors to go back. The parents of the sick child asked and perhaps begged the nurse to stay and attend the child awhile longer. Later, the nurse would be taken back to her people and given many valuable gifts. She agreed and said she wanted a teenage daughter or granddaughter to stay behind with her. **[The Shoshone woman was probably from the family that was adopted by *Sacagawea*'s family.]** Soon the young girl made friends with Crow girls and was quite comfortable and happy with her new friends. When girls go swimming and had races she would easily beat them. The girls would say that she could swim like a frog. Soon she was given the name *Sauk Bia*, Frog Woman.

One day, some Earthen Lodges, now called Hidatsa, came to visit their Crow relatives who were camped up the headwaters of the Missouri River. These visitors came from their villages along the Missouri near the present location of Bismarck, North Dakota. When the (Hidatsa) visitors left, they took *Sauk Bia*, the Frog Woman, apparently with the knowledge and consent of the Crows. There was no account of abduction or what happened to the grandmother. In closing, may I point out an interesting and intriguing semantic question. The two words forming the name of this girl are quite similar in sound but have different meanings: *Sauk-bia*, frog woman in Crow; *Seguak-wia*, bird woman in Hidatsa.

## More Relatives of Sacagawea

*Sacagawea* was probably at Crow from Hidatsa country with her own family and/or Crow relatives and/or with her adopted Shoshone relatives. Her father had an adopted brother/family among the Shoshones, and *Sacagawea*'s family and the Shoshone family visited back and forth and would have been very close. If *Sacagawea* was with a Shoshone woman, it would have helped foster the misconception that she was Shoshone.

*Sacagawea* was probably taken back to Hidatsa country with her own family and/or with Charbonneau, as early informants state that he probably got her at Crow and from her Hidatsa father, which would help to foster the belief that she was taken captive by the Hidatsa. Some believe that her Frog Woman name morphed into *Sacagawea*, Bird Woman, from Eagle Woman. Medicine Crow ended his article with a note that *Sacagawea* was known to have a sister, She Kills, whom the Hidatsa also acknowledge as her "sister."

**Oral tradition places a young *Sacajawea* with Crow.**
— *Billings Gazette*, July 23, 2010

*Sacajawea* may have spent part of her childhood among the Crow, Crow historian, **Elias Goes Ahead**, said. Goes Ahead, who has been researching the Lewis and Clark Expedition from the Crow point of view, said his information came from an old account taken by a nephew of White Dog, who died in the 1930s at the age of 106. He stated, "This girl was good at taking care of sick babies. An older Crow woman took her in and taught her women's work. This girl was athletic. The older Crows always had young women swim in contests. This girl had a nice breast stroke- she used her legs like a frog swimming in the water and she always won. Her swimming style was the inspiration for her Crow name — *Sag-Bia*, translated as Frog woman.

The article does, however, say that she was Shoshone and had been gotten by the Crows from the Hidatsas and then captured back by the Hidatsas. He goes on, "A few years later, visiting Crows recognized her among the Hidatsa in what is now North Dakota. That was where Lewis and Clark found her in 1804." The older Crow woman was probably *Sacagawea*'s own grandmother.

Goes Ahead stated that although there were four Crow bands reportedly on the Yellowstone in the summer of 1806 when Clark set out to explore it, the Crow made no attempt to meet members of the expedition. But Goes Ahead also said that according to one Crow story, *Sacajaw*ea (*Sag-Bia*) had a brother named Cherry Necklace, who married a River Crow and lived among her people. He said that Cherry Necklace, a shaman, met his sister at Pompey's Pillar and presented her with a white buffalo dress.

**No such meeting between the Crows and the Lewis and Clark party was recorded in the journals, but a similar story is told by the Hidatsas. The Hidatsa version states that Cherry Necklace gave Charbonneau a white buffalo horse. There is some disagreement as to when this meeting occurred: the year before the Expedition, during the Expedition, or in 1816-17 when *Sacagawea* and Charbonneau made the trip to the southwest. The Crows are known to commemorate Lewis and Clark events at Pompey's Pillar in Montana, along the route of the expedition and named by Clark after Pomp, *Sacagawea*'s son. In the summer of 2018, the Crow event at Pompey's Pillar recognized *Sacagawea* as being Hidatsa/Crow.**

**William Ware,** whose presentation, "The Prophecy of Old Spotted Horse," in the seminar "A Confluence of Cultures, Native Americans and the Expedition of Lewis and Clark," University of Montana, 2003, stated that there is plenty of information about the arrival of Lewis and Clark, but the historical record lacks detailed information of their meeting with the People of the Long Beaked Bird, the Crow.

## More Relatives of Sacagawea

*River Crow Chiefs on the banks of the Yellowstone, opposite the mouth of the Big Porcupine River, ambrotype by James D. Hutton, traveling with the William F. Raynolds Expedition, August 21 or 22, 1859. Twists His Tail (Wraps Up his Horse's Tail for War), the River Crow Head Chief, is seated at the right. Next to him is his Camp Soldier, Bear's Head. Note the grizzly bear claws on his moccasins.*
— Beinecke Library Collection, Yale University.

Information regarding *Sacagawea*'s relatives and her Crow connection is well documented.

**Now, armed with a great deal of evidence, we can tell our story. The next section outlines our response to journal accounts from the Lewis and Clark Expedition.**

*Crow tribal celebration at Pompey's Pillar, Montana, 2018, with reenactment of meeting the Lewis and Clark Expedition, including Sacagawea.*

## Sources Authored or Provided by MHA Tribal Members:

Black Hawk, Naomi Foolish Bear. "Story of Three Sisters," Unpublished.

Fredericks, Pat. Personal Interview by Marilyn Young Bird, Lewis and Clark Bicentennial

MHA Times, "Gathering," March 18, 2004.

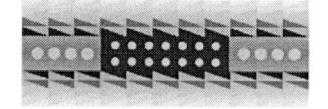

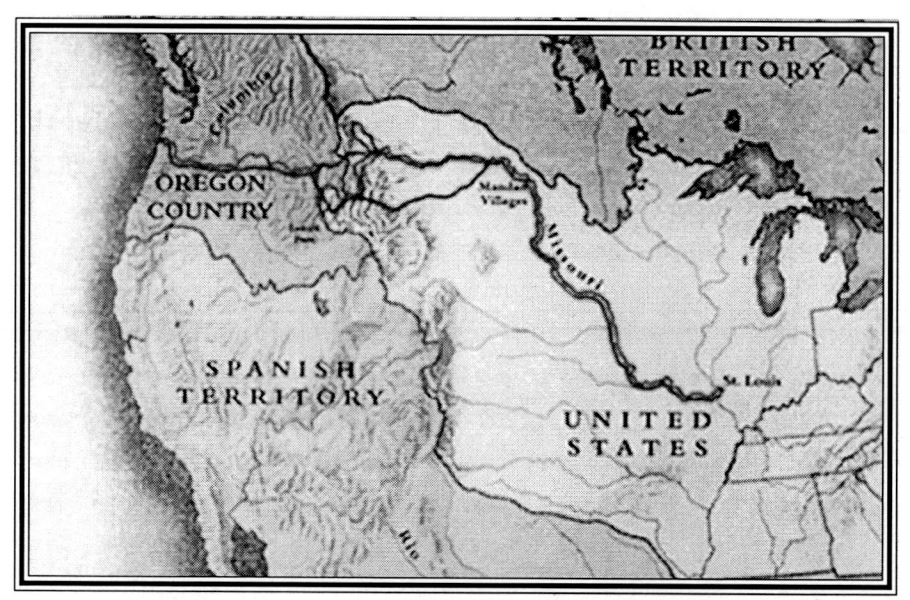

*Map of the Lewis and Clark Expedition, 1803-1806*

## Chapter 9
### *OUR RESPONSE*
*Sacagawea Entries in the Journals*

**N**ext is our response to journal accounts from the Lewis and Clark expedition and, following that, a summary of our evidence and a timeline of *Sacagawea's* life based upon our knowledge of her.

Lewis and Clark entries are taken from Ruben Gold Thwaites, editor (1904 edition), and other named sources. *Sacagawea*-related entries are presented here with explanations from people of the MHA Nation to correct erroneous interpretations. Language interpretation errors most probably resulted in inaccuracies, and there were other reasons for misinterpretation as well.

**Lewis and Clark and company were living in the Mandan Villages for the winter, preparing to leave for the West in the spring.**

**The Indian people were suspicious of them, as were the local fur traders. Rumors that were not favorable for the visitors spread among these two groups who then accused the Lewis and Clark party of taking harmful actions against the locals.**

November 4, 1804 (Clark)
*A fine morning, we continued to cut down trees and raise our houses. A Mr. Chaubonie, interpreter for the Gross Ventre nation came to see us, and informed that [he] came down with several Indians from a hunting expedition up the river, to hear what we had told the Indians in Council. This man wished to hire as an interpreter.*

November 4, 1804 (Ernest Staples Osgood, ed., The Field Notes of Captain William Clark, 1964 edition)
*A French man by name Chabonah, who speaks the Gros Ventre, [Hidatsa] language visit us. He wished to hire and informed us his 2 [wives] were Snake Indians. We engaged him to go on with us and take one of his wives to interpret the Snake language.*

**People of the MHA Nation believe that Charbonneau lied about his wives being Snake (Shoshone) in order to get the job. A second explanation is that someone told that *Sacagawea* had snake medicine, and it was interpreted that she was a Snake Indian. A third explanation stems from the fact that *Sacagawea's* father, Smoked Lodge, had adopted a Shoshone man as his brother. Their families would have considered themselves to be one, and they would have visited back and forth. If Charbonneau used this information to present her as Shoshone, he did not correct the half truth. He kept the inaccuracy going because he was the interpreter. *Sacagawea* may not have seen this as a lie.**

## Sacagawea Entries in the Journals

November 27, 1804 (Clark)

*Many circumstances combined to give force to those [unfavorable] reports, i.e., the movement of the interpreters and their families to the Fort [Mandan], the strength of our work, etc. One report was that the [Lewis and Clark] party would join with the Dacotah to fight the Mandans and Gros Ventres (Hidatsa).*

**The interpreters and their families were moved to the Fort [Mandan] where they were with the Lewis and Clark party who would have gotten to know them. A statement from Ft. Berthold Agency to Charles Eastman stated that Lewis and Clark became fond of *Sacagawea*.**

November 29, 1804 (Clark)

*Heard that Francois Larocque wanted to give medals and flags to certain tribal leaders to make them chiefs. As he denied this, we agreed that one of our interpreters should speak for him on conditions he did not say anything more than what tended [related] to trade alone.*

In a footnote to the journals, Ruben Thwaites wrote:

The interpreter lent to the British was Charboneau. [Charles] MacKenzie, of the Northwest Company, thus describes the method of Lewis and Clark's communications with the Indians: A mulatto, who spoke bad French and worse English, served as interpreter to the Captains, so that a single word to be understood by the party required to pass from the Natives to the woman [*Sacagawea*, Indian wife of Charboneau, who could not speak English], from the woman to the husband, from the husband to the mulatto, from the mulatto to the captains. The mulatto most likely was René Jaussaume.

**The people of Fort Berthold have been concerned about the lack of accurate communication during the expedition because of so many languages being used and the likelihood of misinterpretation. According to Calvin Grinnell, Tribal Historian, Charbonneau was known to be a very poor interpreter.**

Reverend Charles Hall, stationed at Ft. Berthold, stated in *The Village Indians of the Upper Missouri by Meyer, 1925*, "Although he (Charbonneau) was said to speak seven different languages, it was hard to understand him in any." Charles MacKenzie stated that Jessaume [who interpreted from Charbonneau's French to English for Lewis and Clark, and back] spoke English that ranged somewhere between inadequate and nonexistent, and that the Frenchmen, Charbonneau and Jessaume, had disputes about the meaning of every word taken by the captain.

*Sacagawea* spoke Hidatsa and Crow, with her father being Hidatsa, and her mother Crow. She probably also spoke some Shoshone because of her family's connection to them. The Crow people lived near the Shoshones at the time and the tribes interacted regularly. *Sacagawea* lived part of the time among her mother's people. She had also visited the Shoshones a year before with Charbonneau. She most likely also knew sign language. In any case, the language situation surely resulted in inaccuracies all through the journals. Each communication should be seen as a possible misinterpretation.

December 24, 1804 (Patrick Gass Journal)

*At half past 2 another gun was fired, as a notice to assemble at the dance, which was continued in a jovial manner till 8 at night; and without the presence of any females, except three . . . wives to our interpreter, who took no other part than the amusement of looking on.*

This seems to indicate that Charbonneau had three wives at this time. Two of them were *Sacagawea* and her sister, Otter Woman. In *Coyote Warrior* by Paul VanDevelder, it states that *Sacagawea* lived with her sister and Charbonneau. Many accounts name Otter Woman as another wife of Charbonneau. Ft. Berthold records list *Sacagawea* (Eagle

Woman) and Otter Woman as sisters. Coues, who wrote of the expedition in 1893, states that Charbonneau had two other wives besides *Sacagawea* among the Mandans. Bulls Eye stated that Charbonneau had wives among the Mandan, Hidatsa and Arikara, and it is known that he had a 14-year old Ute wife toward the end of his life.

January 13, 1805 (Clark)

*Mr. Chabonee (our interpreter) and one man that accompanied him to some lodges of the Menatarres [Hidatsa]... returned... Chaboneau informs that the Clerk of the Hudson's Bay Co. with the Me ne tar res had been speaking some few expressions unfavorable towards us, and that it is said the NW Co. intend building a fort at the Mene tar res. He saw the grand chief of the Big Bellies [Gros Ventre] who spoke slightly of the Americans, saying if we would give our great flag to him he would come to see us.*

**This indicates the discontent of the Indian people and the fur traders in regard to Lewis and Clark.**

February 11, 1805 (Lewis)

*About five o'clock this evening one of the wives of Charbono was delivered of a fine boy. This was the first child which this woman had borne, and... her labor was tedious and the pain violent. Mr. Jessome informed me that he had frequently administered a small portion of the rattle of the rattle-snake, which he assured me had never failed to produce... hastening the birth of the child. Having the rattle of a snake by me, I gave it to him and he administered two rings of it to the woman broken in small pieces with the fingers and added to a small quantity of water... I was informed that she had not taken it more than ten minutes before she brought forth [a child].*

Coues wrote in his notes: This was *Sacajawea*, the Shoshone captive purchased by Charbonneau, who had two other wives among the Mandan. *Sacajawea* was the only woman taken upon the Expedition.

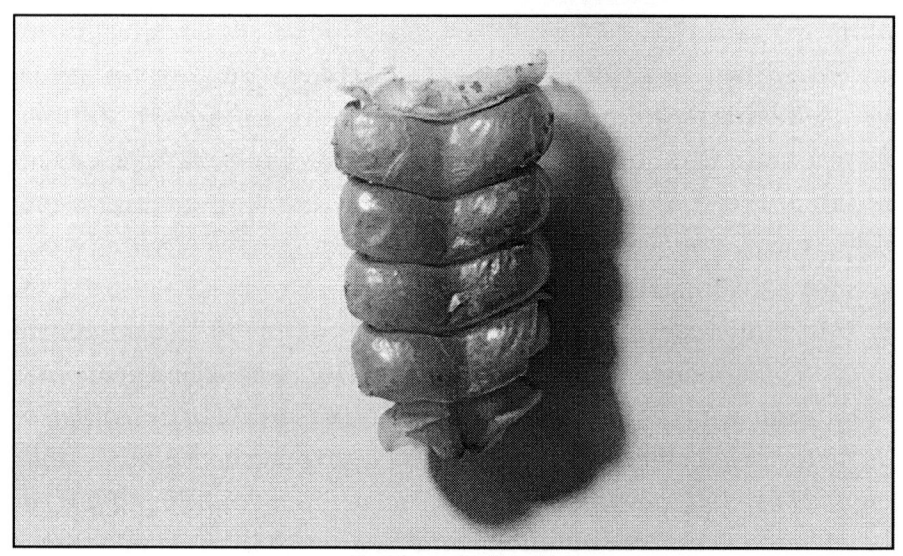

*Rattlesnake Rattle*

**Sacagawea was not a Shoshone captive. She was given to Charbonneau by her Hidatsa father probably at Crow, according to early informants, this helping to foster the idea that she was a captive of the Hidatsa. Her baby, Jean Baptiste or Pomp as Clark called him, became a very accomplished man. His obituary states that his mother was half Crow Indian, and he was returning to Montana to the land of his people when he died in Oregon of Mountain Fever. Sacagawea, herself, had snake medicine like her brother, Cherry Necklace. It is probable that the medicine was her own.**

March 1, 1805

*Sharbonaur returned this evening from the Gross Ventres... He (our Menetarre interpreter) had received a present from Mr. Chaboillez of the N.W. [fur] Company of the following articles: 3 Brace of Cloth, 1 Brace of Scarlet, a pair of Corduroy overalls, 1 Vest, 1 Brace Blue Cloth, 1 Brace Red or scarlet with 3 bars, 200 balls and powder, 2 braces of tobacco, 3 knives. [A brace was the French word brasse, for 5.3 feet of cloth.]*

March 11, 1805 (Clark)

*We have every reason to believe that our Menetarre interpreter (whom we intended to take with his wife, as an interpreter through his wife to the Snake Indians of which nation she is) has been corrupted by the [blank] Company, etc. Some explanation has taken place which clearly proves to us the fact. We give to him tonight to reflect and determine whether or not he intends to go with us under the regulations stated.*

**Charbonneau was playing both sides: the fur companies and the Lewis and Clark party.**

March 12, 1805 (Clark)

*Our Interpreter Shabonah, determines on not proceeding with us as an interpreter under the terms mentioned yesterday.*
*He will not agree to work, let our situation be what it may, nor stand a guard, and if miffed with any man he wishes to return when he pleases, also have the disposal of as much provisions as he chooses to carry. Lewis and Clark found this inadmissible and we suffer him to be off the engagement which was only verbal.*

**Charbonneau appeared to be demanding his own rules for the trip and his role.**

March 17, 1805 (Clark)

*Mr. Chabonah sent a Frenchman of our party [to say] that he was sorry for the foolish part he had acted and if we pleased he would accompany us agreeably to the terms we has proposed and do everything we wished him to do, etc., etc. He had requested me through our French interpreter [Jaussaume] two days ago to excuse his simplicity and take him into the service. . .we called him in and spoke to him on the subject. He agreed to our terms and we agreed that he might go on with us, etc., etc.*

## Our Story of Eagle Woman, Sacagawea

April 1, 1805 (Clark's Field Journals, Ernest Osgood, ed.)

*Our party will consist of one Interpreter & Hunter, one French man as interpreter with his two wives (this man speaks Minnetarre to his wives, who are Skiatars [?] or Snake Indians of the nations through which we shall pass, and to act as interpretresses through him).*

**Only one wife of Charbonneau went along. The wife who stayed behind, Otter Woman, was ill. The two wives spoke Minnetarre (Hidatsa) and Crow, the languages of their parents, and probably some Shoshone because of their family's relationship with the Shoshones.**

April 7, 1805 (Lewis)

*The party included Interpreters, George Drewyer [Drouillard] and Taussant Charbono, also a Black man by the name of York, servant to Captain Clark, an Indian Woman wife to Charbono with a young child, and a Mandan man who had promised us to accompany us as far as the Snake Indians with a view to bring about a good understanding and friendly intercourse between that nation and his own, the Minnetarees and the Amahamis.*

**The Amahamis were an Hidatsa group who were refugees from regional war and pestilence. Note that a Mandan man accompanied the group and was to assist with addressing the Snake Indians as well. The Mandan and Hidatsa people knew the area of the trip and the people along the way. They had made maps for the Lewis and Clark party.**

*The party are in excellent health and spirits, zealously attachedto the enterprise, and anxious to proceed. Not a whisper of murmur or discontent to be heard among them, but all act in unison, and with the most perfect harmony.*

*Captain Clark, myself and two interpreters and the woman and child sleep in a tent of dressed skins.*

**This was a way to protect *Sacagawea* and her child from harm, and from others.**

## Sacagawea Entries in the Journals

April 7, 1805 (Clark)

    *The party included George Drewyer who acts as a hunter and interpreter, Shabonah and his Indian [wife] to act as an interpreter and interpretress for the Snake Indians—one Mandan and Shabonah's infant.*

April 9, 1805 (Clark)

    *When we halted for dinner, [Sacagawea] busied herself in searching for the wild artichokes which the mice collect and deposit in large hoards.*

    *This operation she performed by penetrating the earth with a sharp stick about some small collections of drift wood. . . she procured a good quantity of these roots. The flavor of this root resembles that of the Jerusalem Artichoke.*

    **Sacagawea knew how to find, dig and use plants in this region as she had spent time living among the Crows, her mother's tribe, when she was younger and had also passed through that region before while going to visit the Shoshones.**

April 14, 1805 (Lewis)

    *Passed an Island, above which two small creeks fall in on the larboard [left] side; the upper creek largest, which we call Sharbono's Creek, after our interpreter who encamped several weeks on it with a hunting party of Indians. This was the highest point to which any whiteman had ever ascended, except two Frenchmen (one of whom, Lapage, was now with us) who having lost their way had straggled a few miles further, though to what place precisely I could not learn.*

    Coues' notes state: Lewis and Clark here distinctly state that they have now passed beyond the highest point on the Missouri heretofore explored by white men. Chaboneau had been as far as the creek named for him (probably Indian Creek of today), and Lepage, another recruit from the Mandan towns, had, with one other Frenchman, gone a few miles further. . .

it shows that the quest for furs had not yet been pushed appreciably west of the Mandan villages by the British fur companies.

**Charbonneau indicated that he had gone only that far on the Missouri before, but Bulls Eye stated that Charbonneau and *Sacagawea* had gone to the Salmon River and to the Shoshones the year before when they probably took the easier route by land, going up Knife River thence across the headlands to the Yellowstone Valley.**

April 18, 1805 (Clark)
*After breakfast I ascended a hill and observed that the river made a great bend to the south. I concluded to walk through the point about 2 miles and take Shabono, with me. He had taken a dose of salts, etc. His [wife] followed on with her child. When I struck the next bend of the [river] could see nothing of the Party, left this man and his wife and child on the river bank and went on to hunt.*
**The Charbonneaus were closer to Captain Clark than they were to Captain Lewis.**

April 30, 1805 (Clark)
*I walked on shore today, our interpreter and his [wife] followed. In my walk the [woman] found and brought me a bush something like the currant, which she said bore a delicious fruit and that great quantities grew on the Rocky Mountains. This shrub was in bloom, has a yellow flower with a deep cup; the fruit when ripe is yellow and hangs in bunches like cherries. [This was most probably the gooseberry plant, (Ribes uva-crispa). Again, Sacagawea would have known about the plants and berries along the way.]*

May 8, 1805 (Clark)
*We are willing to believe that this is the River the Minitarres [Gros Ventres, Hidatsas] call the river which Scolds all others [the Marias River] . . . In walking on Shore with the Interpreter &*

his wife, [she] gathered on the sides of the hills wild Lickerish, & the white apple as called by the . . . [engages] and gave me to eat.

The white apple was a tuber that could be eaten fresh in season, or dried and ground into powder to be added to other foods to give it a sweet taste.

**The Hidatsa knew the area and the river.**

May 9, 1805 (Lewis)

*I also killed one buffalo which proved to be the best meat, and from the cow I killed we saved the necessary materials for making what our right-hand cook Charbono calls the boudin blanc, and immediately set him about preparing them for supper. This white pudding we all esteem one of the greatest delicacies of the forest.* Lewis described how Charbonneau stuffed the sausage in a skin, then cooked it fried with bear's oil until it becomes brown, when it is ready.

**Charbonneau was the cook for the group.**

May 14, 1805 (Clark)

*We proceeded on very well until about 6 o'clock [when] a squall of wind struck our sail broad side and turned the pirogue nearly over, and in this situation the pirogue remained until the sail was cut down in which time she nearly filled with water. The articles which floated out was nearly all caught by [Sacagawea] who was in the rear. This accident had like to have cost us dearly, for in this pirogue were embarked our papers, instruments, books, medicine, a great proportion of our merchandise, and in short almost every article indispensably necessary to further the views, and insure the success of the enterprise in which we are now launched to the distance of 2,200 miles.*

**Sacagawea was known to be a tall, athletic, aggressive person as reported by MHA tribal members, Helen Wolf Wilkinson and Esley Thorton, a direct descendant. The Crow stories of her swimming ability attest to this also.**

## May 16, 1805 (Lewis)

By 4 o'clock in the evening our Instruments, medicine, merchandise provision, etc., were perfectly dried, repacked and put on board the pirogue. The loss we sustained was not so great as we had first apprehended; our medicine sustained the greatest injury, several articles of which were entirely spoiled, and many others considerably injured. The balance of our losses consisted of some garden seeds, a small quantity of gunpowder, and a few culinary articles which fell overboard and sunk. The Indian woman to whom I ascribe equal fortitude and resolution, with any person on board at the time of the accident, caught and preserved most of the light articles which were washed overboard.

## May 20, 1805 (Clark)

The hunters returned this evening and informed us that the country continued much the same in appearance as that we saw where we were..., and that about five miles above the mouth of Shell River [the Musselshell River] a handsome river of about fifty yards in width discharged itself into the Shell River on the Starboard or upper side. This stream we called Sah-ca-ger wea, or Bird Woman's river, after our interpreter the Snake woman.

**The honoring was probably because she had saved their items from going overboard. Clark's spelling is very close to the Hidatsa name for Bird Woman, *Sacagawea*. The spelling, *Sacajawea*, with a j, was injected into the journal interpretations by Nicholas Biddle who edited the journals in 1814 after the trip. *Sacajawea* means Boat Launcher in Shoshone.**

## May 29, 1805 (Lewis)

Capt. Clark also saw a large encampment just above the entrance of this river [the Judith] . . . of rather older date, probably they were the same Indians. The Indian woman with us examined the moccasins which we found at these encampments and informed us that they were not of her nation the Snake Indians, but she believed they were some of the Indians who inhabit the country on this side of the Rocky Mountains and North of the Missouri. [This tribe would have been the Atsinai (Gros Ventre of Montana).]

**This was probably a language misinterpretation, or *Sacagawea* may have been referring to her adopted Shoshone relatives. Recall, also, that Charbonneau was the interpreter of *Sacagawea's* words and may have indicated that the Snake nation was her nation. It may also have been that Charbonneau had directed her to continue the story that she was Shoshone. The other interpreters and Lewis and Clark expected to hear that she was from the Snake nation, as they believed this to be the case, and would have intentionally passed that information along.**

May 29, 1805 (Clark)

*I also saw large encampment on the Starboard side at the mouth of a small creek of about 100 lodges which appeared to be 5 or 6 weeks past. The Indian woman examined the moccasins and told us they were the Indians which resided below the Rocky Mountains and to the north of this river. [She said] that her nation make their moccasins differently.*

June 10, 1805 (Lewis)

*Sah-cah-gah wea, our Indian woman, is very sick this evening; Capt. [Clark] bled her.*

**Lewis spelled her name to sound like *Sacagawea*, her Hidatsa name. She was referred to as Bird Woman, *Sacagawea*, throughout the journey, not *Sacajawea*, Boat Launcher.**

June 15, 1805 (Clark)

*Our Indian woman sick and low-spirited. I gave her the bark and apply it externally to her region which revived her much. The Indian woman much worse this evening. She will not take any medicine. Her husband petitions to return, etc.*

June 16, 1805 (Lewis)

*I reached the camp [and] found the Indian woman extremely ill and much reduced by her indisposition. This gave me some concern as well for the poor object herself, then with a young child in her arms, as from the consideration of her being our only dependence for a friendly negotiation with the Snake Indians on whom we depend for horses to assist us in our portage from the Missouri to the Columbia River.*

*I found that two doses of barks and opium which I had given [Sacagawea] had produced an alteration in her pulse for the better; they were now much fuller and more regular. I caused her to drink the mineral water altogether. When I first came down, I found that her pulse [was] scarcely perceptible, very quick, frequently irregular and attended with strong nervous symptoms, that of the twitching of the fingers and leaders of the arm. Now the pulse has become regular, much fuller and a gentle perspiration has taken place. . . . I determined to remain at this camp in order to make some celestial observations, restore the sick woman, and have all matters in a state of readiness to commence the portage immediately on the return of Capt. Clark.*

June 16, 1805 (Clark)

*The Indian woman very bad, and will take no medicine whatever, until her husband, finding her out of her senses, easily prevailed on her to take medicine. If she dies, it will be the fault of her husband as I am now convinced.*

June 19, 1805 (Lewis)

*The Indian woman was much better this morning. She walked out and gathered a considerable quantity of the white apples of which she [eats] so heartily in their raw state, together with a considerable quantity of dried fish without my knowledge that she complained very much and her fever again returned. I rebuked Sharbono severely for suffering her to indulge herself with such food, he being privy to it and having been previously told what she must only eat.*

# Sacagawea Entries in the Journals

June 20, 1805 (Clark)

The Indian woman is quite free from pain and fever this morning, and appears to be in a fair way for recovery. She has been walking about and fishing.

June 29, 1805 (Lewis)

Clark left one man at Willow run to guard the baggage and took with him his black man, York. Shabono and his Indian woman also accompanied Capt. [Clark]. On his arrival at the falls, he perceived a very black cloud rising in the West which threatened immediate rain. He looked about for a shelter but could find none without being in great danger of being blown into the river should the wind prove as violent as it sometimes is on those occasions in these plains. At length about a [quarter] a mile above the falls, he discovered a deep ravine where there were some shelving rocks under which he took shelter near the river with Sharbono and the Indian woman. Laying their guns, compass, etc., under a shelving rock on the upper side of the ravine where they were perfectly secure from the rain.

The first shower was moderate, accompanied by a violent rain the effects of which they did not feel. Soon after a most violent torrent of rain descended, accompanied with hail. The rain appeared to descend in a body and instantly collected in the ravine and came down in a rolling torrent with irresistible force, driving rocks, mud and everything before it which opposed its passage. Capt. [Clark] fortunately discovered it a moment before it reached them and, seizing his gun and shot pouch with his left hand, with the right he assisted himself up the steep bluff, shoving occasionally the Indian woman before him who had her child in her arms. Sharbono had the woman by the hand, endeavoring to pull her up the hill, but was so much frightened that he remained frequently motionless, and but for Capt. [Clark] both himself and his woman and child must have perished.

*So sudden was the rise of the water that before Capt. [Clark] could reach his gun and begin to ascend the bank, it was up to his waist and wet his watch, and he could scarcely ascend faster that it arose until it had obtained the depth of 15 feet with a current tremendous to behold. One moment longer and it would have swept them into the river just above the great cataract of 87 feet, where they must have inevitably perished. Sharbono lost his gun, shot pouch, horn tomahawk, and my wiping rod. Capt. [Clark], his umbrella and compass or circumferenter. They fortunately arrived on the plain safe.*

*The bier in which the woman carries her child and all its clothes were swept away as they lay at her feet, she having time only to grasp her child. The infant was therefore very cold, and the woman also who had just recovered from a severe indisposition was also wet and cold. Capt. [Clark] therefore relinquished his intended tour and returned to the camp at willow run in order also to obtain dry clothes for himself and directed them to follow him.*

**John Rees, in "The Shoshonis' Contributions to the Lewis and Clark Expedition," 1923, stated that *Sacagawea (Sacajawea)* told the Shoshone story of the thunder bird after the cloudburst event. The Hidatsas have a story including a thunder bird, so it was most likely the Hidatsa story, if in fact a story was told.**

July 13, 1805 (Lewis)

*Saw where the natives had peeled the bark off the pine trees about the same season. This the Indian woman with us informs that they do to obtain the sap and soft part of the wood and bark for food.*

July 22, 1805 (Lewis)

*The Indian woman recognizes the country and assures us that this is the river on which her relations live, and that the three forks are at no great distance. This piece of information has cheered the spirits of the party who now begin to console themselves with the anticipation of shortly seeing the head of the Missouri yet unknown to the civilized world.*

## Sacagawea Entries in the Journals

**Sacagawea was most likely referring to the family of her father's adopted Shoshone brother as her relatives. Again, Charbonneau was the interpreter for *Sacagawea's* words. He could have been stressing that she was Shoshone, or *Sacagawea* was giving the impression that she was Shoshone.**

July 22, 1805 (Patrick Gass Journal)
*At breakfast [Sacagawea] informed us she had been at this place before when small.*

**Sacagawea could have been referring to a previous trip made with her family who would have visited back and forth with their Shoshone adopted relatives. This may have been Charbonneau saying this to stress that she was Shoshone or *Sacagawea* emphasizing that erroneous information.**

July 24, 1805 (Lewis)
*I fear every day that we shall meet with some considerable falls or obstruction in the river, notwithstanding the information of the Indian woman to the contrary who assures us that the river continues much as we see it.*

July 24, 1805 (Patrick Gass Journal)
*The morning was fine, and we early prosecuted our voyage, passed a bank of very red earth, which [Sacagawea] told us the natives use for paint.*

July 28, 1805 (Lewis)
*The Shoshones were encamped at the time the Minnetares of the Knife [River] first came in sight of them, five years since. From hence they retreated about three miles up Jefferson's river and concealed themselves in the woods. The Minnetares pursued, attacked them, killed 4 men, 4 women, a number of boys, and made prisoners of all the females and four boys. Sah-cah-gar-we-ah, our Indian woman, was one of the female prisoners taken at that time;*

*though I cannot discover that she shows any emotion of sorrow in recollecting this event, or of joy in being again restored to her native country. If she has enough to eat and a few trinkets to wear, I believe she would be perfectly content anywhere.*

**This was probably a language misinterpretation, or Charbonneau told Lewis the story of the attack by the Hidatsa and taking of prisoners to further the story that *Sacagawea* was Shoshone and a captive of the Hidatsas. It is noted, however, that *Sacagawea* did not show emotions regarding being taken as a prisoner, or those usually associated with a return to home.**

July 28. 1805 (Clark)

*Our present camp is the precise spot [where] the Snake Indians were camped at the time the Minetarries came in sight, attacked and killed 4 men, 4 women, and a number of boys, and made prisoners of all the females and 4 boys.*

July 28, 1805 (Patrick Gass Journal)

*[Sacagawea] informed us that it was at this place she had been taken prisoner by the Grossventers 4 or 5 years ago.*

**Sacagawea may have said it was the place where she had been or camped before, or it was an intentional misinterpretation by Charbonneau, or she may have maintained the story that she was Shoshone and was captured as directed by Charbonneau.**

July 30, 1805 (Lewis)

*Sharbono, his woman, two invalids, and myself walked through the bottom of the Larboard [left] side of the river about 4 ½ miles when we again struck it at the place the woman informed us that she was taken prisoner . . . . We dined and again proceeded on; as the river now passed through the woods the invalids got on board together with Sharbono and the Indian woman.*

# Sacagawea Entries in the Journals

August 6, 1805 (Lewis)

*With Sharbono I directed my course to the main forks through the bottom, directing others to meet us there. The Indian woman recognized the point of a high plain to our right, which she informed us was not very distant from the summer retreat of her nation on a river beyond the mountains which runs to the west.*

*This hill she says her nation calls the beaver's head, from a conceived resemblance of its figure to the head of that animal. She assures us that we shall either find her people on this river or on the river immediately west of its source; which from its present size cannot be very distant. As it is now all important with us to meet with those people as soon as possible . . .*

Beaver's Head Rock, Montana. Its traditional Indian name was explained by Sacagawea.

**Sacagawea and Charbonneau had been to this place before, and she had relatives there.**

August 11, 1805 (Lewis)

*After having marched in this order for about five miles, I discovered an Indian on horseback. . . coming down the plain toward us. With my glass, I discovered from his dress that he was of a different nation of any that we had yet seen, and was satisfied of his being a Shoshone...*

*I now called to him in as loud a voice as I could command, repeating the word tab-ba-bone, which in their language signifies white man.*

Lewis could not have chosen a worse word. In modern Shoshone, tai-va-vone means a stranger or an enemy. Lewis could have learned the word only from *Sacagawea*.

***Sacagawea's* Shoshone language ability was questionable.**

August 14, 1805 (Lewis)

*In order to give Captain Clark time to reach the forks of the Jefferson River, I concluded to spend this day at the Shoshone camp and obtain what information I could with respect to the country... The means I had of communicating with these people was by way of Drewyer [Drouillard], who understood perfectly the common language of gesticulation or signs which seems to be universally understood by all the Nations we have yet seen.*

*This evening Charbono struck his Indian Woman, for which Capt. [Clark] gave him a severe reprimand.*

***Sacagawea* was not the only one whom Lewis and Clark relied upon for interpretation. *Sacagawea* was most likely under constant threat of being struck if she didn't do as Charbonneau said. He may have seen her as not following his cover story that she was Shoshone. Clark was protective of her.**

August 15, 1805 (Clark)

*In walking on shore, I saw several rattle snakes and narrowly escaped at two different times, as also [Sacagawea] when walking with her husband on shore.*

**John Rees, who wrote "The Shoshonis' Contributions to the Lewis and Clark Expedition," 1923, stated that *Sacagawea (Sacajawea)* told the Shoshone story of the snake dominating the country after this event. The Hidatsas have a story about the snake and its domination, so it could well have been the Hidatsa story.**

## Sacagawea Entries in the Journals

August 16, 1805 (Lewis)

*I had mentioned to the [Shoshone] chief several times that we had with us a woman of his nation who had been taken prisoner by the Minnetares, and that by means of her I hoped to explain myself more fully than I could do [by] signs.*

**Lewis says he told the Shoshone chief several times that they had a woman of the Shoshone nation with them, but it appears that the chief was not too interested. If he knew it was *Sacagawea*, he would have known she was not of the Shoshone nation, only an adopted relative.**

August 16, 1805 (Joseph Whitehouse Journal)

*Capt. Clark, our interpreter and wife walked on shore and found a great number of fine berries, which [are] called Service berries. Our interpreter's wife gathered a pail full and gave them to the party at noon, where we halted at a grove of cotton trees . . . We named this place Service Valley, from the abundance of these berries along under the hills, etc.*

August 17, 1805 (Lewis)

*Shortly after Capt. Clark arrived with the Interpreter Charbono, and the Indian woman, who proved to be a sister of the Chief Cameahwait. The meeting of those people was really affecting, particularly between Sah-cah-gar-we-ah and an Indian woman, who had been taken prisoner at the same time with her, and who had afterward escaped from the Minnetares and rejoined her nation.*

**The brother/sister relationship was a result of *Sacagawea's* father previously adopting a Shoshone man as a brother and, according to Bulls Eye, it was Cameahwait himself. Maybelle Good Bird Lone Fight, of the MHA Nation, and descendant of Buffalo Bird Woman, also stated that the brother/sister relationship between *Sacagawea* and Cameahwait was the result of a tribal adoption.**

**Close relatives were referred to as brother or sister in the Hidatsa kinship system and probably in that of other tribes. Non-Indians would have had no understanding of this. The Indian woman *Sacagawea* was glad to see was probably from Cameahwait's family or a friend *Sacagawea* had made on a previous trip. Charbonneau may have said that the Indian woman was a prisoner at the same time as *Sacagawea* was.**

*Accordingly, about 4 P.M. we called them together and through the medium of Labuish [LaBische], Charbono and Sah-cah-gar-weah, we communicated to them fully the objects which had brought us into this distant part of the country, in which we took care to make them a conspicuous object of our own good wishes, and the care of our government.*

**Note that it took several to interpret between the party and the Shoshones, not just *Sacagawea* who was to be the interpreter. She was not fluent in Shoshone.**

*Also to take the Indians, Charbono, and the Indian woman with him [Clark]; that on his arrival at the Shoshone camp he was to leave Charbono and the Indian woman to hasten the return of the Indians with their horses to this place, and to proceed himself with the eleven men down the Columbia in order to examine the river and if he found it navigable and could obtain time to set about making canoes immediately.*

**A main reason for *Sacagawea* to speak to the Shoshones was to acquire horses from them.**

August 17, 1805 (Clark)
*The Interpreter and [Sacagawea] who were before me at some distance danced for the joyful sight, and she made signs to me that they were her nation.*

**Charbonneau and *Sacagawea* were, of course, glad to see the family of her father's adopted brother and friends they had made on a previous trip. Charbonneau may have been overreacting to ensure that the party believed *Sacagawea* was Shoshone.**

## Sacagawea Entries in the Journals

*The great chief of this nation proved to be the brother of the woman with us and is a man of influence, sense, and easy and reserved manners. [He] appears to possess a great deal of sincerity.*

August 19, 1805 (Lewis)

Lewis spoke of how Shoshone fathers gave their daughter in marriage, in exchange for gifts. *Sah-car-gar-we-ah had been thus disposed of before she was taken by the Minnetares, or had arrived to the years of puberty. The husband was yet living with this band. He was more than double her age and had two other wives. He claimed her as his wife, but said that as she had had a child by another man, who was Charbono, that he did not want her.*

**Because *Sacagawea's* family had been close to the Shoshones, such an arrangement might have been made for her marriage when she was a young girl. This may also have been more of Charbonneau's trying to prove that *Sacagawea* was Shoshone.**

August 20, 1805 (Lewis)

*At 3 P.M. Capt. Clark departed, accompanied by his guide and party, except one man whom he left with orders to purchase a horse if possible and overtake him as soon as he could. He left Charbono and the Indian woman to return to my camp with the Indians.*

August 22, 1805 (Lewis)

*Charbono, the Indian Woman, Cameahwait and about 50 men with a number of women and children arrived. They encamped near us.*

*I gave him [Cameahwait] a few dried squashes which we had brought from the Mandans. He had them boiled and declared them to be the best thing he had ever tasted except sugar, a small lump of which it seems his sister, Sah-cah-gar Wea had given him.*

## Our Story of Eagle Woman, Sacagawea

August 25, 1805 (Lewis)

*Sometime after we had halted, Charbono mentioned to me with apparent unconcern that he expected to meet all the Indians from the camp on the Columbia tomorrow on their way to the Missouri. I was out of patience with the folly of Charbono, who had not sufficient sagacity to see the consequences which would eventually flow from such a movement of the Indians, and although he had been in possession of this information since early in the morning when it had been communicated to him by his Indian woman, yet he never mentioned it until after noon.*

**Lewis was upset with the behavior and work of Charbonneau.**

October 19, 1805 (Lewis)

*As soon as they saw the . . . wife of the interpreter, they pointed to her and informed those who continued yet in the same position I first found them, they immediately all came out and appeared to assume new life. The sight of this Indian woman, wife to one of our interpreters, confirmed those people of our friendly intentions, as no woman ever accompanies a war party of Indians in this quarter.*

***Sacagawea's* presence helped when meeting groups of Indians along the way.**

November 3, 1805 (Lewis)

*A canoe arrived from the village below the last rapid with a man, his wife, and 3 children, and a woman whom had been taken prisoner from the Snake Indians on Clark's River [on a river from the south which we found to be Mulknoma]. I sent the interpreter's wife, who is a So so ne or Snake Indian of the Missouri, to speak to this [woman]. They could not understand each other sufficiently to converse.*

**Another example of *Sacagawea* not speaking Shoshone as well as was expected.**

*Sacagawea Entries in the Journals*

November 20, 1805 (Clark)

*One of the Indians had on a robe made of 2 sea otter skins, the fur of them more beautiful than any fur I had ever seen. Both Capt. Lewis and myself endeavored to purchase the robe with different articles. At length we procured it for a belt of blue beads which the . . . wife of our interpreter, Shabono, wore around her waist.*

**Sacagawea had a belt of blue beads, the kind made by the Hidatsas. The decorations on the belts were insignias of the person's memberships or accomplishments. Sacagawea would have earned the right to wear the beads by having accomplished certain tasks required by Hidatsa women and assigned to her by one of her Hidatsa clan aunts.**

November 21, 1805 (Patrick Gass Journal)

*The season being so far advanced, we wished to establish our winter quarters as soon as possible. One of the natives here had a robe of sea-otter skins, of the finest fur I ever saw, which the Commanding Officers wanted very much, and offered two blankets for it, which the owner refused, and said he would not take five. He wanted beads of a blue color, of which we had none, but some that were on a belt belonging to our interpreter's [wife]. So they gave him the belt for the skins.*

November 21, 1805 (Clark)

*We gave [Sacagawea] a coat of Blue Cloth for the belt of Blue Beads we gave for the Sea otter skins purchased of an Indian.*

November 24, 1805 (Lewis and Clark Journals)

When Lewis and Clark took the vote about winter quarters on the Columbia River, Reuben Gold Thwaites noted that *Sacagawea* was "in favor of a place where there is plenty of potatoes." [Roots which she would be finding and digging, to help provision the camp.]

## Our Story of Eagle Woman, Sacagawea

November 30, 1805 (Clark)

[Sacagawea] gave me a piece of bread today made of flour she had reserved for her child, and carefully kept until this time, which has unfortunately got wet, and a little sour. This bread I ate with great satisfaction, it being the only mouthful I had tasted for several months.

December 3, 1805 (Clark)

After eating the marrow out of two shank bones of an elk, [Sacagawea] chopped the bones, fine-boiled them, and extracted a pint of grease, which is superior to the tallow of the animal.

December 25, 1805 (Clark)

I received a [Christmas] present of a fleece hosiery vest, drawers and socks of Capt. Lewis, [a] pair of moccasins of Whitehouse, a small Indian basket of Guterich, and 2 dozen white weasel's tails of the [wife] of Sharbono, and some black roots of the Indians.

January 6, 1806 (Lewis)

Capt. Clark set out after an early breakfast with the party in two canoes as had been concerted the last evening. Charbono and his Indian woman were also of the party. The Indian woman was very importunate to be permitted to go, and was therefore indulged. She observed that she had traveled a long way with us to see the great waters, and that now that monstrous fish was also to be seen, she thought it very hard she could be permitted to see either (she had never yet been to the Ocean).

March 23, 1806  Starting home

April 23, 1806 (Clark)

Shabono made a bargain with one of the Indian men going with us, for a horse for which he gave his shirt, and two of the leather suits of his wife.

## Sacagawea Entries in the Journals

April 28, 1806 (Lewis)

*We found a Sho-sho-ne woman, prisoner among these people, by means of whom and Sah-cah-gah-weah, Shabono's wife, we found means of conversing with the Wallahwallars. We conversed with them for several hours and fully satisfy all their enquiries with respect to ourselves and objects of our pursuit. They were much pleased.*
**The women must have used sign language to converse with the Walla Walla people.**

May 11, 1806 (Lewis)

*To this end we drew a map of the country with a coal on a mat in their way and by the assistance of the Snake boy and our interpreters were enabled to make ourselves understood by them, although it had to pass through the French, Minnetare, Shoshone and Choppunish languages. The interpretation being tedious, it occupied nearly half the day before we had communicated to them what we wished. They appeared highly pleased.* [This was a council of tribal leaders of the Nez Percé.]

May 11, 1806 (Clark)

*The One-Eyed Chief, Yoom-park-kar-tim arrived and we gave him a medal of the small size, and spoke to the Indians through a Snake boy, Shabono, and his wife. We informed them who we were, where we came from, and our intentions towards them, which pleased them very much.*

May 16, 1806 (Clark)

*Shabono's [wife] gathered a quantity of fennel roots which we find very palatable and nourishing food. The onion we also find in abundance, and boil it with our meat.*

May 18, 1806 (Clark)

*The . . . wife to Shabono busied herself gathering the roots of the fennel called by the Snake Indians Year-pah for the purpose of*

259

drying to eat on the Rocky Mountains. Those roots are very palatable, either fresh roasted, boiled or dried and are generally the size of a quill and that of a man's finger, and about the length of the latter.

May 22, 1806 (Lewis)
Charbono's child is very ill this evening. He is cutting teeth, and for several days past has had a violent lax, which having suddenly stopped he was attacked with a high fever, and his neck and throat are much swollen this evening. We gave him a dose of cream of tartar and flour of sulphur, and applied a poultice of boiled onions to his neck as warm as he could well bear it.

May 26, 1806 (Lewis)
The clyster given the child last evening operated very well. It is clear of fever this evening, and is much better. The swelling is considerably abated, and appears as if it would pass off without coming to a head. We still continue fresh poultices of onions to the swollen part.

June 5, 1806 (Clark)
The child is recovering fast. I applied a plaster of salve made of the resin of the long-leafed pine, Beeswax and Bear's oil-mixed, which has subsided the inflammation entirely, the part is considerably swelled and hard.

July 1, 1806 (Lewis)
Capt. [Clark], with the remaining ten, including Charbono and York, will proceed to the Yellowstone river at its nearest approach to the three forks of the Missouri. Here he will build a canoe and descend the Yellowstone river with Charbono, the Indian woman, his servant, York, and five others to the Missouri River, where should he arrive first he will wait my arrival.

## Sacagawea Entries in the Journals

July 3, 1806 (Clark)

We collected our horses and after breakfast I took my leave of Capt. Lewis and the Indians, and at 8 A.M. set out . . . Met interpreter Shabono and his wife and child (as an interpreter and interpretess for the Crow Indians and the latter for the Shoshoni) with 50 horses.

July 6, 1806 (Clark)

The Indian woman, wife to Shabono, informed me that she had been in this plain frequently and knew it well, that the creek which we descended was a branch of Wisdom river, and when we ascended the higher part of the plain, we would discover a gap in the mountains in our direction to the canoes, and when we arrived at that gap we would see a high point of a mountain covered with snow in our direction to the canoes. [Sacagawea] pointed to the gap through which she said we must pass, which was south 56 degrees, East. She said we would pass the river before we reached the gap.

**Sacagawea knew this because she had been there before.**

July 9, 1806 (Clark)

[Sacagawea] brought me a plant, the root of which the natives eat. This root resembles a carrot in form and size and something of its color, being of a paler yellow than that of our carrot, the stem and leaf is much like the common carrot, and the taste not unlike. It is a native of moist land.

July 13, 1806 (Clark)

The Indian woman who has been of great service to me as a pilot through this country recommends a gap in the mountain more south which I shall cross. The footnote says, Sacagawea recommended the Bozeman [pass], the one chosen for the Northern Pacific Railway.

## Our Story of Eagle Woman, Sacagawea

July 14, 1806 (Clark)

*The Indian woman informs me that a few years ago, Buffalo was very plenty in those plains and valleys quite as high as the head of Jefferson's river, but few of them ever come into those valleys of late years owing to the Shoshones who are fearful of passing into the plains west of the mountains, and subsist on what game they can catch in the Mountains principally, and the fish which they take in the East Fork of Lewis' river.*

July 18, 1806 (Clark)

*I observed a smoke rise to the S.S.E. in the plains toward the termination of the Rocky Mountains in that direction. This smoke must be raised by the Crow Indians in that direction, as a signal for us or other bands.*

July 25, 1806 (Clark)

*I proceeded on after the rain, lay a little, and at 4 p.m. arrived at a remarkable rock situated in an extensive bottom on the starboard side of the river... This rock I ascended and from its top had a most extensive view in every direction. This rock, which I shall call Pompey's Tower...I marked my name and the day of the month and year...*

**The people of Fort Berthold and of Crow both tell the story that *Sacagawea* met her brother, Cherry Necklace, along this way, and he gave Charbonneau a white horse. She gave him gifts also. This is not recorded in the journals. Some believe that it was on the trip made the year before by Charbonneau and *Sacagawea* or was during an 1816-17 trip. The Crows have a memorial every year commemorating the meeting of Lewis and Clark and the Crows at Pompey's Pillar.**

August 17, 1806 (Clark)

*Settled with Toussaint Charbono for his services as an interpreter, the price of a horse and lodge purchased of him for public service, in all amounting to $500.33. [This was the tent of*

*Pompey's Pillar, Montana, named for Sacagawea's son.*

dressed skins they camped in during the journey.] Directed [that two] of the largest of the canoes be fastened together with poles tied across them so as to make them steady for the purpose of conveying the Indians and interpreter and their families.

We also took our leave of T. Chabono, his Snake Indian wife and their child [son] who had accompanied us on our route to the Pacific Ocean in the capacity of interpreter and interpretess. T. Chabono wished much to accompany us in the said capacity if we could have prevailed upon the Menatarre chiefs to descend the river with us to the U. states. But as none of these chiefs of whose language he was conversant would accompany us, his services were no longer of use to us, and he was therefore discharged and paid up.

We offered to convey him down to the Illinois [river] if he chose to go. He declined, proceeding on at present, observing that he had no acquaintance or prospects of making a living below, and must continue to live in the way that he has done. I offered to take his little son, a beautiful promising child who is 19 months old, to which they, both himself and his wife, were willing, provided the child had been weaned. They observed that in one year the boy would be sufficiently old to leave his mother, and he would then take him to me if I would be so friendly as to raise the child for him in such a manner as I thought proper, to which I agreed.

*Our Story of Eagle Woman, Sacagawea*

*William Clark's carving on Pompey's Pillar, 1806*

Around 1809, Charbonneau, *Sacagawea* and Jean Baptiste (Pomp) went to St. Louis and stayed for a while. In 1811 Charbonneau took a job in North Dakota at Ft. Manuel. Pomp was left, at age five, with Captain Clark to raise and educate in St. Louis.

In a letter to Toussaint Charbonneau, August 20, 1806, Captain Clark wrote, *Your woman [Sacagawea]...deserved a greater reward for her attention and service on that route than we had in our power to give her.*

Again, although they have been taken as gospel, the journals undoubtedly contain misinformation. The language barrier, the fact that Charbonneau was stretching the truth, the fact that the journals were written and interpreted through the perspectives of people who did not understand the context and cultures they were dealing with

– all of this should require historians to take another look at this story. These things, coupled with the information provided herein, provide the groundwork and evidence.

The next chapter includes a summary of our evidence and a timeline story of *Sacagawea's* life according to the MHA Nation.

**Sources:**

Thwaites, Reuben Gold, editor, *Original Journals of the Lewis and Clark Expedition*, 1804-1806. New York: Antiquarian Press, 1959.

Some entries were taken from journals and writings of others as noted.

On the next page is a 1910 statue of *Sakakawea (Sacagawea)* by Leonard Crunelle erected on the grounds of the state capitol building in Bismarck, ND. Mink Woman or Hannah Levings, an Hidatsa woman, but not the granddaughter of *Sacagawea* as has been reported previously, posed for the statue. She was the mother of George, Guy, and Albert Fox and Susie Fox Lone Fight. A replica of this statue was placed in Washington, DC, in Statuary Hall of the United States Capitol in 2003.

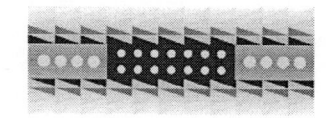

*Our Story of Eagle Woman, Sacagawea*

*Sacagawea bronze sculpture by Leonard Crunelle, 1910.* — Colin Archibald

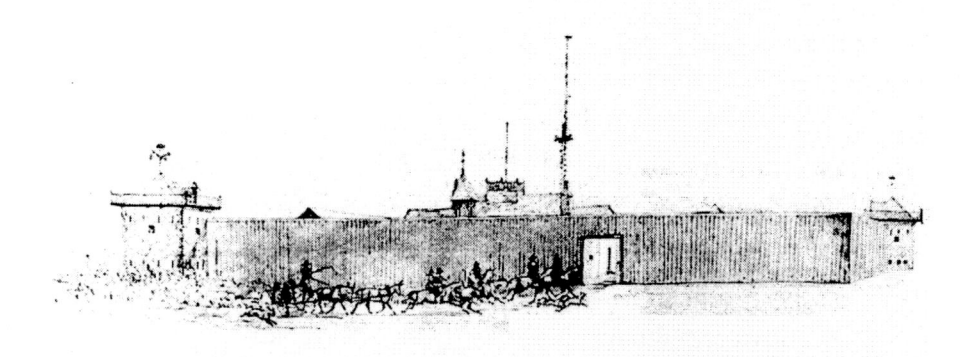

*Fort Union, at the mouth of the Yellowstone. Charbonneau and Sacagawea moved here during the smallpox epidemic of 1837. Their three daughters, Otter Woman, Cedar Woman and Different Breast, were born here or nearby.*
*— Drawing by Rudolph F. Kurz, 1852. National Anthropological Archives.*

# Chapter 10
## *OUR STORY*
### Timeline of the Life of Maeshuwea (Sacagawea)

***In summary, after doing research** and reviewing the Journals, the evidence supporting our claim that Maeshuwea, Sacagawea, was Hidatsa/Crow, and one of us, is extensive.*

Following is a listing of such:

• Oral stories and recollections have been handed down indicating that *Sacagawea* was Hidatsa/Crow.

• Stories from Crow indicating that *Sacagawea* was at Crow when she was a teenager support Hidatsa accounts that Charbonneau got her at Crow from her Hidatsa father. This would also have helped foster the idea that she was an Hidatsa captive.

- DNA matches exist of *Sacagawea* descendants (Parshalls) with descendants of Cherry Necklace, Hidatsa/Crow, who early informants confirmed was *Sacagawea's* brother.

- There is a story from both Crow and Ft. Berthold that *Sacagawea* met her brother, Cherry Necklace, on her way back from a trip to the West.

- Alfred Bowers, who studied the Hidatsa extensively, stated that *Sacagawea* lived closely with the Cherry Necklace family.

- Jean Baptiste's obituary and other accounts state that his mother was half Crow Indian and he was part Crow Indian.

- DNA matches exist of *Sacagawea* descendants (Parshalls) with descendants of the Young Bird, Fredericks and Pease families who oral history states were/are related to *Sacagawea*.

- There is recognition from the descendants of Cherry Necklace, the Parshall, Young Bird, Pease, and Fredericks families that they are all related to one another.

- *Sacagawea* had a sister named Otter Woman after their mother who was also Otter Woman.

- BIA Agency and MHA Tribal records support all of the above relationships.

- The likelihood of misinterpretation, with so many languages being used during the expedition, is great.

- Charbonneau and Jessaume were known to be poor interpreters.

- Charbonneau most likely lied to get a job on the expeditiion.

*Timeline of the Life of Maeshuwea (Sacagawea)*

- Lewis and Clark both spelled her name close to *Sacagawea*, Hidatsa meaning Bird Woman, not *Sacajawea*, Shoshone meaning Boat Launcher. (Shoshone has no word "wea.")

- While on the expedition, *Sacagawea* was not a fluent Shoshone speaker.

- Adoption of members of other tribes was and is common among the Hidatsa and Crow people. This tradition supports Bulls Eye's report that *Sacagawea's* family had an adopted Shoshone brother who they had visited before.

- *Sacagawea* did not act as if she was home or wanted to stay with the Shoshones.

- *Sacagawea* wore a belt of blue beads, signature of the Hidatsa and awarded to young women who earned the right to wear one by an Hidatsa clan aunt.

- Editors of the Journals changed or made up details.

- DNA matches of *Sacagawea* descendants (Parshalls) with Toussaint Charbonneau's family exist.

- DNA matches of *Sacagawea* descendants and relatives with members of the descendants of Toussaint Charbonneau and Otter Woman exist. Otter Woman (2) was *Sacagawea's* older sister and the first wife of Charbonneau.

- Evidence from non-Indian sources supports the Ft. Berthold stories and recollections.

- The Wyoming story has been widely discredited.

- There is evidence that *Sacagawea* lived beyond 1812, discounting the belief that she died then at Ft. Manuel.

- The naming of Lake *Sakakawea* and a statue of *Sacagawea* in North Dakota would not have been requested or sanctioned by the Three Affiliated Tribes if she had not been Hidatsa.

**FOLLOWING IS A TIMELINE OF *SACAGAWEA*'S LIFE, BASED UPON OUR KNOWLEDGE OF HER.**

1758   Toussaint Charbonneau was born in or near Montreal, Canada.

1778   Cherry Necklace, *Sacagawea's* brother, was born. His father was Smoked Lodge, Hidatsa, and his mother was Girl Woman, Crow.

1787   *Maeshuwea (Sacagawea)* was born in an Hidatsa village. Her father was Smoked Lodge, Hidatsa, and her mother was Otter Woman, Crow, sister to Girl Woman. The family lived back and forth between the two tribes.

1796-99   Toussaint Charbonneau settled among the Mandans and Hidatsas.

1787-1800   *Sacagawea* lived mainly among the Hidatsas, her tribe on her father's side. She learned to accomplish tasks required of Hidatsa women and earned a belt of blue beads as evidence of these skills.

1800   Crow stories put *Maeshuwea (Sacagawea)* at Crow as a teenager. When at Crow, she and her family would visit back and forth with the Shoshones. Her father, Smoked Lodge, had adopted a Shoshone brother (in the tribal way).

## Timeline of the Life of Maeshuwea (Sacagawea)

1803   Smoked Lodge agreed, at Crow, for *Sacagawea* to marry Charbonneau. They went to live in the Hidatsa village now referred to as *Sakakawea* Village. Otter Woman, *Sacagawea's* sister, had married Charbonneau at least two years before.

1803   Charbonneau, *Sacagawea* and possibly Smoked Lodge made a trip which included to or passing through the Shoshone country.

Oct. 1804   Lewis and Clark arrived at the Mandan village where they spent the winter preparing for the Expedition to continue to the West.

*Lewis and Clark meeting Sacagawea and Charbonneau by Vernon Erickson*
*— State Historical Society of North Dakota A4466-00001*

Nov. 1804   Toussaint Charbonneau requested to be hired as an interpreter for the trip. Charbonneau was hired and was to take his mistakenly-called "Shoshone" wife to interpret and help acquire horses from the Shoshone.

## Our Story of Eagle Woman, Sacagawea

Feb. 1805     Jean Baptiste, *Sacagawea's* son, was born at Fort Mandan where *Sacagawea* was with Charbonneau and her sister, Otter Woman (who was another wife of Charbonneau), and the Lewis and Clark party.

1805-1806     *Sacagawea* and her baby accompanied thirty-one men west on the Lewis and Clark journey. She was an invaluable member of the party by assisting in many ways while also taking care of her baby son.

*Encampment of the Travellers on the Missouri. — Karl Bodmer*
— Joslyn Art Museum Enron Art Foundation

1803, 1806 or 1817 *Sacagawea* met her brother Cherry Necklace as she and Charbonneau passed through the Crow country on their way back from the West. Cherry Necklace gave Charbonneau a white buffalo horse.

Aug. 1806     A group led by Lewis and another led by Clark returned and met at Reunion Bay, near New Town, North Dakota.

## Timeline of the Life of Maeshuwea (Sacagawea)

1806   Charbonneau and *Sacagawea* went back to live in *Sakakawea (Sacagawea)* Village. Clark wrote Charbonneau a letter expressing his gratitude for the services of Charbonneau and *Sacagawea*. He expressed his desire to have Pomp (Jean Baptiste) live with him to be educated.

*Hannah Levings posing for the statue of Sakakawea in Bismarck, ca. 1906*
— State Historical Society of North Dakota

1809   Charbonneau, *Sacagawea* and Jean Baptiste went to St. Louis. Charbonneau farmed a piece of land but was not satisfied with life there.

1811   Charbonneau took a job at Fort Manuel in North Dakota. Jean Baptiste (Pomp) remained with William Clark in St. Louis.

1812   Otter Woman, *Sacagawea's* sister, died at Fort Manuel from putrid fever. Some believed it was *Sacagawea* who died. Otter Woman's two children, Toussaint (2) and Lisette, were taken to St. Louis and raised as wards of William Clark.

1813   Charbonneau and *Sacagawea* moved back to *Sakakawea* Village.

1815   *Sacagawea* and Charbonneau went to St. Louis to check on Jean Baptiste, then ten years old.

1816-1817 While in St. Louis, Charbonneau was hired by August Chouteau as part of a fur-trapping expedition westward along the Arkansas River to the vicinity of Santa Fe. The party, including *Sacagawea*, spent the winter in the mountains near the Great Salt Lake, then continued north across Wyoming, down the Bighorn, Yellowstone and Missouri rivers, returning to the Knife River Villages in late-summer, 1817. Charbonneau continued downriver to St. Louis, where he collected his pay for the two years, in December.

1823-1829   German Duke Friedrich Paul Wilhelm of Wurttemberg met 18-year-old Jean Baptiste Charbonneau while traveling in the West and invited him to travel with him back to Europe where Charbonneau remained six years.

1825   *Sacagawea* was reported to be at the Mandan village when her father Smoked Lodge or Black Lodge signed the Atkinson-O'Fallon Treaty for the Hidatsa. Charbonneau was a witness.

## Timeline of the Life of Maeshuwea (Sacagawea)

*Two young men, dressed in their best clothes for courting, stand under a corn-drying stage in one of the small plazas at Like-A-Fishhook Village.*
— Stanley J. Morrow, 1871. State Historical Society of North Dakota.

## TREATY WITH THE BELANTSE-ETOA OR MINITAREE TRIBE
*7 Stat. 261, July 20, 1825, Proclaimed February 6, 1826*

Done at the Lower Mandan Village, this thirtieth day of July, A. D. 1825, and of the independence of the United States the fiftieth.

In testimony whereof, the commissioners, Henry Atkinson and Benjamin O'Fallon, and the chiefs and warriors of the said Belantse-etea or Minnetaree tribe of Indians, have hereunto set their hands and affixed their seals.

### Commissioners:
H. Atkinson, brigadier-general U. S. Army,
Benj. O' Fallon, United States agent, Indian affairs,

### Chiefs:
Shan-sa-bat-say-e-see, the wolf chief, his x-mark,
E-re-ah-ree, the one that make the road, his x-mark,
Pas-ca-ma-e-ke-ree, the crow that looks, his x-mark,
E-tah-me-nah-ga-e-she, the guard of the red arrows, his x-mark,
Mah-shu-ca-lah-pah-see, the dog bear, his x-mark,
Oh-Sha-lah-ska-a-tee, his x-mark,
Kah-re-pe-shu-pe-sha, the black buffalo, his x-mark,
Ah-too-pah-she-pe-sha, the black mocasins, his x-mark,
Mah-buk-sho-ok-oe-ah, the one that carries the snake, his x-mark,

### Warriors:
**At-ca-chis, the black lodges,** his x-mark,
Nah-rah-ah-a-pa, the color of the hair, his x-mark,
Pa-ta-e-she-as, the wicked cow, his x-mark,
Kee-re-pee-ah-too, the buffalo head, his x-mark,
Lah-pa-ta-see-e-ta, the bear's tail, his x-mark,
Pa-ta-lah-kee, the white cow, his x-mark,
Ah-sha-re-te-ah, the big thief, his x-mark,
Bo-sah-nah-a-me, the three wolves, his x-mark,
San-jah-oe-tee, the wolf that has no tail, his x-mark,
Sa-ga-e-ree-shus, the finger that stinks, his x-mark,
Me-a-cah-ho-ka, the woman that lies, his x-mark,
Ah-mah-a-ta, the missouri, his x-mark,
E-sha-kee-te-ah, the big fingers, his x-mark,
Mah-shu-kah-e-te-ah, the big dog, his x-mark,
Be-ra-ka-ra-ah, the rotten wood, his x-mark,
E-ta-ro-sha-pa, the big brother, his x-mark,

*Timeline of the Life of Maeshuwea (Sacagawea)*

**In the presence of:**

A. L. Langham, secretary to the commission,
H. Leavenworth, colonel, U. S. Army,
G. H. Kennedy, United States sub-In-dian agent,
John Gale, surgeon, U. S. Army,
D. Ketchum, major, U. S. Army,
John Gantt, captain, Sixth Infantry,
Wm. Day, lieutenant, First Infantry,
R. B. Mason, captain, First Infantry,
Jas. W. Kingbury, lieutenant, First Regiment Infantry,
R. Holmes, lieutenant, Sixth Infantry,
J. Rogers, lieutenant, Sixth Infantry,
W. S. Harney, lieutenant, First Infantry,
Levi Nute, lieutenant, Sixth Infantry,
B. Riley, captain, Sixth Infantry,
R. M. Coleman, assistant surgeon, U. S. Army,
George C. Hutter, lieutenant, Sixth Infantry,
Colin Campbell,
P. Wilson, United States sub-Indian agent,
**Touissant Chaboneau,** interpreter, his x-mark,
S. W. Kearny, brevet major, First Infantry.
Wm. Armstrong, captain, Sixth Regiment Infantry.

\*\*\*\*\*

1834   Sioux raiders burned and destroyed *Sakakawea* Village.

Mid-1830s James Beckwourth lived with the Crow tribe for eight years. In his autobiography, he mentioned that Jean Baptiste's mother was Crow, and he spoke highly of her.

1837   Smallpox once again struck the Knife River Villages, greatly reducing the population of the Hidatsa and Mandan tribes.

1837-1838   Due to the smallpox, *Sacagawea* and Charbonneau moved to the Fort Union area, according to Wolf Chief.

1838   *Sacagawea* gave birth to her second child, Otter Woman, during the tribe's effort to restore the population because of the smallpox ravages. Otter Woman was Bulls Eye's mother.

1839   A third child, Cedar Woman, was born to *Sacagawea* and Charbonneau. Cedar Woman's daughter, Medicine Arm, was George Parshall's mother.

1840   A fourth child, Different Breast, was born.

In mid-1839, when Toussaint Charbonneau was 81 years old, he was fired from his position as interpreter at Fort Clark. He then canoed all the way downriver to St. Louis to collect his last paycheck. No one ever saw him again. In 1843, Jean Baptiste had his father declared dead, and probated his estate.

1845 – *Maeshuwea (Sacagawea)* moved to Like-A-Fishhook Village. She lived there with her daughters and with Cherry Necklace. There was a garden plot at Like-A-Fishhook that belonged to Eagle Woman *(Maeshuwea)* and one belonging to Cedar Woman, another daughter of *Sacagawea*, according to the account of Buffalo Bird Woman.

## Timeline of the Life of Maeshuwea (Sacagawea)

1864  Bulls Eye was born, son of Otter Woman, daughter of *Sacagawea*.

*In Bowers' book, Mandan Social and Ceremonial Organization, 1950, it is recorded that Eagle Woman (Sacagawea), Otter Woman and Cedar Woman, Sacagawea's daughters, attended a Mandan ceremony at Like-A-Fishhook Village.*
— State Historical Society of North Dakota

1864  *Sacagawea's* mother and other close female relatives came to Like-A-Fishhook Village from Crow. *Sacagawea's* mother and her mother's niece, All Moves or Moves Along, went back to Crow. Moves Along's granddaughter, Goes Between, stayed among the Hidatsas, married James Walker, and had a family there. Descendants are the Young Bird, Pease and Fredericks families.

1866  Jean Baptiste Charbonneau died and was buried near Danner, Oregon. His obituary states that he was half Crow Indian and that he was on the way to Montana, the land of his mother, when he died. He was important in American history as a trapper, guide, a miner, a scout for the Mormon Battalion, and was for about a year the alcalde of the Mission San Luis Rey de Francia near San Diego, California.

## Our Story of Eagle Woman, Sacagawea

*Joseph Young Bird Family*
— State Historical Society of North Dakota 01076-00074

**1869** *Sacagawea*, her daughter Otter Woman, and Bulls Eye, Otter Woman's son, went to buy coffee at a trading post at Sand Creek in Montana near Wolf Point. One account says that they were on their way to visit Crow relatives with a group. Their party was attacked. Otter Woman was killed and *Sacagawea* was severely wounded and died seven days later. *Sacagawea* was wrapped in canvas and buried at or near Ft. Buford.

**1870-1895** Cedar Woman, Bulls Eye's aunt or "mother" lived with Bulls Eye in Crow Flies High Village near her mother's grave at Ft. Buford and later with Bulls Eye in Shell Creek. She told him the stories about his grandmother's life.

**1873** *Sacagawea's* brother, Cherry Necklace, died at the age of 95. He was a powerful medicine person who cured many during the smallpox epidemic. He and *Sacagawea* had snake medicine. Foolish Bear took Bulls Eye to his grandmother *Sacagawea's* grave.

280

## Timeline of the Life of Maeshuwea (Sacagawea)

**1904-06** The Centennial of the Lewis and Clark Expedition brought renewed interest in the event.

**1910** A statue of *Sakakawea (Sacagawea)* was erected on the grounds of the state capitol building in Bismarck, ND. Hannah Levings, Mink Woman, posed for the statue.

**1923** Bull's Eye told the history of *Sacagawea* to Major Welch.

**1925** Charles Eastman submitted his report from his investigation done to determine the identity and burial place of *Sacajawea (Sacagawea)*. He determined the location to be Fort Washakie, Wyoming, and that she was Shoshone.

*Hannah Levings, Mink Woman, 1906 — State Historical Society of North Dakota A4413-00001*

**1955** A note in William Clark's personal papers saying "dead" by *Sacagawea's* name was considered proof that she had died in 1812 at Ft. Manuel.

**1967** Lake *Sakakawea* was named after *Sacagawea*. It resulted after completion of the Garrison Dam. The Tribal Council of the Three Affiliated Tribes requested that it be named so in 1956.

**2000** Papers of Major A. B. Welch, supporting the Bulls Eye story, surfaced and were recovered by people at Ft. Berthold.

2000  A coin with *Sacagawea's* image on it was issued by the United States government as part of the celebration of the Lewis and Clark Bicentennial.

2001  The Three Affiliated Tribes (Now referred to as the MHA Nation) issued a proclamation stating that the Bulls Eye story of *Sakakawea (Sacagawea)* was the official position of the tribe.

2002  The Three Affiliated Tribes' Tribal Council passed a resolution stating that *"Sacagawea"* would be the correct Hidatsa pronunciation of her name.

2003  A replica of the statue of *Sacagawea* in Bismarck was placed in the National Statuary Hall as part of the Lewis and Clark bicentennial celebration. The MHA Nation played a major role in the event.

In 2015 the MHA Tribal Council began funding a research project to gather evidence to confirm that *Sacagawea* was Hidatsa.

### "Remembering Ma Ishu Wea" in Dakota Lakota Journal, September 8-15, 2006.

Four Bears Park - Clad in her grandmother's beaded buffalo-hide dress, Jessica Grinnell [a relative of *Sacagawea*] expressed her feelings with the crowd that gathered to hear her talk about *Sakakawea (Sacagawea)*.

Speaking of *Sakakawea*, or "Bird Woman," Grinnell said, "She did a heroic thing but wouldn't have been able to do that without the

## Timeline of the Life of Maeshuwea (Sacagawea)

language, stories, history, without listening to her people."

Grinnell shared a song before she began telling the story of this "sister" of history who many Hidatsa claim was *Maa-Ishu Wea* or "Eagle Woman."

Grinnell said that at one time the Crow and Hidatsa were one tribe. *Sakakawea* was with the group that became known as the Hidatsa at the mouth of the Missouri River with her brother, Cherry Necklace, a medicine man.

For months she said *Sakakawea* accompanied Lewis and Clark, providing the explorers with knowledge of plant medicines, wild foods, as well as cultural knowledge critical to the expedition's success. For those months, life on the trail was all she and her infant son, Pomp, would know, Grinnell said.

Grinnell went to a medicine person with kidney fat and dried meat stew, and he taught her the song and story of *Sakakawea* in Hidatsa and English.

When Jessica Grinnell was asked how she would record her own history, as *Sakakawea's* was recorded by Lewis and Clark, she said, "Our women today are educated and outspoken; are hard workers." Adding, "by knowing traditional women's roles: getting up early, tending to the garden, the children, and your husband."

For further reading on the life of Hidatsa girls and women of *Sacagawea's* time, the following are recommended:

*Buffalo Bird Woman's Garden* as told to Gilbert L. Wilson, St. Paul, Minnesota Historical Society Press, 1987.

*Waheenee: an Indian Girl's Story*, Gilbert L. Wilson, St. Paul, MN, Webb Publishing Company, 1921.

*Women of the Earth Lodges: Tribal Life on the Plains,* Virginia Bergman Peters, Norman, University of Oklahoma Press, 1995.

*Our Story of Eagle Woman, Sacagawea*

This document contains what we know about *Maeshuwea, Sacagawea,* an Hidatsa/Crow woman who accompanied the Lewis and Clark Expedition.

<u>They got it wrong!</u> This is Our Story.

It is noted that *Sacagawea* would never have wanted to be portrayed as she has been. She would not have seen her actions as extraordinary.

In the next chapter we discuss DNA evidence that verifies our claim regarding *Sacagawea's* heritage.

Major Welch stated that the Bulls Eye story would "eventually lead a person of research to the true light." We hope we have succeeded in doing that. Further research would reveal more evidence. We encourage it.

— *Sacagawea* Project Board of the MHA Nation

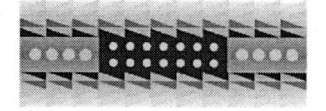

# Chapter 11
# *BLOOD PROOF*
# *DNA Study*

*T*he *Sacagawea Project Board did far more* than others to study the background and life of *Sacagawea* using a mix of family and tribal stories, interviews, documents, texts, diaries, journals, other research, and scientific data. The Board was willing to examine every source that came to light. The two popular stories of *Sacagawea*, the Wyoming and the Ft. Manuel stories, are based on less evidence than we have provided, yet they are believed. Our story deserves as much attention!

At midpoint in the development of this book, it appeared that we had found and documented the many stories of Fort Berthold tribal elders, past and present, showing that *Sacagawea* was Hidatsa. We had also found historical written evidence and linguistic evidence that *Sacagawea* was more likely an Hidatsa than a Shoshone. So, at this point, Jerry "Bird" Birdsbill Ford, whose grandfather was the commanding scout at the memorial day event when Bulls Eye told the Hidatsa story of *Sacagawea,* suggested using DNA evidence as proof. Bird and her daughter, Rebecca Burbridge, had knowledge of DNA requirements and its use. Bird talked with the project board about the use of DNA in our research.

It was determined that the group would attempt to locate **descendants of Jean Baptiste Charbonneau,** *Sacagawea's* son. If found, they would then be DNA tested relative to Ft. Berthold descendants of *Sacagawea*. Further, we would use DNA to determine other *Sacagawea*-related evidence if found. If successful in this effort to show biological relationships, we believed that we could greatly enhance our findings and finally put the matter of her heritage to rest. We did recognize the limitations of DNA programs in that they would only be as good as what was entered in them.

The project board did invest in an effort to have Ancestry DNA, a specialized offshoot of Ancestry.com, perform professional research to help in our effort and to especially locate descendants of Jean Baptiste Charbonneau. Unfortunately, shortly after the contract was signed, the Ancestry.com organization made a unilateral decision to cancel the contract as they felt that it was too large a project and that there was too much research that needed to be done. Although we disagreed, they stopped work and referred us to a university DNA laboratory which did conduct large DNA research projects. However, we found this lab was closed, not only due to the Covid-19 pandemic of 2020-21, but also because their professor director was on sabbatical for two years. Therefore, we performed our own research to determine potential DNA connections.

We DNA tested, through Ancestry.com, members of the *Sacagawea* Project Board, all of whom were related to *Sacagawea*. We also found that many younger generations of *Sacagawea* descendants and other relatives [See page 225] had already tested either with Ancestry or 23 and Me. We then tested other direct descendants of *Sacagawea;* direct descendants of *Sacagawea's* brother, Cherry Necklace; and direct descendants of the Fredericks, Pease and Young Bird families who were all related to *Sacagawea*. We found that all of the forenamed were indeed related as shown in our sections of this book on *Sacagawea's* relatives. Most appeared as each other's DNA matches. We purposely included the DNA of Crow relatives and those whose ancestors were mainly white. Other members of these families also submitted their DNA and family trees to Ancestry, and we cross checked their matches also. This reinforced our findings. All of the above families strongly acknowledge that they are related, and Fort Berthold and Crow Agency records confirm it.

Some believe that *Sacagawea* was adopted by Cherry Necklace, and that's how she became an Hidatsa. If *Sacagawea* was really "Sacajawea" and was Shoshone, it's possible that her descendants married into the Hidatsa Tribe that she was supposedly adopted into.

However, her descendants would remain related to Shoshones of her original line and would also be related to descendants of Toussaint Charbonneau. They would not necessarily be related to descendants and relatives of her supposedly "adopted" brother, Cherry Necklace. We have found that *Sacagawea's* descendants are clearly related to Cherry Necklace's descendants and to the descendants of relatives All Moves and She Kills, ancestors of the Fredericks, Pease and Young Bird families. For example, *Sacagawea* direct descendant D.S. was matched to E. L., descendant of Cherry Necklace, sharing 48 DNA centimorgans. Further, D. S. was matched to C. G., descendant of All Moves and She Kills, sharing 35 DNA centimorgans. The higher the centimorgans, the more closely related individuals are.

Our project required basic research as well as genealogy and the use of DNA technology. We began to study the life of Jean Baptiste Charbonneau, the baby "Pomp" who accompanied Lewis and Clark and his parents to the West Coast, and who grew up to lead an extraordinary life of adventure in his own right. He was born in 1805 and died in 1866. Initially schooled by Captain William Clark in St Louis, he ventured off with German Prince Paul of Wurttemberg at age 18 to reside there in his castle for six years as a hybrid guest and worker.

We learned that while in Germany Jean Baptiste fathered a male child named **Anton Fries** who died in infancy and is buried in Germany. Anton Fries was born on February 20, 1829, to Jean Baptiste and Anastasia Katharina Fries in Mergentheim, Germany. Anton died three months later, with no documentation available other than a reference in the diary of Duke Paul Herzog of Wurttemberg with whom Jean Baptiste had lived for the previous six years. The reference to Anton Fries appears in several sources on Jean Baptiste's life in Europe. Among these is Paul Wilhelm, Duke of Wurttemberg, *Travels in North America, 1822-1824,* translated by Robert Nitske, edited by Savoie Lottinville (Norman, OK: University of Oklahoma, 1973).

## Our Story of Eagle Woman, Sacagawea

We found that Jean Baptiste returned to America at age 25 and became an invaluable frontiersman. He spoke German, French, Hidatsa, English and Crow, among other languages. He hired himself out to fellow adventurers, similar to what his father did. He later served as hireling, trapper, adventurer, a mayor, and even a wagon driver (teamster) with the Mormon Battalion which traveled to California.

Dr. Michael Welsh, researcher for the *Sacagawea* project, pursued the account that Jean Baptiste married a Cheyenne woman and there was a child born at Bent's Fort, near La Junta, Colorado, on March 20, 1846, to Jean Baptiste Charbonneau and a woman known as "Rufine." This information was recorded in the diary of Alexander Barclay who served as the superintendent of Bent's Fort in the years 1845-1849. The child, **"Louise,"** reappears in the Barclay journals in December, 1847, when she and her mother were mentioned as leaving the camp of the Cheyenne chief, The Whirlwind, and going down to Bent's Fort alone and afoot. Jean Baptiste had left them in 1846 for Santa Fe to join the US Army of the West as it advanced to Southern California. He worked as a driver on Mormon Battalion wagon trains where he was known for going ahead of the wagons not only to hunt for food but also to create a new path through the desert to Southern California. The best source for the information on Louise is George P. Hammond, editor, *The Adventures of Alexander Barclay, Mountain Man,* Denver: Old West Publishing Company, 1976.

Complicating this story is the fact that a **Luisa Shahuano** (Charbonneau phoneticized by the census taker) is shown as 13 years old, born in 1837 on the Arkansas River, and living in the household of Kit Carson and his wife, Maria Josefa Jaramillo. This is recorded in the 1850 census for Taos County, New Mexico, found on Ancestry.com. Other researchers have referred to this finding as evidence of a child of Jean Baptiste. Luisa did not appear in the census records after that, and she was not found in the Ancestry.com database after many hours and hours of searching and reaching out to historians and families who may have had pertinent information.

Therefore, no descendants of Luisa were located. Indian census reports included in Ancestry.com began in 1885 so were not helpful in our search either.

The search for descendants of Jean Baptiste Charbonneau continued. Dr. Michael Welsh, researcher for our book project and University of Northern Colorado professor, and Bird Ford, MHA Tribal member assisting with the book project, met separately with Dr. John Johnson, Curator of Anthropology, Santa Barbara Museum of Natural History, in California. Welsh met with him in the summer of 2018 and Ford in September, 2019. Dr. Johnson had found the baptismal certificate of **Maria Catarina Charguana,** child of Jean Baptiste Charbonneau, in the records of the Plaza Church of Los Angeles as part of his larger study, entitled, "Descendants of Native Communities in the Vicinity of Marine Corps Base Camp Pendleton: An Ethnohistoric Study of Luiseño and Juaneño Cultural Affiliation" (December 2001). Dr. Johnson and his research team had reviewed documents from numerous research libraries in California, including the Federal National Archives.

It was hoped that Dr. Johnson had information about Jean Baptiste's child after her birth. Although he had extensive research files related to his 2001 study of Camp Pendleton, no records concerning Maria Catarina Charguana could be found after 1848. It was believed she did not survive, or possibly her name was changed when her mother later married Gregorio Trujillo and had ten other children. Both Ms. Ford and Welsh met either in person or by telephone with members of the Luiseno Tribe and particularly with Mel Vernon, a tribal official, but no one there knew about this child or her family.

No new information was uncovered regarding this child when Bird Ford met with Dr. Johnson a year later. However, Ms. Ford noticed that Dr. Johnson had numerous Ancestry DNA boxes throughout his office. He began to discuss DNA in depth and provided the papers that he had written concerning DNA.

He was thrilled that our project was moving towards using DNA, and he highly recommended that we pursue a contract with Ancestry DNA or another DNA entity to locate any descendants of Jean Baptiste. Dr. Johnson provided copies of his papers, "A Land of Diversity: Genetic Insights into Ancestral Origins" and "Genetics Linguistics and Prehistoric Migrations: An Analysis of California Indian Mitrochrondrial DNA Lineage." These documents support the concept that research into families can be greatly enhanced by the use of DNA.

At the time that Jean Baptiste arrived in Southern California, it was under the Mexican flag. He briefly worked as the Alcalde, or "mayor", in 1847-48 while living at San Luis Rey Mission. He fathered Maria Catarina (or Cantarina) with a Luiseno lady named Margarita Sobin after her villages of Sobinish. This child was born in February, 1848, and she was baptized at the Plaza Church in downtown Los Angeles under the last name Charguana, in May, 1848. Charbonneau had already left his position by that time to head north to the gold fields of California. The child's godmother was Felipa Pico, from the influential Mexican Governor Pico family who would later give a large ranchero estate to Margarita which was passed down to her heirs through the turn of the century. Following is Maria Catarina's baptismal certificate.

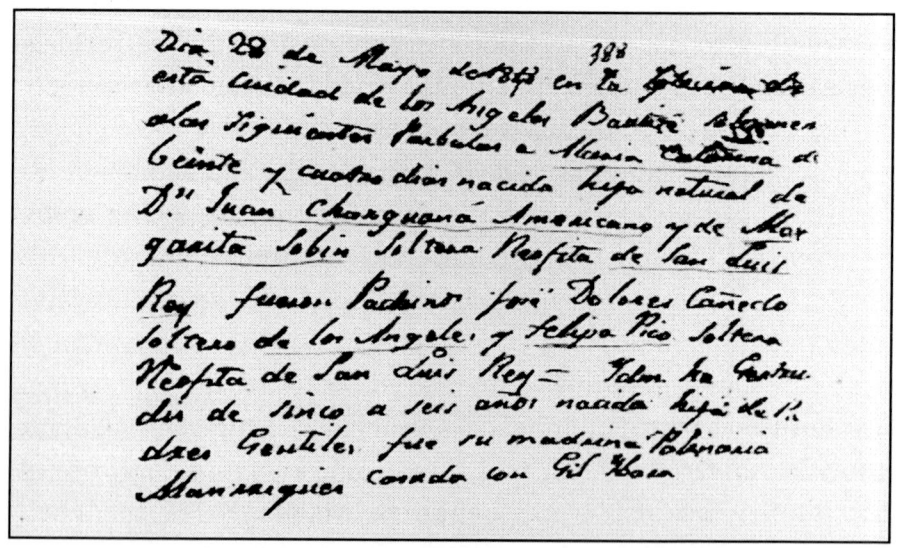

*Baptismal record of Maria Catarina Charguana (Charbonneau)*

Further research utilizing the Ancestry.com database did find Maria Cantarina as a member of her mother's family in California. Her mother, Margarita Sobin, married someone named "Holcomb" and, later, someone named "Gregorio Trujillo." She had children from both marriages. Ancestry listed both marriages and the children from them. Maria was listed as a half sibling but as having no known children in the Life Story section.

An article, "Toussaint Charbonneau in the Pacific North in 1805," by Chalk Courchane in *Early Pioneer Families of the Northwest,* online, date unknown, states that a family of Charbonneaus at Ft. Totten, North Dakota, claimed to be descendants of *Sacagawea*. Their story was told in the Bismarck Tribune of October 8, 1939, and stated that Bird Woman *(Sacagawea)* and Baptiste Charbonneau had a son named Toussaint. This son was a trapper and, in Manitoba, he married Mary Victoria Vandell who like him was a French-Indian half-blood. In 1848 the family came to Dakota Territory and helped in building Fort Totten. Toussaint died there in 1869. Mary, Toussaint and Victoria's daughter, was born August 8, 1856. In 1878 she married Alexander Bouret and they moved to a point near Sheyenne, North Dakota. Mr. Bouret died in 1903, and in 1904 she married Fritz Hillstrom. Mary Charbonneau Hillstrom also had a brother, Robert Charbonneau of Fort Totten. Some of the relatives and descendants of Toussaint Charbonneau (2) and Victoria Vandell still live in North Dakota.

We believe that their story is not quite right. *Sacagawea* was married to Toussaint Charbonneau (1), not Baptiste. Baptiste was their son. Otter Woman, *Sacagawea's* sister and another wife of Toussaint (1), did have a son named Toussaint (2). Other descendants of the son, Toussaint (2), have posted this relationship. John Luttig of Ft. Manuel took Otter Woman's children, Lisette, age 1, and Toussaint, age 10, to St. Louis after Otter Woman died at the fort in 1812. The children were taken in by Captain William Clark, just as Jean Baptiste was. It is reported that Toussaint (2) left St. Louis and became a fur trapper and trader.

*Our Story of Eagle Woman, Sacagawea*

# FORT BERTHOLD/FORT TOTTEN SACAGAWEA CONNECTION

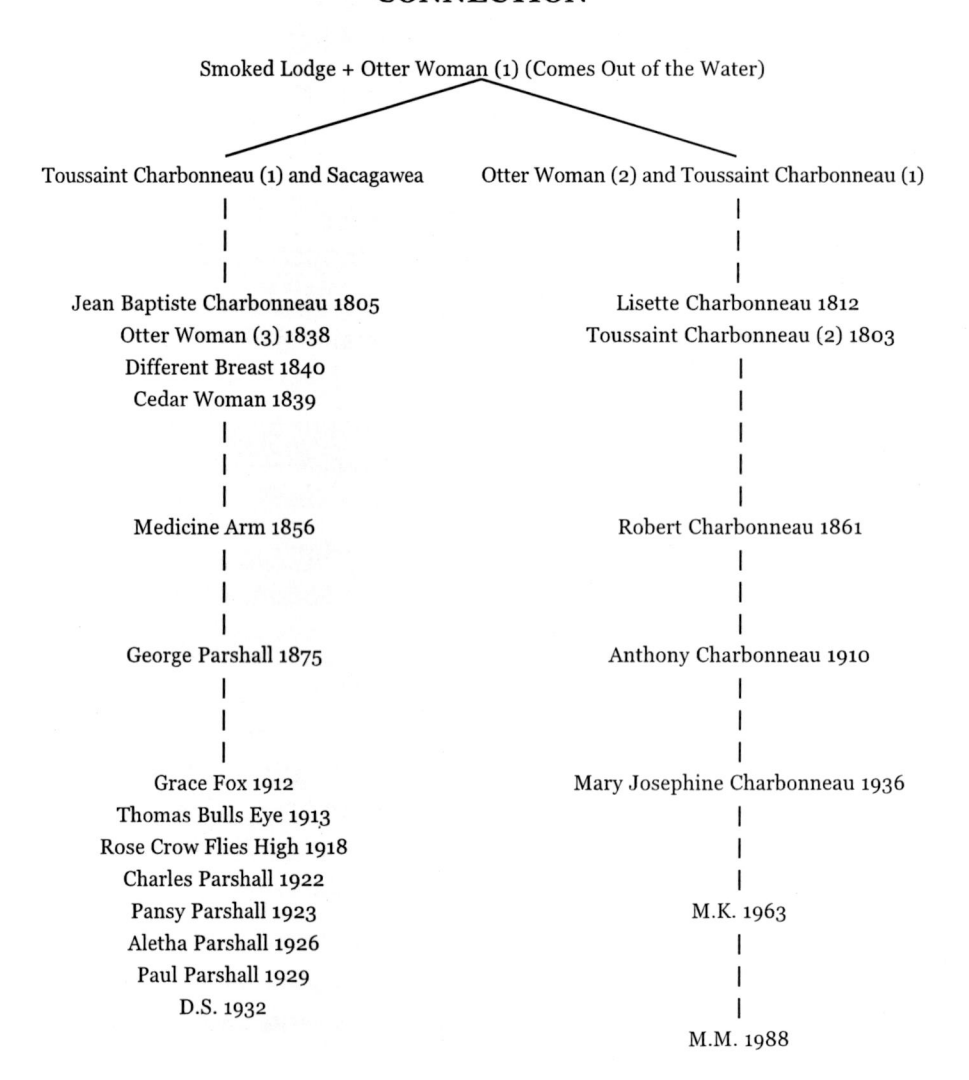

Smoked Lodge + Otter Woman (1) (Comes Out of the Water)

Toussaint Charbonneau (1) and Sacagawea     Otter Woman (2) and Toussaint Charbonneau (1)

| | |
|---|---|
| Jean Baptiste Charbonneau 1805 | Lisette Charbonneau 1812 |
| Otter Woman (3) 1838 | Toussaint Charbonneau (2) 1803 |
| Different Breast 1840 | |
| Cedar Woman 1839 | |
| | |
| Medicine Arm 1856 | Robert Charbonneau 1861 |
| | |
| George Parshall 1875 | Anthony Charbonneau 1910 |
| | |
| Grace Fox 1912 | Mary Josephine Charbonneau 1936 |
| Thomas Bulls Eye 1913 | |
| Rose Crow Flies High 1918 | |
| Charles Parshall 1922 | |
| Pansy Parshall 1923 | M.K. 1963 |
| Aletha Parshall 1926 | |
| Paul Parshall 1929 | |
| D.S. 1932 | |
| | M.M. 1988 |

*DNA Study*

# FORT TOTTEN CHARBONNEAUS - FAMILY TREE

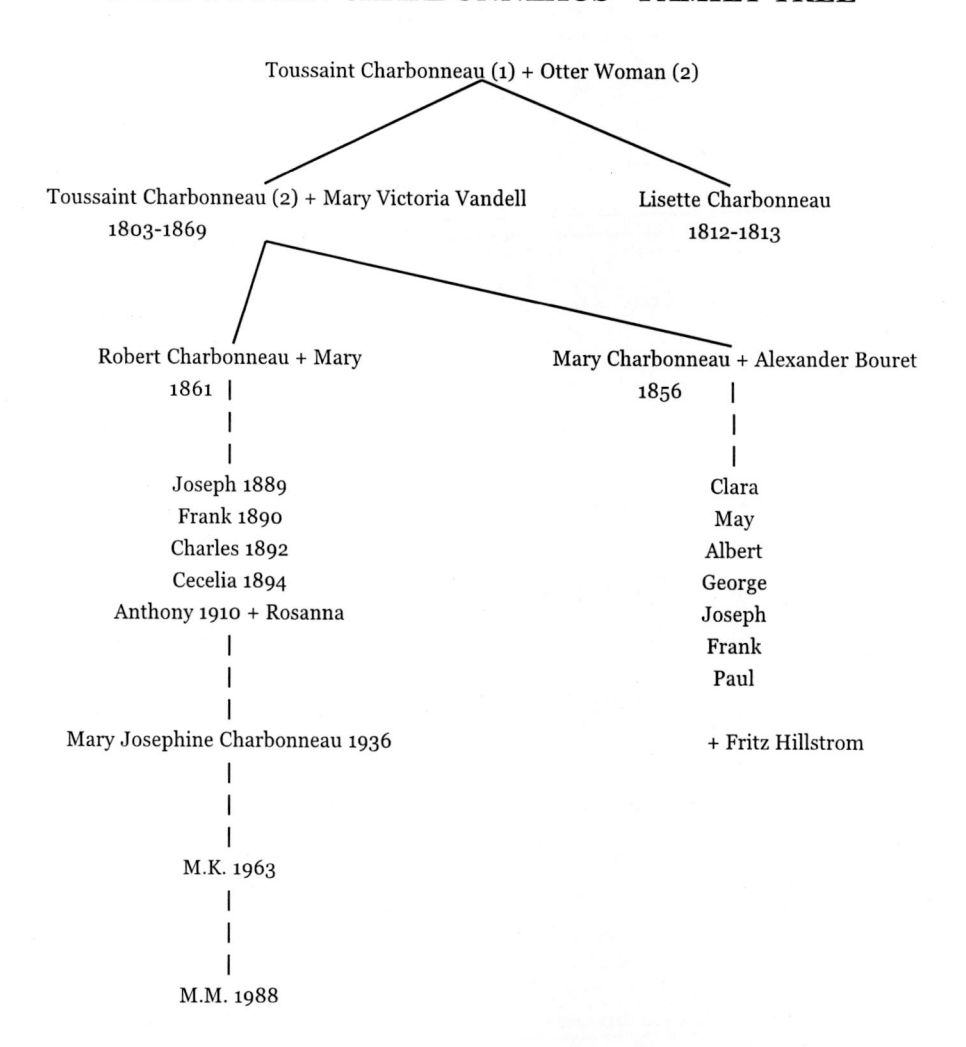

Toussaint Charbonneau (1) + Otter Woman (2)

Toussaint Charbonneau (2) + Mary Victoria Vandell      Lisette Charbonneau
1803-1869      1812-1813

Robert Charbonneau + Mary      Mary Charbonneau + Alexander Bouret
1861      1856

Joseph 1889      Clara
Frank 1890      May
Charles 1892      Albert
Cecelia 1894      George
Anthony 1910 + Rosanna      Joseph
     Frank
     Paul

Mary Josephine Charbonneau 1936      + Fritz Hillstrom

M.K. 1963

M.M. 1988

*Fort Totten Charbonneau Family*

A DNA match of D. S., direct descendant of *Sacagawea*, with a descendant of this Fort Totten family, M. M., was revealed on Ancestry.com so the Charbonneau relationship was established. The 23 and Me DNA program was enlisted in order to help further determine if members of the Ft. Totten family were DNA matches with others on *Sacagawea's* family tree to determine if a relationship existed between D. S. and Otter Woman, *Sacagawea's* sister, in addition to a relationship with the Charbonneaus.

We have found that, indeed, there was a DNA blood relationship between members of the Ft. Totten Charbonneaus and representatives of *Sacagawea's* descendants; representives of Cherry Necklace's descendants; and with representatives of the Pease, Young Bird, and Fredericks families. M. M., a young descendant of the Fort Totten family, shared 7 DNA centimorgans with D. S., direct descendant of *Sacagawea*. Other examples of evidence are that M. M. also had matches with E. L., a Cherry Necklace descendant, and P. F., a descendant of the Fredericks family. These findings occurred before Ancestry limited its results in August 2020 to elderly relatives with 8 centimorgans or higher. We are confident that the Charbonneau family members of Ft. Totten are related to the Fort Berthold relatives of *Sacagawea* through Charbonneau, *Sacagawea* and Otter Woman.

It is important to show a relationship not only to other Charbonneaus but also to the original Charbonneau, Olivier Charbonneau. Many of his descendants will have mostly French Canadian blood. We found that D. S., direct descendant of *Sacagawea*, had over 70 DNA matches on Ancestry.com with individuals with a Charbonneau surname in their family trees and with the relationship readily traceable. There were many more individuals who were DNA matches with French backgrounds back to Quebec, Canada, where Toussaint Charbonneau was from. We are confident D. S. is a descendant of Toussaint. Following is a family tree tracing her relationship (and her siblings') to Olivier Charbonneau. Her DNA matches to elderly relatives A.E. and R.C. in Ancestry.com were 22 centimorgans.

*DNA Study*

# CHARBONNEAU/PARSHALL FAMILY TREE

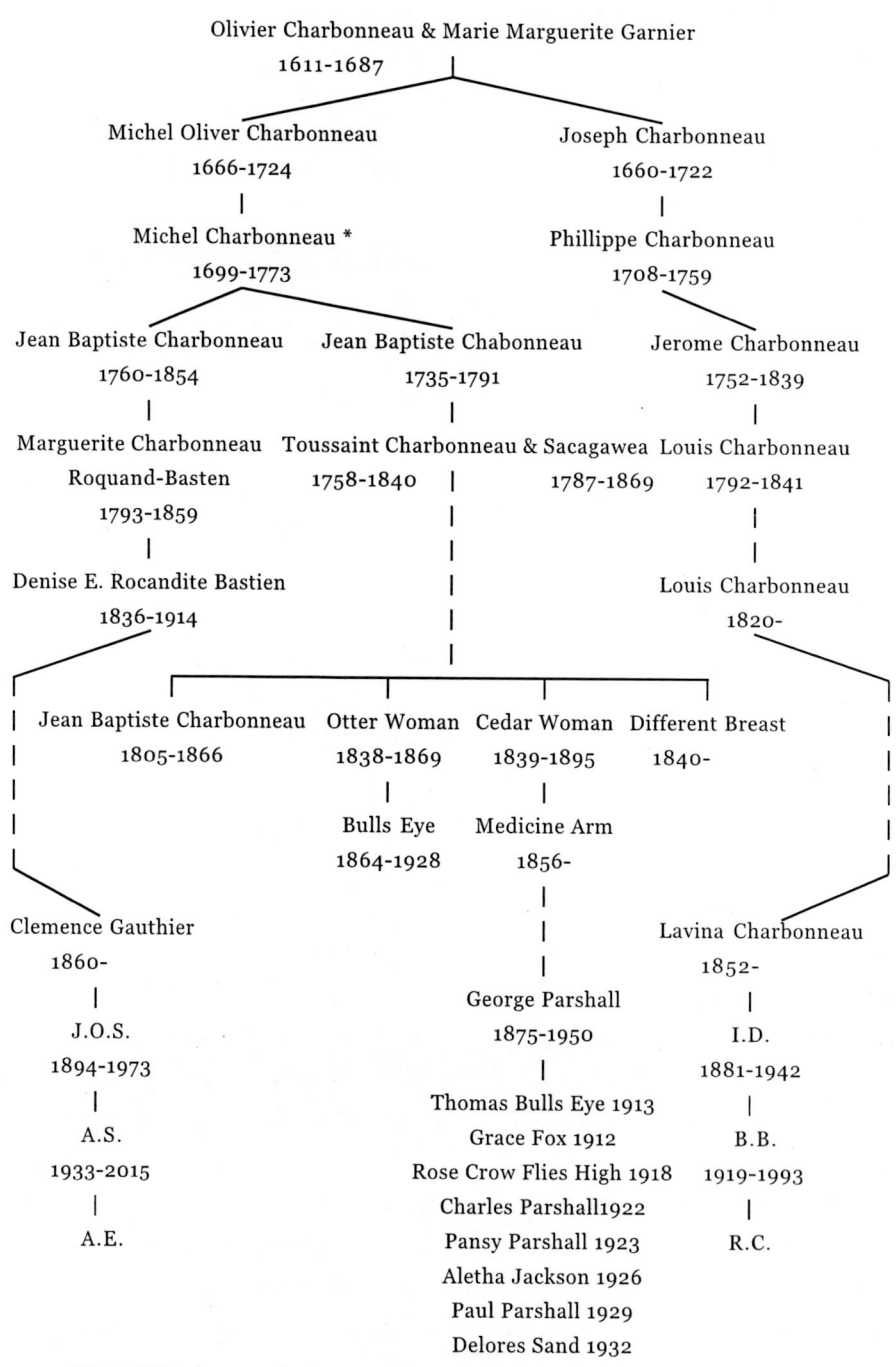

Olivier Charbonneau & Marie Marguerite Garnier
1611-1687

Michel Oliver Charbonneau
1666-1724

Joseph Charbonneau
1660-1722

Michel Charbonneau *
1699-1773

Phillippe Charbonneau
1708-1759

Jean Baptiste Charbonneau
1760-1854

Jean Baptiste Chabonneau
1735-1791

Jerome Charbonneau
1752-1839

Marguerite Charbonneau
Roquand-Basten
1793-1859

Toussaint Charbonneau & Sacagawea
1758-1840         1787-1869

Louis Charbonneau
1792-1841

Denise E. Rocandite Bastien
1836-1914

Louis Charbonneau
1820-

Jean Baptiste Charbonneau
1805-1866

Otter Woman
1838-1869

Cedar Woman
1839-1895

Different Breast
1840-

Bulls Eye
1864-1928

Medicine Arm
1856-

Clemence Gauthier
1860-

Lavina Charbonneau
1852-

J.O.S.
1894-1973

George Parshall
1875-1950

I.D.
1881-1942

A.S.
1933-2015

Thomas Bulls Eye 1913
Grace Fox 1912
Rose Crow Flies High 1918
Charles Parshall 1922
Pansy Parshall 1923
Aletha Jackson 1926
Paul Parshall 1929
Delores Sand 1932

B.B.
1919-1993

A.E.

R.C.

* Michel Charbonneau had two sons named Jean Baptiste from different mothers.

295

We are convinced we are correct in our determination that *Sacagawea* was an Hidatsa/Crow Indian, primarily due to DNA matches but also due to other evidence included in this document.

Our manuscript demonstrates the century-long efforts of the Hidatsa to overcome the power of the Lewis and Clark journals. Only tribal members could make the statements contained in each chapter about the errors of historical fact. They always knew who *Sacagawea* was. This made the rejection of their stories all the more frustrating. No matter who it was who told them, they were considered wrong. The use of DNA shows the due diligence that the *Sacagawea* Project Board performed to find any and all proof of the merits of the Hidatsa and Crow stories.

Finally, it is hoped that sometime in the future some of our readers will decide to conduct further research on this subject. We would encourage college students to perform research for a potential thesis or even for an update to this book. They could contact a DNA research organization to proceed further in that area. The MHA Interpretive Center will continue to monitor DNA findings.

**We have seen that Ancestry.com and 23 and Me DNA matches exist between and among those in the databases including Ft. Berthold descendants of *Sacagawea*; descendants of Cherry Necklace; and Fredericks, Pease, and Young Bird family members. There is solid DNA evidence that Ft. Berthold descendants of *Sacagawea* are biologically related to the Charbonneau family. Further, we have found that the Ft. Berthold descendants and relatives of *Sacagawea* are DNA matched to descendants of Toussaint (1) and Otter Woman (2), *Sacagawea's* sister. Therefore, we state that *Sacagawea* (Eagle Woman) was an Hidatsa/Crow Indian and was not Shoshone.**

**They got it wrong!**
— Jerry Birdsbill "Bird" Ford
— Dr. Michael Welsh

# Appendix
## Other Sources

### Chapter 1

Ahler, Stanley A., Thiessen, Thomas D. and Trimble, Michael K. People of the Willows: *The Prehistory and Early History of the Hidatsa Indians, Grand Forks:* University of North Dakota Press, 1991.

Bowers, Alfred W. *Hidatsa Social and Ceremonial Organization.* Lincoln: University of Nebraska Press, 1992.

Cash, Joseph H. and Wolff, Gerald W. *The Three Affiliated Tribes (Mandan, Arikara, and Hidatsa).* Phoenix: Indian Tribal Services, 1974.

Curtis, Edward S. *The Apsaroke or Crows, The Hidatsa. The North American Indian Series,* North American Book Distributor, LLC, 2015.

Demallie, Raymond J., volume editor, and Sturtevant, William C., general editor. *Handbook of North American Indians, Volume 13.* Plains. Washington, DC: Smithsonian Institution Press, 2001. Entries -- Hidatsa / Frank Henderson Stewart -- Mandan / W. Raymond Wood and Lee Irwin -- Arikara / Douglas R. Parks -- Three Affiliated Tribes / Mary Jane Schneider.

Freedman, Russell. *An Indian Winter.* Holiday House, 1992.

Hearings before the Subcommittee on Indian Affairs of the Committee on Public Lands, House of Representatives, Eighty-First Congress, First Session on House Joint Resolution 33 Providing for the Ratification by Congress of the Contract to Purchase Indian Lands by the United States from the Three Affiliated Tribes of Fort Berthold, North Dakota, 1949.

Lowie, Robert H. *Anthropological Papers of The American Museum of Natural History,* Vol. XXI, Part I, "Notes on the Social Organization and Customs of the Mandan, Hidatsa, and Crow Indians." New York: The American Museum of Natural History, 1917.

Matthews, Washington. *Ethnography and Philology of the Hidatsa Indians.* Government Printing Office, 1877.

Meyer, Roy W. Fort Berthold and the Garrison Dam. *North Dakota History, Journal of the Northern Plains.* Vol. 35, Nos. 3 & 4, 1968.

National Park Service. *Like-A-Fishhook Village and Fort Berthold Garrison Reservoir North Dakota.* Washington: U.S. Department of the Interior, 1972.

Potter, Tracy. *Sheheke, Mandan Indian Diplomat: The Story of White Coyote, Thomas Jefferson, and Lewis and Clark.* Washburn, ND: Fort Mandan Press, 2003.

Ronda, James P. *Lewis and Clark among the Indians.* Lincoln: University of Nebraska Press, 1984.

Schneider, Mary Jane. *The Hidatsa.* New York: Chelsea House Publishers, 1989 and Gilman, Carolyn. *The Way to Independence: Memories of a Hidatsa Indian Family, 1840-1920.* St. Paul: Minnesota Historical Society Press, 1987.

Sullivan, Nicole and Vrooman, Nicholas Peterson. *The Knife River Indian Villages.* Theodore Roosevelt Nature & History Association. Helena, MT: SkyHouse Publishers, 1995.

Welch, A. B. Col. and Cox, Everett, et. al. *War Drums of the 1800's: Warriors of the Sioux, Mandan, Arikara and Hidatsa Nations Speak of the Battles.* Amazon Digitl Services, LLC, 2014.

Wilson, Gilbert. *Buffalo Bird Woman's Garden, Agriculture of the Hidatsa Indians.* Minneapolis: University of Minnesota Press, 1917. *Goodbird the Indian.* Andecite Press, 2015. and *Waheenee: an Indian Girl's Story.* St. Paul: Webb Publishing Co., 1921.

Wood, W. Raymond and Thiessen, Thomas D., editors. *Early Fur Trade on the Northern Plains: Canadian Traders among the Mandan and Hidatsa Indians, 1738-1818.* Norman: University of Oklahoma Press, 1985.

## Chapter 2

Bowers, Alfred W. *Hidatsa Social and Ceremonial Organization.* Lincoln, NE: University of Nebraska Press, 1992.

Connolly, James B. Article in *North Dakota Motorist.* July-August, 1975, Vol. 21, No. 1.

Eastman, Doris. "Sakakawea: Hidatsa or Shoshone?" *Fargo Forum.* October 1975.

Garcia, Louis. "Hidatsa Place Names," Unpublished paper, 2006.

## Chapter 3

Cowdrey, Mike. Letter to Ken Burns. January, 1997.

Welch, Major Albert B. *Welch Dakota Papers.* Lacey, Washington.

# Other Sources

## Chapter 4

Hearings Before the Subcommittee on Indian Affairs of the Committee on Public Lands, House of Representatives, Eighty-First Congress, First Session, on House Joint Resolution 33, Providing for the Ratification by Congress of the Contract to Purchase Indian Lands by the United States from the Three Affiliated Tribes of Fort Berthold, North Dakota, 1949.

Potter, Tracy. *Sheheke, Mandan Indian Diplomat: The Story of White Coyote, Thomas Jefferson, and Lewis and Clark*. Washburn, ND: Farcountry Press, Fort Mandan Press, 2003.

## Chapter 5

Ahler, Stanley A. and others. *The Prehistory and Early History of the Hidatsa Indians*. Grand Forks: University of North Dakota Press, 1991.

Barbour, Barton H. *Ft. Union and the Upper Missouri Fur Trade*. University of Oklahoma Press, 2001

Beckwith, Martha Warren, editor. *Mandan-Hidatsa Myths and Ceremonies. American Folk Lore Society,* New York, 1937.

Bowers, Alfred W. *Mandan Social and Ceremonial Organization*. University of Chicago, 1950.

Eastman, C.A. Shoshone—January 2, 1925 File, Box 64, E-953 HM 1992, Record Group 75, Records of the Bureau of Indian Affairs, Inspection Division, Inspection Reports, 1908-1940, Shoshone to Siletz Files, National Archives and Records Administration, Washington, DC.

Gilman, Carolyn and Schneider, Mary Jane. *The Way to Independence: Memories of a Hidatsa Indian Family, 1840-1920*. St. Paul: Minnesota Historical Society Press, 1987.

Lowie, Robert. "Notes on the Social Organization and Customs of the Mandan, Hidatsa and Crow Indians," 1917.

Stevens, Michael. *Biographical Dictionary of the Mandan, Hidatsa and Arikara*. online.

Welch, Major A. B. *Welch Dakota Papers*. Lacey, Washington.

Wilson, Gilbert. *Agriculture of the Hidatsa Indians: An Indian Interpretation*. Minneapolis: University of Minnesota Press, 1917.

Wilson, Gilbert. *The Hidatsa Earthlodge*. American Museum of Natural History, New York, 1934.

Wilson, Gilbert. *Buffalo Bird Woman's Garden: Agriculture of the Hidatsa Indians*. With a new introduction by Jeffrey R. Hanson. St. Paul: Minnesota Historical Society Press, 1987.

## Chapter 6

American Indigenous Research Association Meeting Agenda, 2018, Polson, MT.

Atkinson, General Henry. Diary. Missouri Historical Society.

Barbour, Barton H. *Fort Union and the Upper Missouri Fur Trade.* University of Oklahoma Press, 2001.

Beckwourth, James P. and Bonner, Thomas D. *The Life and Adventures of James P. Beckwourth as Told to Thomas D. Bonner.* Lincoln: University of Nebraska Press, 1972 reprint of 1856 ed.

Bowers, Alfred W. *Hidatsa Social and Ceremonial Organization.* Lincoln, NE: University of Nebraska Press, 1992.

Bowers, Alfred W. Letter to James Connolly, 1975.

Case, Rev. and Mrs. Harold. *100 Years at Ft. Berthold,* 1977.

Chardon, F. A. *Chardon's Journal at Fort Clark, 1834-1839.* Pierre, SD: South Dakota Historical Society, 1834.

Colby, Susan M. *Sacagawea's Child: The Life and Times of Jean-Baptiste (Pomp) Charbonneau.* Spokane: The Arthur H. Clark Company, 2006.

Eastman, C.A. Shoshone — January 2, 1925 File, Box 64, E-953 HM 1992, Record Group 75, Records of the Bureau of Indian Affairs, Inspection Division, Inspection Reports, 1908-1940, Shoshone to Siletz Files, National Archives and Records Administration, Washington, DC.

Engelhardt, Zephryn. *San Luis Rey Mission,* San Francisco, CA: The James H. Barry Company, 1921.

Fremont, John C. *Narrative of the Exploring Expedition to the Rocky Mountains and to Oregon and North California.* Washington, DC: Gales and Seaton, Printers, 1845.

Ft. Buford 6th Infantry Regiment Association. *A Chronological Record of Events at the Missouri-Yellowstone Confluence Area from 1805 to 1896 and A Record of internments at the Fort Buford Dakota Territory Post Cemetery 1866 to 1895,* 1971.

Hafen, Leroy R., editor, *The Mountain Men and the Fur Trade of the Far West.* Glendale, CA: Arthur H. Clark Company, 1965-1972.

Hebard, Grace Raymond. Papers, American Heritage Center, University of Wyoming.

Hebard, Grace Raymond. *Sacajawea, a Guide and Interpreter of the Lewis and Clark Expedition with an Account of the Travels of Toussaint Charbonneau and Jean Baptiste, the Expedition Papoose.* Glendale: Arthur H. Clark Co., 1933.

Hosmer, James. *History of the Expeditions of Captains Lewis and Clark, 1804-06.* Chicago: A.C. McClurg, 1902.

Howard, Harold P. "The Two Versions." *Sacajawea.* Norman: University of Oklahoma Press, 1971.

*Indian Country Today.* Lakota Storytelling Tradition. August 4, 2004.

Jager, Rebecca K. *Malinche, Pocahontas, and Sacagawea: Indian Women as Cultural Intermediaries and National Symbols.* Norman: University of Oklahoma Press, 2015.

Kessler, Donna J. *The Making of Sacagawea: A Euro-American Legend.* Tuscaloosa, AL: University of Alabama Press, 1996.

Matson, William B. Crazy Horse: *The Lakota Warrior's Life & Legacy,* The Edward Clown Family, as told to William Matson. Layton, UT: Gibbs Smith, 2016.

Matthews, Washington. *Ethnography and Philology of the Hidatsa Indians.* Government Printing Office, 1877.

Montana Historical Society. *Montana Place Names.* Helena: Montana Historical Society Press, 2009.

Ottoson, Dennis R. "Toussaint Charbonneau, A Most Durable Man." *South Dakota History* 6, Spring, 1976.

Rain Bird, Manu. "With each discovery, remember Pueblo struggles." *Albuquerque Journal,* December 28, 2018.

Reading, Mrs. James. "Jean Baptiste Charbonneau." *The Journal of San Diego History,* San Diego Historical Society Quarterly, March 1965, Vol. 11, Number 2.

Reid, Russell. Letter to Mr. E.C. Jacobsen, October 5, 1933.

Robinson, Doane. *Papers.* South Dakota State Historical Society, Pierre.

Sacagawea File. American Heritage Center, University of Wyoming.

Sanderson, George B. Quote from unpublished transcript of Sanderson's diary by Ken R. Henson and Laura Anderson, University of Utah.

Schroer, Blanche. *Papers,* American Heritage Center, University of Wyoming.

St. George Cooke, Phillip. *The Conquest of New Mexico and California: An Historical and Personal Narrative.* Albuquerque: Horn and Wallace, 1964.

von Sachsen-Altenburg, Hans. *Duke Paul of Wurttemberg on the Missouri Frontier: 1823, 1830, and 1851.* Boonville, MO: Pekitanoui Publishers, 1998.

Webb, George Washington. *Chronological List of Engagements Between the Regular Army of the United States and Various Tribes of Hostile Indians Which Occurred During the Years 1790 to 1898*. St. Louis: Wing Publishing, 1939.

Welch, Major A. B. *Welch Dakota Papers*. Lacey, Washington.

Wurtemburg, Prince Paul of. *Travels to North America*. Henry E. Huntington Library, San Marino, California.

### Chapter 7

Beckwith, Martha Warren, editor. "Medicine Men and Medicine Ceremonies, Cherry Necklace." *Mandan-Hidatsa Myths and Ceremonies*. New York: Kraus Reprint Co., 1969.

Beckwourth, James Pierson. *The Life and Adventures of James P. Beckwourth as Told to Thomas D. Bonner*. Lincoln, NE: University of Nebraska Press, 1972 reprint of 1856 edition.

Bowers, Alfred W. *Hidatsa Social and Ceremonial Organization*. Lincoln, NE: University of Nebraska Press, 1992.

Bunnell, Paul. *French and Native North American Marriages, 1600-1800*. Westminster, MD: Heritage Books, 2007.

Colby, Susan M. *Sacagawea's Child: The Life and Times of Jean-Baptiste (Pomp) Charbonneau*. Spokane, WA, Arthur H. Clark, 2006.

Hafen, Leroy R., editor, *The Mountain Men and the Fur Trade of the Far West*. Glendale, CA: Arthur H. Clark Company, 1965-1972.

Josephy, Alvin M., editor "Obituary of Jean Baptiste Charbonneau, Son of Sacagawea." *Lewis and Clark Through Indian Eyes*. New York: Knopf, 2006.

Lowie, Robert. "Religion of the Crow Indians." *Anthropological Papers*. American Museum of Natural History, Vol. XXV, 1922.

Meyer, Roy W. *The Village Indians of the Upper Missouri: The Mandans, Hidatsas and Arikaras*. Lincoln: University of Nebraska Press, 1977.

Sanderson, George B. Quote from unpublished transcript of Sanderson's diary by Ken R. Henson and Laura Anderson, University of Utah.

Thorp, Daniel. *An American Journey, Lewis and Clark*. New York: MetroBooks, 1998.

VanDevelder, Paul. *Coyote Warrior*. New York: Little, Brown, 2004.

*Other Sources*

Wood, W. Raymond and Thiessen, Thomas, eds. *Early Fur Trade on the Northern Plains: Canadian Traders among the Mandan and Hidatsa Indians*. Univ. of Oklahoma Press, 1985.

### Chapter 8

Bowers, Alfred W. *Hidatsa Social and Ceremonial Organization*. Lincoln, NE: University of Nebraska Press, 1992.

Goes Ahead, Elias. "Oral tradition places a young Sacajawea with Crow," Billings Gazette, July 23, 2010.

Lewis, Meriwether. *The Travels of Captains Lewis and Clark*. London: Longman, Hurst, Rees and Arme, 1809.

Medicine Crow, Joe, Tribal Historian. "Story of *Sacagawea*," Unpublished.

Ware, William. "The Prophecy of Old Spotted Horse," A Confluence of Cultures, Native Americans and the Expedition of Lewis and Clark. University of Montana, 2003.

Wolf, Helen Pease. "My Mother, Sarah Walker Pease," Reaching Both Ways.

### Chapter 9

Thwaites, Reuben Gold, editor, *Original Journals of the Lewis and Clark Expedition, 1804-1806*. New York: Antiquarian Press, 1959.

### Chapter 10

*Buffalo Bird Woman's Garden* as told to Gilbert L. Wilson, St. Paul, Minnesota Historical Society Press, 1987.

*Waheenee: an Indian Girl's Story*, Gilbert L. Wilson, Waheenee, St. Paul, MN, Webb Publishing Company, 1921.

*Women of the Earth Lodges: Tribal Life on the Plains*, Virginia Bergman Peters, Norman, University of Oklahoma Press, 1995.

The 1806 map details on pages 28 and 50 are from: Kevin O'Briant, "Too-Nee's World: The Arikara Map and Native American Cartography," *We Proceeded On*, Vol. 44, No 2, May 2018.

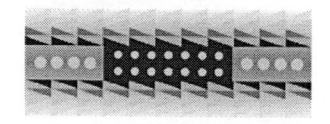

*Our Story of Eagle Woman, Sacagawea*

# Appendix
## *Illustrations List*

### FOREMATTER

The cover depicts Eagle Woman, *Sacagawea*   Dennis Fox, Jr.
Cover
Hidatsa Design   Dennis Fox, Jr.   throughout
MHA Emblem   Dennis Fox, Jr.   i
Lucy Bulls Eye Evans, great-granddaughter of *Sacagawea*   State Historical Society of North Dakota.   v
*Sacagawea* Project Board   Bernie Fox   xviii

### CHAPTER 1

Hidatsa Earthlodge Villages on the Knife River, 1810   Sitting Rabbit, Mandan, 1905,   State Historical Society of North Dakota   1
Oscar H. Will Company Seed Catalog. 1908   North Dakota State Archives   4
William Clark, 1810, and Meriwether Lewis, 1807   Charles Willson Peale, National Park Service   5
Lewis and Clark meeting *Sacagawea* and Charbonneau at Mandan Village, 1804   Vernon Erickson, Historical Society of North Dakota.   5
Mandan Chief Sheheke (White Coyote), 1807   Charles Balthazar de Saint Memin, copy by Charles Bird King, 1837, McKenny & Hall   6
Hidatsa & Crow Territory during the 19th Century   Barry Lawrence Ruderman Antique Maps   8
Yellow Cloud Woman, Hidatsa, in a Bull Boat on the Missouri River, 1911   G.L Wilson   10
Bull Boat and carved paddle, 1879   Orlando Scott Goff, both State Historical Society of North Dakota   10
Like-A-Fishhook Village, 1871-72   Stanley J. Morrow / State Historical Society of North Dakota   12
Xoshga Hidatsa Chief Crow Flies High, 1879,   Orlando Scott Goff, Smithsonian Institution   14

*Illustrations List*

Signing of the Garrison Dam Project   1948, National Archives and Records Administration   16

### CHAPTER 2

The Little Missouri River   National Park Service   9
Big Hidatsa Village site on the north side of Knife River   National Park Service   20
Wolf with the leg of a deer   National Park Service   23
Wolf Headdress   National Museum of Natural History   25
Knife River Villages. Ink drawing by Inquida Necharo (Riding Chief), 1806   Kevin O'Briant. "Too Ne's World: The Arikara Map and Native American Cartography." We Proceeded On, Vol. 44, No. 2, May 2018.   Bibliotheque national de France, Paris   28
Remains of the Awatixa Hidatsa village on Knife River 1837   National Park Service   30
Aerial view of Night Walker's Butte Village.   Missouri Basin Project, Smithsonian   31
Awatixa Hidatsa Village on the Knife River   National Park Service   34
The Little Missouri River   National Park Service   42
Bears Arm   Everett R Cox/Welch Dakota Papers   43
Gerard Baker   MHA Interpretive Center   43

### CHAPTER 3

Reconstructed Fort Mandan, 1804   National Park Service   45
Major A. B. Welch giving the Memorial Day address at Shell Village, N.D., 1923   Everett R Cox   46
Toussaint Charbonneau, Prince and Karl Bodmer at Fort Clark, 1833   Karl Bodmer/Denver Art Museum   49
Knife River Villages. Ink drawing by Inquida Necharo (Riding Chief), 1806   Kevin O'Briant. "Too Ne's World: The Arikara Map and Native American Cartography." We Proceeded On, Vol. 44, No. 2, May 2018. Bibliotheque national de France, Paris   50
Ceremonial earthlodge of Hairy Coat, at Shell Creek, ca. 1910   State Historical Society of North Dakota   53

Major Welch, Bulls Eye and Interpreter Stanley Deane at Sanish
   N.D., 1927   Welch Family                                    54
Shell Village Announcement, 1923   Everett R Cox/Welch Dakota
   Papers                                                       55
Interpreter Burr, Chief Birds Bill, Foolish Bear and Coffee, 1924
   B. L. Brigham                                                57
Major Welch with Ft. Berthold men   Everett R Cox/Welch Dakota
   Papers                                                       58
Henry Bad Gun, 1910   Fred Olson Collection, State Historical
   Society of North Dakota                                      61
Helen Wolf Wilkinson on horseback, 1935   Leo D. Harris/North
   Dakota State Historical Society                              63
Montana Territory, 1879   State Historical Society of North
   Dakota/Library of Congress                                   69
Fort Buford, 1871   State Historical Society of North Dakota    70
Joseph Packineau and Family, 1902   L.A. Huffman, at
   Elbowoods, North Dakota                                      74
Hidatsa Medicine Lodge at Like-A-Fishhook Village, D.T.   Stanley
   J. Morrow                                                    77
Fort Berthold, D.T., 1872   Stanley J. Morrow                   78

## COLOR SECTION

*Sacagawea* with infant son Jean Baptiste   Dennis Fox, Jr.     79
Big Hidatsa Village on Knife River, 1832   George Catlin        80
Winter Village of the Hidatsas, 1834   Karl Bodmer              81
Earthlodge Interior view (Mandan), 1834   Karl Bodmer           82
Toussaint Charbonneau, husband of Sacagawea, 1833
   Karl Bodmer                                                   3
Pehriska-Ruhpa (Two Ravens),1833   Karl Bodmer                  84
Hidatsa buffalo robe, 1833-34   Ethnology State Museum, Berlin,
   Germany                                                      85
Two Ravens, 1833   Karl Bodmer                                  86
E'e-a-chin-che-a (Red Thunder), 1832   George Catlin            87
River Crow Chiefs at Knife River, 1833   Karl Bodmer            88
Pa-ris-ka-roo-pa (Two Crows), 1832   George Catlin              89
Wife of Two Crows, 1832   George Catlin                         89

*Illustrations List*

Four Wolves at Fort Union, 1832   George Catlin               90
Woman Who Lives in a Bear Den, 1832   George Catlin           90
Seet-se-be-a (The Midday Sun), 1832   George Catlin           91
Addih-Hiddisch (He Makes the Road to War), 1833   Karl Bodmer 92
Ba-da-ah-chon-du (The Man Who Jumps Ahead of All), 1832
    George Catlin                                             92
Birohka (Beautifully-Furred Robe), 1833   Karl Bodmer         94
War Party of River Crows, 1832   George Catlin                95
Ahschupsa Masihichsi (Chief of the Pointed Horn), 1832   Karl
    Bodmer                                                    96
Hidatsa Scalp Dance, 1833   Karl Bodmer                       97
Buffalo Chase, 1832   George Catlin                           98
Teenage Hidatsa boys at Like-A-Fishhook Village, 1870   Lion Boy
    Ledger                                                    99
Indians Killing Buffalo in the Missouri River, 1874   William de
    la Montagne Cary                                          99
Fort Berthold and Like-A-Fishhook Village, 1870   Count Philippe
    Regis de Trobriand, State Historical Society of North Dakota   100
Hidatsa Burials near Fort Berthold, 1870   Dr. Washington
    Mathews, U.S. National Museum of Natural History          101
The newly-rising Lake Sakakawea, 1954   State Historical Society
    of North Dakota                                           102

**CHAPTER 4**

Lake *Sakakawea* from Crow Flies High Butte west of New Town,
    ND   Trina Locke                                          103
Calvin Grinnell   Bernie Fox                                  110
Marilyn Hudson   Chuck Hudson                                 110
Pat Fredericks   Lovina Fox                                   110
Wanda Fox Sheppard   Shyla Sheppard                           110
Chairman Martin Cross   State Historical Society of North Dakota
                                                              113
Chairwoman Rose Crow Flies High   MHA Interpretive Center  113
Chairman Tex G. Hall   Robin Blankenship                      113
Sakakawea," Leonard Crunelle statue at the U.S. Capitol Building,
    Washington, D.C., 2003   Architect of the Capitol         115

## CHAPTER 5

River Crow young woman visiting Like-A-Fishhook Village, 1851
   Rudolph F. Kurz / Berne Historical Museum    121
Buffalo Bird Woman, Waheenee   State Historical Society of North
   Dakota    123
Like-A-Fishhook Village, 1917   Buffalo Bird Woman / Gilbert L.
   Wilson / Minneapolis: University of Minnesota Press    124
Wolf Chief at Fort Buford, D.T., 1874   Orlando Scott Goff/State
   Historical Society of North Dakota    125
Goodbird and family.   State Historical Society of North Dakota
   00086-00547    127
Hidatsa Earthlodges in Like-A-Fishhook Village   Goodbird (G.L.
   Wilson)    128
Thomas Bulls Eye   MHA Interpretive Center    131
Foolish Bear   MHA Interpretive Center    146
Poor Wolf or Lean Wolf   Historical Society of North Dakota    148

## CHAPTER 6

Fort Manuel, Dakota Territory, 1812   W.O. Bassford    149
Charles Easman Telegram, 1920   National Archives    150
Cemetery at Fort Washakie, WY, ca. 1933   MHA Interpretive
   Center    152
Tombstone dedicated to Baptiste Charbonneau, Fort Washakie,
   WY.   Phil Konstantin    153
The Travels of Charbonneau and *Sacagawea*, 1815-1817   Barry
   Lawrence Ruderman Antique Maps    159
Birds Bill of the Gros Ventre (Hidatsas)   Everett R Cox/Welch
   Dakota Papers    167
James P. Beckwourth, ca. 1850   T. D. Bonner    174
The old Post Trader's store at Fort Buford, D.T., ca. 1870-71    175
The Xoshga Hidatsa village of Chief Crow Flies High, near Fort
   Buford, D.T. 1874   A.C. Leighton    176

## CHAPTER 7

Bulls Eye, 1927   Welch Dakota Papers    177
Jean Baptiste Charbonneau, 1823   Duke Paul of Wurttemberg   182
Mergentheim Castle, Wurttemberg    183

*Illustrations List*

Charbonneau Obituary, Auburn, CA, 1866   Placer Herald      184
Signboard    Oregon State Park Dept.                         185
Bulls Eye's children, George and Lucy Evans, 1902   State
    Historical Society of North Dakota                       189
George Parshall at Shell Creek, N.D.,ca.1902   State Historical
    Society of North Dakota                                  191
Delores Parshall Sand    James Ford                          192
Bulls Eye, Individual History Card, 1928   MHA Interpretive
    Center                                                   193
Cedar Woman, Census 1891    MHA Interpretive Center          194
Delores Sand, Pansy Parshall, Rose Crow Flies High    MHA
    Interpretive Center                                      195
Grace Parshall Fox    MHA Interpretive Center                196
Aletha Jackson    Ziggy Jackson                              196
Charles Parshall    MHA Interpretive Center                  196
Paul Parshall    MHA Interpretive Center                     196
Cherry Necklace tattoo, 1851.    Rudolf Friedrich Kurz/Berne
    Historical Museum                                        198
Individual History Card, son of Cherry Necklace.    MHA
    Interpretive Center                                      205
George Parshall and Fred Gunn    MHA Interpretive Center     207
Many Bears, 1898    Rev. Harold Case/State Historical Society of
    North Dakota                                             207

## CHAPTER 8

Otter Woman, 1906    W.A. Petzoldt/McCracken Research Library,
    Cody, WY                                                 209
Relatives Naomi Foolish Bear Black Hawk, Cora Young Bird Baker,
    Fred Gunn, Naomi and Fred,   MHA Times, MHA Interpretive
    Center                                                   211
Anna Dawson, Carrie Anderson & Sarah Walker, 1878   Hampton
    University Archives                                      215
Anna Dawson, Sarah Walker & Carrie Anderson, 1878   Hampton
    University Archives                                      216
Mary Young Bird Lone Fight, She Kills   MHA Interpretive Center   220
Individual History Card for Mary Fredericks,    MHA Interpretive
    Center                                                   221

## Our Story of Eagle Woman, Sacagawea

Mary Walker Fredericks and Susie Nagle   MHA Interpretive Center   222
Sara Walker Pease, Susie Walker Young Bird and Mary Walker Fredericks.   MHA Interpretive Center   223
Family tree of the Fredericks, Young Bird and Pease families. Morrison Family   224
Sacagawea *(Maeshuwea)* Family Tree   225
River Crow Chiefs on the banks of the Yellowstone, 1859   James D. Hutton/Beinecke Library Collection, Yale University   231
Crow tribal celebration at Pompey's Pillar, MT, 2018   232

### CHAPTER 9
Map of the Lewis and Clark Expedition, 1803-1806   233
Rattlesnake Rattle   238
Beaver's Head Rock, MT   251
Pompey's Pillar, MT   263
William Clark's carving on Pompey's Pillar, 1806   264
*Sacagawea* bronze sculpture by Leonard Crunelle, 1910   Colin Archibald   266

### CHAPTER 10
Fort Union, at the mouth of the Yellowstone, 1852   Rudolph F. Kurz/National Anthropological Archives   267
Lewis and Clark meeting *Sacagawea* and Charbonneau   Vernon Erickson/State Historical Society of North Dakota   271
Encampment of the Travellers on the Missouri.   Karl Bodmer/Joslyn Art Museum Enron Art Foundation   272
Hannah Levings, ca. 1906   Historical Society of North Dakota   273
Two young men, Like-A-Fishhook Village, 1871   Stanley J. Morrow/State Historical Society of North Dakota   275
Treaty with the Belantse-Etoa Minitaree Tribe, 1826   276
Like-A-Fishhook Village   State Historical Society of North Dakota   279
Joseph Young Bird Family   State Historical Society of North Dakota   280
Hannah Levings, Mink Woman, 1906   State Historical Society of North Dakota   281

*Illustrations List*

Gold Dollar coin with *Sacagawea's* image, 2000   US Govt.   282

## CHAPTER 11
Baptismal record of Maria Catarina Charguana (Charbonneau)   290
Fort Berthold/Fort Totten *Sacagawea* Connection   292
Fort Totten Charbonneaus - Family Tree   293
Charbonneau/Parshall Family Tree   295

*Our Story of Eagle Woman, Sacagawea*

# Appendix
## *Index*

Except where otherwise noted, Ft. Berthold personal names listed are understood to be members of the Three Affiliated Tribes (MHA Nation). Specific tribes are included if stated in the text. Numerals printed in bold type indicate an illustration on that page.

**A**

*Addih-Hiddisch*, see He makes the Road to War

Adoption customs   9, 51, 108, 125, 153, 162, 172, 197, 213, 253-254, 268, 270

*Ahschupsa Masihichsi*, see Chief of the Pointed Horn

Allard, LaDonna Brave Bull (Tribal Curator, Standing Rock Reservation)   169-170

All Moves/ Moves Along, Hidatsa/Crow (cousin of *Sacagawea* & Cherry Necklace)   xvi, 210, 213, 215, **224**, 279, 287

Allotment Act, 1891   13

American Fur Company, operate Fort Union   121

American River, California   186

Ancestry.com   286, 288, 294, 296

Ancestry DNA   286, 289-290

Anderson, Carrie   **215-216**

Antelopes Dance Hall, 45

Arkansas River, Kansas   158-**159**

Arikara Tribe (*Sahnish*—Original People)   1, 2-3, 7, **171**, **174**
  as accomplished farmers   3-**4**
  as premier traders   3-4
  Earthlodge Villages at Grand River, S.D., 1800-1825   **8**

Atkinson, Henry (Brigadier-General, U.S. Army, 1825)   **276**

Atkinson-O'Fallon Treaty, 1825   3, 48, 104, 157-158, 179, 274, **276-277**

Auburn, California   186

*Awatixa*   see Hidatsa Villages

**B**

*Ba-da-ah-chon-du*, see Man Who Jumps Ahead of All

Bad Gun, Henry, Mandan   52, **61**

Bad Horn   **128**

312

## Index

Bad Lodge, Hidatsa, see Black Lodge/Smoked Lodge   205
Baker, Dr. Gerard (Yellow Wolf), Mandan-Hidatsa   ii, ix, xiii, **xviii**, 29, **43**, 222
Baker, Cora Young Bird, Hidatsa   **211**, 222
Baker, James   **16**
Baker, Paige, Sr., Mandan   28, 29, 83, 202
Baker, Quincy (Rattling/Shaking Medicine)   vi, x, xiii
Baptiste (Shoshone son of Porivo) grave rifled and moved by Charles A. Eastman, 1924   **124, 126-127**
Bateman, Earl, Arikara   **16**
Bazil/Bazile (Shoshone son of Porivo), grave rifled and moved by Charles A. Eastman, 1924   **124, 126**, 127
Bear Ceremony, Hidatsa (owned by Cherry Necklace; sold to Black Shield)   210
Bear-heart   **128**
Bear-nose   **128**
Bear's Arm, Hidatsa   27, 28, **43**, 61, 121-122, 146, 199-201
Bear's Head, River Crow   **231**
Bear Sits, elevation opposite Wolf Point, Montana   65, 68
Bear's Tail, Hidatsa, 1825   **276**
Bear Woman, Hidatsa/Crow   **205, 221**,
Beautifully-Furred Robe (*Birohka*), Hidatsa Chief   **94**
Beaver Creek, Arikara community   13
Beaver's Head Rock, Montana   251-**252**
Beckwith, Martha Warren, folklorist   122, 146, 199
Beckwourth, James P. (trapping partner of Jean Baptiste Charbonneau)   173-**174**, 184, 186, 278
*Belantse-Etoa* (People of the Willows), an Hidatsa name for their own tribe, 1825   **276**
Benson, Ben, Mandan   **58**
Bent's Fort, Colorado   288
Biddle, Nicholas, 1st editor of Lewis & Clark Journals (invented spelling of *"Sacajawea"*)   162
Big-black   **128**
Big Brother, Hidatsa, 1825   **276**
Big-bull   **128**
Big Dog, Hidatsa, 1825   **276**

Big Fingers, Hidatsa, 1825   **276**
Big Head, Hidatsa (half-brother of Bulls Eye)   **193**
Bighorn Mountains, Montana   13
Bighorn River, Montana   118, **159**, 219
Big Magpie, Crow   190
Big Porcupine River, Montana   231
Big Thief, Hidatsa, 1825   **276**
Bird, Pansy Parshall, Hidatsa   190
Bird Woman (*Sacagawea*), recognized Hidatsa name   ix, 106
Bird Woman's River, Montana   244
Birds Bill (*Tsakakapi*), Anthony, Mandan-Hidatsa (WW I veteran & Chief of Old Scouts Society) **1873-**   47, 52, **57**, 166-169, **167**, 170, 171 ; helped to survey Fort Berthold Reservation with A.B. Welch   167
Birds Bill, Lawrence, aka Dressed Buffalo (*Gidipi E Gigshish*), Mandan-Hidatsa   166
Bird Bear, Cora Snow, Hidatsa   179
*Birohka*, see Beautifully-Furred Robe
Black Chest, Hidatsa   52
Black Bear, Hidatsa   xvii, 47
Black Buffalo, Hidatsa chief, 1825   **276**
Black Hawk, Naomi Foolish Bear   xvii, 108-109, 122, 210, **211**
Black Hawk, Plain House, wife of Birds Bill   166
Black-horn   **128**
Black Lodge/ Smoked Lodge/ Bad Lodge, Hidatsa (father of *Sacagawea* & Cherry Necklace)   48, 104, 163, 179, 197, 209, 270, 271, **276**, **292** signed 1825 Atkinson-O'Fallon Treaty, as leading Hidatsa War Chief 104, 157, 179, 274, **276**
Black Moccasins, Hidatsa chief, 1825   **276**
Black-panther   **128**
Blacks-his-shield   **128**
Black Shield, Hidatsa/Crow (probably the same as preceding)   210, **221**
Blankenship, Robin   113
Bloody-mouth   **128**
Blue/Green Blanket (wife of Bulls Eye)   187, **194**
Blue-stone   **128**

*Index*

Boarding schools   9, **215-216**, 218-220

Bobtail Bull, *Xoshga* Hidatsa Chief   13, 187

Bodmer, Karl, Swiss artist   4, **49**, **81**, **82**, **83**, **84**, **86**, **88**, **92**, **94**, **96**, **97**, **272**

Bolman Family (descendants of Cherry Necklace)   199

Bonds Unitarian Christian Industrial School, Crow Reservation, Montana 219- 220

Bouret, Alexander, Metis son-in-law of Toussaint Charbonneau (2)   291, **292**

Bouret family, part of extended Charbonneau family   291, **292**

Bowers, Alfred W., ethnologist   20, 35, 40, 122, 125, 140, 146, 161, 162, 171, 197, 201, 214, 279

Bowl   **128**

Brave, Crow   186

Brave, John, Hidatsa   212-213

Breckenridge, Henry (riverboat traveler, 1811)   meets Charbonneau & "Snake" wife   155, 157

Brings the Pipe (Wife of Bulls Eye)   187, 190, **194**

Brown Bear, Hidatsa (son of Cherry Necklace)   198, **205**

Buffalo Bird Woman, *Maxidiwiac/ Waheenee,* Hidatsa (sister of Wolf Chief)   7, 108, **123-124**, 127, 279

Buffalo Head, Hidatsa, 1825   **276**

Buffalo hunting   4, **98**, **99**

Buffalo robes, painted, Hidatsa   v, **83**, **84**, **85**, **94**, **97**, **188**
   River Crow   **88**

Bug Woman, Hidatsa, (grandmother of Joseph Packineau)   60, **205**

Bull boats   9, **10**, **80**, **99**

Bull Facing the Wind, Hidatsa (grandson of *Sacagawea*)   65

Bull-has-spirit   **128**

Bull Gets Up, Hidatsa (nephew of Bulls Eye)   **194**

Bulls Eye/Bulls Eyes, Hidatsa (grandson of *Sacagawea*), **1864-1928**
   ix, xi, xiii, 42, 47-59, **54**, 60, 62, 73, 104, 107, 122, 168, 171, **177**, 179, 187, 190, 191, **193**, **194**, 197, 237, 278-282, **295**
   was raised by Cedar Woman at Crow Flies High Village, ca. 1870-1884   129
   post-1884, they lived at Shell Creek   129, **194**, 280,
   children of   187, **194**

315

Lucy & George Evans   187-**188**
see also George Parshall & Thomas Bulls Eye
respected medicine man   190
Bulls Eye's story of *Sacagawea*'s life and death   42, 45-55, 65-71, 80, 106, 136-137, 161-166, 166-171, 282
garbled versions of, reported to Charles A. Eastman   130-134, 144-146
Bulls Eye, Thomas, Hidatsa (son of George Parshall, adopted and raised by Bulls Eye)   **131**, 187, 190, **292, 295**
Burbridge, Rebecca   285
Burke, Charles, Commissioner of Indian Affairs (orders report on life & death of *"Sacajawea"*)   149-150, 156
Burns, Ken, documentary film about the Lewis & Clark Expedition   71-75
Burr, Interpreter   **57,**
Butterfly, Mandan   127-128

# C

Caddoan language group of Arikara   2
Calf Woman, Mandan (knew *Sacagawea* and her daughters, ca.1860)   122
*Cameahwait*, Shoshone Chief   xvi, 37-38, 162, 163, 254-256
Camp, Dr. Charles L, geologist, saves portrait of Jean Baptiste Charbonneau   182
Carlisle Indian School, PA,   111
Carries the Snake, Hidatsa chief, 1825   **276**
Carson, Kit (may have adopted a daughter of Jean Baptiste Charbonneau) 288
Cary, William de la Montagne, American artist 99
Catches Enemy, Crow   190
Catlin, George, American artist   4, **80**, 87, **89, 90, 91, 93, 95, 98**
Cedar Woman, Hidatsa (daughter of *Sacagawea*), **ca.1839-1894**   48, 56, 106, 122, 123, 126, 129, 171, 180, 186, 188, **267**, 278-279, 281, **292, 295**
lived with Bulls Eye at Crow Flies High Village, and later lived in the home of Bulls Eye at Shell Creek,   129, 135, **194**, 280, 281
Chaboillez, Charles (Northwest Company fur trader)   238

# Index

Charbonneau family descendants, related by DNA testing to *Sacagawea* family descendants   269, 291-296, **292**, **293**, **295**, 296

Charbonneau, Montana, abandoned ghost town near Fort Union   103

Charbonneau, Jean Baptiste (son of *Sacagawea*), **1805-1866**   45, 74-75, **79**, 106, 111, 155, 158, 161, **182**-186, 237-238, 260-261, 264-265, 272-274, 285-**292**, **295**

   called "Pomp" by William Clark   180, 182, 230, 238, 283

   children of   187, 287-291

   considered himself half-Crow   75, 172, 185, 268, 280

   death & burial near Jordan Valley, Danner, Oregon, 1866   74, 182, **185**, 280

   fake headstone for, placed in Fort Washakie Cemetery, Wyo., 1920s   **152-153**

   Hidatsa names, Plain Track and Cherry Necklace   133, 136, 137, 142

   leads Mormon Battalion to California, 1847   74, 173, 185, 288

   lived in Germany six years with Duke Paul of Wurttemberg, 1823-1829   182-**183**, 185, 274, 278, 287

   obituary of   **184-185**, 196, 238

   Pompey's Pillar, Montana, named for by Willian Clark, 1806   263

   trapping partner of James P. Beckwourth, ca. 1835-1845   173-**174**

Charbonneau, Lisette/Lizette, daughter of Toussaint(1) & Otter Woman (2) 61, 274, **292-293**

Charbonneau, Louise/Luisa (dit "Shahuano", possible daughter of Jean Baptiste Charbonneau)   288

Charbonneau, Maria Catarina, see Charguana

Charbonneau, Maria Louisa, see Shahuano

Charbonneau, Marie Marguerite Garnier (Quebecois great-great-grandmother of Toussaint Charbonneau   191, **295**

Charbonneau, Olivier (Quebecois great-great-grandfather of Toussaint Charbonneau)   191, 294, **295**

Charbonneau, Robert (son of Toussaint Charbonneau (2)   291, **292-293**

Charbonneau, Toussaint (husband of *Sacagawea*), **1758 – ca.1840**

   ix, xvi, xvii, **5**, 36, 38, 39, 45, 48-**49**, 52, **83**, 129, 158, 162-163, 179-181, **193**, 234-266, 267-278, 287, 291, **292-293**, 294, **295**

   at Fort Manuel, D.T., 1811-1812   1, 155-157, 274

   inept interpreter 36, 47, 51, 60, 103, 104, 105, 138, 162, 181, 235-236, 268

317

called "Gay Wood" by Hidatsa   126, 172
died ca.1840   129, 181, 278
leaves *Sacagawea*, ca. 1839   96, 126, 278
marries Ute woman, 1816   144
moves with *Sacagawea* to Fort Union area after 1837 smallpox   126, 129, 147, **267**, 278
philanderer   59-60, 158, 236
trip with *Sacagawea* to Idaho, 1803-04   48-49, 61, 109, 112, 271
trip with Lewis & Clark Expedition, 1805-1806   **5, 45, 50**-51, 179, 233-266, 271-272
trip with *Sacagawea* to St. Louis, then the Southwest, 1815-1817   133, 136-137, 143-145, 158-**159**, 160, 262, 274
Charbonneau, Toussaint (2), son of Toussaint (1) and Otter Woman (2) **1803-1869**   161, 274, **292-293**
Chardon, Francois A. (Factor at Fort Clark, D.T.)   158
Charging, Cleo Stone   83
Charging Eagle, Mandan (son of Four Bears)   52
Charging Eagle, Mandan community   13
Charging, George   **16**
Charguana, Maria Catarina, (Spanish slant-spelling of "Charbonneau"; Luiseno daughter of Jean Baptiste Charbonneau, 1848)   187, 289-291
Cherry (or Choke-cherry, or Berry) Necklace, *Madzu-Awbaesh*, Hidatsa/Crow (brother of *Sacagawea*) **1778-1873**   xvi, 11, 48, 51, 64, 77, 79, 105, 107, 112, 114, 121, 122, 126, 177-178, 197-**205**, 209-215, 268, 270, 278, 281, 283, 286-287, 296
adopted into Alkali Lodge Clan (*Maxoxati*) of Hidatsa   214
children of 178, 198, **206-207**, 209-215
geographical knowledge of Montana & Idaho   204
gives white horse to Toussaint Charbonneau, 51, 65, 75, 76, 103, 107, 133, 230, 262, 272
had two wives, in separate earthlodges at Like-A-Fishhook Village   127-**128**, 198
respected medicine man   107, 180, 197, 199, 281
bear medicine of   204, 210
black-tail deer medicine of   200
neck tattoos of   **198**, 201

*Index*

otter medicine of   199-200
snake medicine of   64, 103, 105, 107-108, 197, 201-202, 281
treated smallpox victims   125, 203, 214, 281
Chicken (Prairie chicken) clan of Hidatsa   125
Chief of the Pointed Horn (*Ahschupsa Masihichsi*), Hidatsa Chief   **96**
Chippewa, kill Hidatsas   63
*Choppunish*, see Nez Perce Tribe
Chouteau, Auguste P., fur trader (hires Toussaint Charbonneau & *Sacagawea*, 1816-1817   **159-160**
Clam Necklace, Mandan (presented gifts to *Sacagawea* and her daughters, ca.1860)   122
Clans, and clan customs   xv-xvii, 197, 213-214, 216
Clark, William   viii, **5**, 39, 60, 157, 161, 162, 181-182, 233-266, 268, 273-274, 282, 287
Coffee, Hidatsa   **57**
Cold Wind, Crow   190
Coleharbor, N.D.   200
Colors the Hair, Hidatsa, 1825   **276**
Comanche Tribe, visited by Charbonneau & *Sacagawea*, 1816   144, 158
Comes Out of the Water, Crow, see Otter Woman (1)   213
Commissioner of Indian Affairs, hires Charles A. Eastman to investigate *Sacajawea*'s history, 146, 149-150, 152
Conklin Family (descendants of Cherry Necklace)   199
Connolly, James B., historian   36-39, 145
Cowdrey, Mike, 1997 letter to film maker Ken Burns   71-75
Crawford, Lewis (North Dakota State Historian)   156
Crazy Horse, Lakota   165
Cross Family (descendants of Cherry Necklace)   199
Cross, Martin, Hidatsa, Tribal Chairman   112, **113**, 114, 178
Crow Flies High Butte   **103**
Crow Flies High, *Xoshga* Hidatsa Chief   ii, 13, **14**, 126, 187
Crow Flies High, Rose Parshall, Hidatsa, Tribal Chairwoman   112, **113**, 190, **195**, **292**, **295**
Crow Flies High Village, *Xoshga* Hidatsa, near Fort Buford   **8**, **176**, 281
Crow-heart   **128**
Crows Breast Village (Mandan)   45
Crow's Paunch, Hidatsa Chief   13, 102

319

Crow That Looks, Hidatsa chief, 1825   **276**
Crow Tribe, see also River Crow Tribe & Mountain Crow Tribe   xi, xv, 48, 85-86, 188
Crunelle, Leonard (sculptor of *Sakakawea* statue), **89**, 265-**266**
Culbertson, Montana   62
Culbertson, name of trader at post where *Sacagawea* died   61, 121; called "Yellow Hair"   58
Custer, Lt. Col. George A.   48, 142, 218

**D**

Dances at Four Places, Crow   **224**
Dancing Bull, Jerome   viii
Dawson, Anna   **215-216**
Dead Grass Hall, at Shell Creek Village   142
Deane, Stanley, Hidatsa, interpreter   52, **54**, 62
DeMun, Jules, fur trader (hires Toussaint Charbonneau & *Sacagawea*, 1816-1817)   **159**-160
Devil's Lake/ Spirit Lake, N.D., origin point of Hidatsa Tribe   2
Different Breast, Hidatsa (daughter of *Sacagawea*), **ca. 1840-1895** (?) 48, 106, 123, 143, 180, 186, **193**, 267, 278, **292**, **295**   see also Pretty Breast
DNA evidence that *Sacagawea* and Cherry Necklace are Hidatsa & Crow   xiii, 171, 191, 197, 209, 268, 269, 285-296
Doesn't Run Away, Hidatsa, rescues young Bulls Eye   68-70
Dog, *Xoshga* Hidatsa, see George Parshall   187, **194**
Dog Bear, Hidatsa chief, 1825   **276**
Dog-cries   102
Dog Dance, Hidatsa ceremony   **86**
Dog's-urine   **128**
Drags Wolf, Hidatsa Chief   **58**, 61
Dressed Buffalo (*Gidipi E Gigshish*), see Birds Bill, Lawrence   140
Dried-squash   102
Driver, James   15, 65-71
Drouillard/Drewer, George (crew member with Lewis & Clark)   240, 241, 252
Dry-of-milk   **128**
Duck Woman, Hidatsa (daughter of Bulls Eye)   **194**

## Index

**E**

Eagle, Hidatsa (Interpreter at Fort Berthold Agency for Charles A. Eastman, 1924)  136

Eagle-trapping rights, owned by Bear's Arm  121

Eagle Woman (*Maeshuwea/ Ma-eshu-weash*), formal name of *Sacagawea*  xi, xiv, xv, xvii, 17, 61, 62, 64, 107, 108, 122, 123-**124**, 142-143, 179, **193**, **205**, 214, 270, 278, 283

Earthlodges  1, **5**, 7, 47, **53**, 77, **80**, **81**, **82**, **87**, **91**, **275**

Eastman, Dr. Charles A., government investigator promoted "*Sacajawea*"
  story of Grace Hebard  40, 56, 58, 121, 149-150, 235, 281
  his conclusions discounted by many others: Alfred W. Bowers  130; Stephen Janus, Supt. At Fort Berthold Agency, 1924  135; Eastman's own wife, Elaine Goodale Eastman  154
  interviews conducted by, at Fort Berthold Agency  130-148, 154
  conflict with other statements by the same people  113-114, 120, 154, 163; or contain obvious errors  141-146, 148
  rifled & moved graves at Fort Washakie, Wyo., looking for "evidence"  **150-153**

Elbowoods, Fort Berthold Reservation Agency, 13, 112

End-rock  **128**

Erickson, Vernon (artist)  **5, 271**

Evans, George Bulls Eye, Hidatsa (great-grandson of *Sacagawea*) **1895-1912**  187-188

Evans, Lucy Bulls Eye, Hidatsa (great-granddaughter of *Sacagawea*) **1893-1909**  v, 187-**188**

Ewald, Paul A.  36, 72

Extra Corn Growth Woman  62-63

Eye-has-no-water  **128**

**F**

Feather  **128**

Finger That Stinks, Hidatsa, 1825  **276**

Finley Family (descendants of Cherry Necklace)  199

First, Crow (mother of Cherry Necklace, in Indian tradition)  51, 197

Five Villages, on Knife River, 1600-1838  xvii, **8**, **50**, 105, 181, 202-203

Flags, given to chiefs   235, 237
Flying-eagle   **128**
Foolish Bear, Hidatsa   **57**, 59, 120, 121, 281
Foolish Bear Family (descendants of Cherry Necklace)   199
Foolish Bear, Naomi, Hidatsa   xvii
Ford, James   192
Ford, Jerry "Bird" Birdsbill (Cornsilk)   vi, x, xiii, 166-171, 285-296
Fort Abraham Lincoln, D.T.   46, 48
Fort Berthold Reservation, N.D.   viii, xiv, 1, 9, 17, 45, **101**, **102**, **103**, 106, 187, 217
Fort Berthold Trading Post, 1845-1874   **8**, 11, **78**, **100**, **101**, **102**
Fort Buford Army Post, 1866-1895   **8**, 13, **69**, **70**, 107, 173, **175-176**, 187, 280
   many Indian attacks nearby in 1868-1869   173, 175
Fort Clark Trading Post, 1830-1861   **8**, **49**, **83**, **96**, 129, 158
Fort Laramie, Treaty of, 1851   200
Fort Mandan (Lewis & Clark winter post, 1804-05)   **8**, **45**, 234-235
"Fort Manuel Story"   see *Sacajawea*
Fort Manuel Trading Post, 1812-1813   **8**, 71, **149**, 155, 265, 270, 274
Fort Peck Trading Post   173
Fort Pine Trading Post, Assiniboine River, Manitoba   180
Fort Union Trading Post, 1829-1867   **8**, 13, **69**, **90**, 126, 129, 147, **267**,
Fort Washakie, Wyoming, Agency of Shoshone Reservation   130, 281
   Cemetery at, where "*Sacajawea*" is alleged to be buried   **150**, **152-153**
Four Bears, Hidatsa Chief   7, 11, 102, 199-200, 201
Four Bears (Mato Topa), Mandan Chief   3, 7, 52
Four Bears Park, New Town   283
Four Dance, Lula, Hidatsa   108
Four Dances, Hidatsa   56, **58**
Four Times /Came Four Times, Crow   210, **220-221**, **224**
Four Wolves, River Crow Chief   **90**
Foolish Bear, Hidatsa   55, **58**, 146-147
Fox, Albert   265
Fox, Bernard (Yellow Dog)   ii, ix, **xviii**, 110
Fox, Dennis, Jr.   ii, ix, **79**
Fox, Dr. Dennis, Sr.   vi, xii, xiii
Fox, Dr. Sandra, wife of Dr. Dennis Fox, Sr.   vi, xii, xiii

*Index*

Fox, George   265
Fox, Gerald Tex   41
Fox, Grace Parshall, Hidatsa   190, **196**, **292**
Fox, Guy   265
Fox, Lovina   110
Fox, Mark N. (MHA Tribal Chairman)   vi, 91
Fox, Tex   178
Fredericks, Buzz   40
Fredericks families, related to *Sacagawea* & Cherry Necklace   209, 213, 215, **224**, 268, 279, 286, 287, 296
Fredericks, Irene (Black Medicine, *Kobodie Shibisha*)   105-106
Fredericks, Mary Walker, Hidatsa   210, 217, **221-222**, **223**
Fredericks, Pat   41, **110**, 204, 226-227
Fredericks, Pete   109
Freeman, Royce   vi
Fries, Anastasia Katharina (German paramour of Jean Baptiste Charbonneau)   187, 287
Fries, Anton (infant son of Jean Baptiste Charbonneau; 1st grandchild of *Sacagawea*, 1829)   187, 287
Frog Woman (*Sauk Bia*)   228, 229
Frost-mouth   **128**
Full-of-honor-marks   **128**

**G**

Garcia, Louis, historian   41
Garrison Dam, N.D.   xii, 3, 15, 16, 86, 222, 282
Gass, Patrick (crewman with Lewis & Clark)   236, 249-250, 251, 258
Gillette, Austin, Arikara   91
Gillette, George, Arikara   **16**
Girl Woman, Crow (sister of Otter Woman (1); mother of Cherry Necklace; aunt of *Sacagawea*)   195, 197, **205**, 209, 270
Glasgow, Montana (*Sacagawea* & Otter Woman (3) attacked nearby, 1869)   53, 136, 142
Goes Ahead, Elias, Crow   229-230
Goes Along the Bank, Hidatsa (2nd wife of Good Chaser)   60
Goes Between/ Travels in the Middle, Hidatsa   210, 214-215, 217, **223**, 279

Goes First, Crow  **224**
Goes Towards Other Woods, Hidatsa  193
Goff, Orlando Scott (photographer)  **10, 14, 125**
Good Bear, Hidatsa  200
Good Bear Family (descendants of Cherry Necklace)  199
Good Bird, Crow  **224**
Good Bird, Edward, Hidatsa (son of Buffalo Bird Woman)  **127, 128**
Good Chaser, (French trader, grandfather of Joseph Packineau), killed by Sioux  60
Goodrich/Guterich, Silas (crewman with Lewis & Clark)  259
Goose  **128**
Grady, Emma (2nd wife of Birds Bill)  166
Gravelines, Joseph, French trader  28
Green Blanket, see Blue Blanket
Grinnell, Calvin (Running Elk), MHA Tribal Historian  ii, ix, x, xiii, **xviii**, 104, 107, **110**, 116, 171, 204
Grinnell, Jessica, Hidatsa  283
Gros Ventre Tribe (French trader name for Hidatsa)  2, 47
Guard of the RedArrows, Hidatsa chief, 1825  **276**
Gunn Family (descendants of Cherry Necklace)  199
Gunn, Fred, Hidatsa  **206, 211**
Guts, see Intestines

# H
Hairy Coat, Hidatsa  **53**
Hall, Diane  x
Hall, Eddie  169-170
Hall, James, Hidatsa (Vice-Chairman)  **16**
Hall, Tex G., Hidatsa (Tribal Chairman)  112, **113**, 114
Hampton Normal & Agricultural Institute, Hampton, VA  **215-216**, 218-219
Hanging Gun, (named site along Missouri river, above mouth of Little Missouri River)  212
Has-a-game-stick, had three wives, in separate earthlodges, at Like-A-Fishhook Village  **128**
Has Many Medicine, see Plenty Medicine (daughter of Cherry Necklace)  213-214

## Index

Has the Otter, Hidatsa   214
Hawk   **128**
Head, Hidatsa, see Pan   186
Heart River, N.D.   2
Hebard, Grace R., novelist promoted *"Sacajawea"* story   40, 62, 72, 75, 151-154
   bribed & invented Shoshone "testimony" about *Porivo*, a deceased Shoshone woman   151-152
   fake headstones for *"Sacajawea"* family placed at Fort Washakie, Wyo., cemetery, 1920s   151-154
Helphrey, Juanita J.   40
He Makes the Road to War (*Addih-Hiddisch*), Hidatsa War Chief   92, **276**
Her Scalp, Crow   **224**
He-raises-all-hearts   **128**
Hidatsa/ Crow adoption customs   xvi, xvii
Hidatsa/ Crow clan relationships   xv-xvii, 99
Hidatsa/ Crow relationship   xiv, xv, 2, 13, 112, 222, 226, 227, 283
Hidatsa/ Crow territory   xv, **8**   greatly reduced in size   3
Hidatsa language (tone sensitive; difficult to translate accurately)   xvii, 162
Hidatsa, Mandan & Arikara resources, homes and graves destroyed by creation of Garrison Dam and Lake *Sakakawea*   15-17, **101**, **102**
Hidatsa Tribe (People of the Willows)   ii, 2-3, 7, **83**
   as accomplished farmers   3-**4**, 7
   as premier traders   ix, xi, xvii, 3-4, 227
   tipis of   176, 240-241, 264
Hidatsa villages on Knife River, D.T. (*Hidatsaati*)   57, 159
   Big Hidatsa Village   **1, 20, 28, 50, 80, 87, 91**
   *Awatixa* Village   xi, **1**, 6, **20, 28, 30, 34-35, 50**, 179, 271
   destroyed by Sioux, 1834   129, **267**, 278
   *Awaxawi* (*Amahami*) Village   30, 35, (French name: Les Siffleurs, or Moccasin Makers)   **50**, 240
   Winter villages   **81**   See also, Like-A-Fishhook Village
High Rump, also High Hump, Hidatsa (son of Cherry Necklace)   200, 201, **205**
Hillstrom, Fritz (son-in-law of Toussaint Cahrbonneau (2)   291-**292**

His-red-stone **128**
Hoffman, Charles W. (Interpreter, Fort Berthold Agency, for Charles A. Eastman, 1924)   136, 173
Holy Women Society, Hidatsa   201
Horn, Hidatsa   56
Hosmer, James (editor, added speculation to Lewis & Clark Journals)   163
Hudson, Chuck, Hidatsa   110
Hudson, Marilyn Cross, Hidatsa (Curator Fort Berthold Tribal Museum)   v, 105, 108, **110**, 114, 116, 170, 178
Hudson's Bay Company   237
Huffman, L.A. (photographer)   **74**
Hunts Along/ Looking (Thad Mason)   52
Hunts Along, Casey, Hidatsa   x
Hurt, Hidatsa   214
Hutton, James D., photographer   **231**

**I**
Independence, Mandan & Hidatsa community   13, 99
Indian Claims Commission   114
Indian Reorganization Act, 1934   15
Intestines   102
In the Water, Hidatsa (daughter of Cherry Necklace)   198, **205**
Iron Necklace, Crow   190

**J**
Jackson, Aletha Parshall, Hidatsa   62, 186, 190, **196**, **292**, **295**
Jackson, Ziggy   **196**
Janus, Stephen (Supt. At Fort Berthold Agency, 1924)   109
Jefferson, President Thomas   4, 6, 28, 50
Jefferson River, Montana   37, 250, 252, 262
Jessaume/Jusseaume/Jessome, Rene, (French trader, interpreter for Lewis & Clark)   162, 235-236, 239, 268
Johnson, Annika, Joslyn Museum   vi
Johnson, Dr. John (museum curator)   289-290
Johnson, President Lyndon B.   116
Jones, Sam   **61**

# Index

Joslyn Museum   vi

## K
Kansas River, Kansas   159, 182
Kansas River Trading Post   180
Killdeer Mountains, N.D.   21, 26-27
Kipp, James, fur trader   11
Kit-fox-fat   **128**
Knife River, N.D.   xiv, xv, **1**, 28, **50, 170**
Knife River Flint, trade resource   3
Krug, Julius, U.S. Secretary of the Interior   **16**
Kurz, Rudolph, Swiss artist   **121, 198, 267**

## L
Labiche, Francois (crewman with Lewis & Clark)   254,
Lajolla Band, Mission Indians   187
Lake Sakakawea, N.D.   77, 90, 116,   Creation of, destroys communities, homes, graves and resources of Fort Berthold Reservation   15-17, **101, 102, 103**, 270, 282
Larocque, Francois (Northwest Company fur trader)   235
Lean Bull/ Poor Bull *(I-ti-in-pu-i-tas),* Hidatsa (son-in-law-of *Sacagawea*/ father of Bull's Eye)   48, 126, 187, **193**
Lean Wolf, see Poor Wolf   114
LeForge, Mrs. Thomas, Wind, Crow   190
LePage/LaPage, Jean Baptiste (crewman with Lewis & Clark)   241
Levings, Hannah (Mink Woman), Hidatsa   265-**266, 273, 281**
Lewis, Meriwether   viii, 5, 37, 78, 181, 227, 233-266, 268,
Lewis & Clark Bicentennial   103, 106, 108, 121, 171, 177-178, 226, **282**
Lewis & Clark Centennial   95, 281
Lewis & Clark Expedition (1804-1806)   ix, xi, xiv, xv, xvi, xvii, 4-6, **5**, 17, 30, **45**, 47, **50**, 57, 64, 71-75, 117, 179, 181, 230, **232, 233**-266, **271**-272
  keelboat of   **50**
Lewis & Clark Journals   viii, xiii, xv, xvii, 162, 178, 226, 296
  confusion & speculation throughout, due to poor translation   234-236, 265
Lewis' River, Montana   262

327

Like-A-Fishhook Village, **1845-1888**   xiv, 7, **8**, 11, **12**, 13, 77, **100, 102,** 121, 123, **124**-126, 198, 210-214, **275**, 278-**279**
   Composed of 70 earthlodges   127-**128**
Little-bear   **128**
Little Missouri River, N.D.   **19**, 21, 28, 31-32, 35, **42-43**, 45, 203
Lion Boy Ledger drawing, Hidatsa   **99**
Locke, Trina   **103**
Lone Bear Family (descendants of Cherry Necklace)   199
Lone-buffalo   **128**
Lone Fight, Edward, (MHA Tribal Chairman)   108
Lone Fight, Mary Young Bird, Hidatsa   **220**
Lone Fight, Maybelle Goodbird   108
Lone Fight, Susie Fox   265
Lone Fight III, Ted   ix
Lone Man, Mandan culture hero   2
Long Bear, Hidatsa   198, **205**
Looks Down, Crow (father of Cherry Necklace, in Indian tradition)   51, 197
Louisiana Purchase   xv, 4, 7
Low Cap Clan of the Hidatsa   xvii, 213-214
Lowie, Robert Henri, ethnologist   123
Lucky Mound, Hidatsa community   13
Luiseno Tribe, CA   289
Luttig, John, fur trader recorded death of "Charbonneau's wife," at Fort Manuel, 1812   62, 72, 155, 157

# M
MacKenzie, Charles (Northwest Company fur trader)   235
*Maeshuwea/ Maeshuweash*, see Eagle Woman
Magic-bird   **128**
Mahto, Mark, Mandan   **16**
Mandan, Arthur, Mandan, son of Scarred Face   52
Mandan, Claryca (Peppermint Woman) Executive Director Hidatsa, Heritage Center   vi, x, xiii, xvii
Mandan, Hidatsa & Arikara Nation (MHA Nation)   iii, viii, xiii, 1, 90, 91, 106, 282
Mandan, N.D.   56

# Index

Mandan Tribe (*Nueta*—Our People)   2-3, 7, **82**, 157-158, 233-234
   as accomplished farmers   3-**4**
   as premier traders   ix, 3-4
   Villages on the Missouri at Knife River   5, 30, **50**, 132, **276-277**
Mandaree,   viii, 15, 29, 41, 177, 222
Man-has-long-hair   **128**
Man-smells-bad   **128**
Man Who Jumps Ahead of All (*Ba-da-ah-chon-du*), River Crow Chief   **93**
Many Bears, Hidatsa (son of Cherry Necklace)   178, 198, **207**
Many Comes Up, Hidatsa (daughter of Cherry Necklace)   198, **205**
Marias River, Montana   243
Mason, Matthew   109
Mason, Thad, see Hunts Along
Mathews, Dr. Washington, surgeon/ethnologist   136, **101**
Maximilian, German Prince of Wied-Nieuwied   4, **49**, **83**, **85**
Medals, given to chiefs   **150**, 235, 260
Medicine Arm, Hidatsa (granddaughter of *Sacagawea*), **1856-?**   106, 186,187, 188, 189, 278, **292, 295**
Medicine Bull, (uncle, by marriage, of *Sacagawea* & Cherry Necklace)   209, **224**
Medicine Calf, Crow   **224**
Medicine Crow, Gloria Morrison, Crow   **224**
Medicine Crow, Joe, Crow Chief & Tribal Historian   227
Mergentheim Castle, Wurttemberg, Germany (home of Jean Baptiste Charbonneau, 1823-1829)   **183**, 287
MHA Nation, see Mandan-Hidatsa-Arikara Nation
Midday Sun (*Seet-se-be-a*), Hidatsa   **91**
*Mide-shaw-ashish,* named site along lower Yellowstone River   211
*Mih-tutta-hang-kush,* Mandan village near Fort Clark   132
Minnitaree/ Manitari, Mandan name for Hidatsa   37, 62, **276-277**
Mink Woman, Hidatsa, see Hannah Levings
Mission San Fernando Rey de Espagna, Los Angeles, California   187
Mission San Luis Rey de Francia, San Diego, California   182, 187, 280, 290
Missouri River   **8**, 11, 15-16, **28**, 30, 49, **50**, 69, **99-103**, **128**, 144, 155, **159**, 242, **272**

329

Missouri-River (personal name), Hidatsa  **128, 276**
Mobridge, S.D., false monument at, marking the "burial" of *Sacajawea* 161
Montreal, Quebec, Canada (original seat of Charbonneau family)  270
Mormon Battalion, 1847  74, 173, 280, 288
Morrison, Alvan, J., Crow  **224**
Morrison, Alvin, Sr., Crow  **224**
Morrison, Ethel Hannah, Crow  **224**
Morrison, Hannah, Crow  **224**
Morrison, Thomas, Crow  **224**
Morrow, Stanley J. (photographer)  **12, 77, 78, 275**
Mossett, Amy (MHA Tribal Tourism Director)  116
Mountain Crow Tribe  13, 227, 263
Moves Along, Hidatsa/Crow, see All Moves  213
Mussel-necklace  **128**
Musselshell River, Montana  244

## N

Naming customs  xv-xvi,
*Naxpike* Ceremony, Hidatsa  11
Newman, Carol Ann Fredericks (Sweet Grass)  ii, x, xiii, **xviii**, 65
Newman Family (descendants of Cherry Necklace)  199
New Town, headquarters of MHA Tribe  3, 15, 36, **103**
Nez Perce Tribe  260
Nightwalker/ Twilight Walker, Hidatsa  31
Nightwalker's Butte Village  **31**
*Nishu*, Arikara community  13
*Noos*, Hidatsa (sister of Bulls Eye)  193
Northwest Fur Company  180, 237
*Nutadokie*  **128**

## O

O'Fallon, Benjamin (U.S. Indian Agent, 1825)  **276**
Okipa Ceremony, Mandan  11
Okipa Ceremonial Lodge at Like-A-Fishhook Village  122
Old Coyote, Dr. Barney, Crow  226
Old Crow, Newton V., Jr., Crow  **224**

## Index

Old Dog, Hidatsa   178
Old Woman, Crow   **224**
Old Woman Crawling, Hidatsa (mother of Bear's Arm)   121
Old-woman-crows   **128**
Old Scouts Society   **46**, 47, 52, **55**, 57, 167-169
One Buffalo, Hidatsa/Crow (brother of Cherry Necklace & *Sacagawea*)   48, 201, **205**
One-Eyed Chief (*Yoom-park-kar-tim*), Nez Perce chief   260
One-horn   **128**
Oral History, vital importance of to many tribes   viii, xiii, xiv-xv, 19-35, 47-70, 103-117, 267, 268
    too often discounted by academic historians   156, 164-165
Ordaz, Fr. Blas (Spanish priest)   187
Other-kind-of-wolf   **128**
Otter medicine of Cherry Necklace, 197-198
Otter Woman (1), aka, Comes Out of the Water, Crow (mother of *Sacagawea*)   xvi, 48, 179, 209-215, 268, 270, 279, **292**
    adopted into Low Cap clan of Hidatsa   313
    adopted-into Prairie Chicken clan of Hidatsa   125
Otter Woman (2), Hidatsa/ Crow (sister of *Sacagawea*/ co-wife of Toussaint Charbonneau), **ca. 1783-1812**   xvi, 115-116, 152-155, 180, **205**, 236, 268, 272, **292-293**, 294, 296
    death of at Fort Manuel, D.T., 1812   152, 154-155, 161, 274
    children of, in guardianship by William Clark   161, 274
Otter Woman (3) *Mida-bow-gay* (daughter of *Sacagawea*/ mother of Bulls Eye), Hidatsa, **ca. 1838-1869**   xvi, 48, 13 3-134, 153, 180, 186, 187, **193**, 214, **267**, 278-279, **292**, **295**
    murder of, 1869   48, 53-54, 56, 66-6, 70, 133-134, 136, 180, 280

**P**

Packineau, Charles, fur trader called Powder Horn, father of Joseph Packineau)   60
Packineau, Joseph, Hidatsa Interpreter   **16**, 60, 73, **74**
Painted Woods   xiv
Paints His Gun Yellow, Crow   **224**
Paints-shoulder-yellow   **128**
Paints-tail-red   **128**

Pan, Hidatsa   186, **205**
*Pa-ris-ka-roo-pa*, see Two Crows
Park, Indrek   65
Parshall, Charles, Hidatsa (great-grandson of *Sacagawea*)   188, 189, **292**, **295**
Parshall Charles (2), Hidatsa,   190, **196**
Parshall families, related to Crow families   268
Parshall, George (Dog/ Plenty Dogs/White Raven), Hidatsa (great-grandson of *Sacagawea*), **1874-1950**   48, 52, **58**, 104, 105, 107, 122, 186, 187, 189-**191**, 192, **193**, **194**, **206**, 213, 278, **292**, **295**
Parshall, Nettie (Berries), Hidatsa (great-granddaughter of *Sacagawea*)   188, 189
Parshall, N.D., named for George Parshall   189-191
Parshall, Pansy, Hidatsa   107, **195**, **292**, **295**
Parshall, Paul,  Hidatsa   190, **196**, **292**, **295**
Parshall, Ruby White Bear, Hidatsa   105, 107, 190
Parshall, William Dennis, (soldier, married Medicine Arm)   106, 188, 189
Paul Wilhelm, Duke of Wurttemberg (German traveler/ mentor of Jean Baptiste Charbonneau)   **182-183**, 274, 287
Pawnee, related to Arikara   2
Pease families, related to *Sacagawea* & Cherry Necklace   209, 215, **224**, 268, 279, 286-287, 296
Pease George, Crow   220
Pease, Sarah Walker, Hidatsa/Crow   210, **215-216**, 217-221, **223**
*Pehriska-Ruhpa*, see Two Ravens
Petzoldt, W.A., photographer   209
Pfaller, Rev. Louis, O.S.B.   39
Phelan, Randy (MHA Tribal Vice-Chairman)   viii, x, 91
Pico, Gov. Pio family (Mexican California)   290
Pine Ridge Reservation, S.D.   123
Pink, Hidatsa (daughter of Cherry Necklace)   198, **205**
Placer County, California   186
Plain Blossom, Hidatsa (paternal aunt of Bulls Eye)   **193**
Plain House Black Hawk, wife of Birds Bill, died 1924   140
Platte River, Wyoming   134
Plenty Dogs, Crow   **224**

# Index

Plenty Dogs, *Xoshga* Hidatsa, see George Parshall
Plenty Medicine, Hidatsa (daughter of Cherry Necklace)   198, **205**, 213-214
Pointed Horn (*Ahschupsa Masihichsi*), Hidatsa Chief   **96**
Pomeroy, Earl, North Dakota Congressman   88
Pompey's Pillar, Montana   230, **232**, **263-264**
Poor Bull, see Lean Bull
Poor Wolf, Hidatsa Chief, 1820-1899   13, **92**, 140
Porcupine-pemmican   **128**
*Porivo*, Shoshone woman buried at Fort Washakie, Wyo. (selected by Grace R. Hebard & Charles A. Eastman as "*Sacajawea*")   125-127, 158
   graves of her sons excavated by Charles A. Eastman, and the bodies moved to Fort Washakie cemetery   **124-127**
Prairie-chicken-cannot-swim, had two wives in separate earthlodges at Like-A-Fishhook Village   **128**
Prairie-chicken-tells-lies   **128**
Pratt, Col. R.H.   218-219
Pretty Breast, Hidatsa (daughter of *Sacagawea*) see Different Breast   117
Pueblo tribes,   139

## R

Rabbit Head (KIA, World War I)   46-47
Raises His Arm, Hidatsa (son of Cherry Necklace)   198, **205**
Raises the Heart, Hidatsa   **205**
Rattlesnakes   **238**, 253
Rattling Medicine, Hidatsa (daughter of Poor Wolf)   114
Raynolds, William F., Expedition, 1859   **231**
Red-belly   **128**
Red Butte, Mandan community   13
Reddening-a-knife   **128**
Red Head, Hidatsa   **205**
Red-thigh   **128**
Red Thunder (*E'e-a-chin-che-a*), Hidatsa Chief   **87**
Reid, Russell (State Historical Society of North Dakota)   157
Rides a White Horse, Crow   **224**

Rides the Bear, Douglas, Crow   228
Riding Chief (*Inquida Necharo*), Arikara Chief, also called Whipporwill (*Too Nee*)   28, 50
River Crow Tribe   xv, 13, 51, **88**, **90**, **93**, **95**, **121**, 227, **231**
River Crow Earthlodge Villages on Little Missouri River, 1790s   **8**, 13, 21-22, **28**, 51
Road Maker, Hidatsa War Chief, see He Makes the Road to War
Robinson, Doane (South Dakota State Historian)   155, 165
Robinson, Will (South Dakota State Historical Society)   154
Rocky Mountains   139, 242, 245, 263
Rolfsrud, Erling N., historian   40
Rotten Wood, Hidatsa, 1825   **276**
Rough-arm   **128**
Rufine paramour of Jean Baptiste Charbonneau, ca. 1845-1847   288
Running (*Hidatsa Adish*), favorite hunting ground near mouth of Yellowstone River   211

# S

*Sacagawea* (Bird Woman), Hidatsa/ Crow, **1787-1869**. See also Eagle Woman.   ii, viii, xi, xiii, xvi, xvii, **5**, 6, 17, 29, 31-36, 47-59, 64, 74, 75, **79**, 109-118, 121, 123-126, 130-148, 149, 155-158, 179-191, **193**, 214, 215, 228-229, **233**-266, 267-284, 285-**292**, 294-**295**, 296

   abandoned by husband Toussaint Charbonneau, ca. 1839   122, 126, 278

   children of   see Jean Baptiste Charbonneau; Otter Woman (3); Cedar Woman; & Different Breast

   coffee, fondness for   ii, 53, 103, 108, 280

   coin (1 dollar) honoring *Sacagawea*, issued by U.S. Mint, 2000   **282**

   death of, 1869   52-55, 58, 62, 66-67, 69, 73, 133-134, 136, 142, 146-147, 180, 280

   formal name was Eagle Woman (*Maeshuwea/Maeshuweash*)   xi, xiv, xv, xvii, 17, 61, 62, 64, 81, 82

   genealogy of   xvi, 48, 76, 79, 80, 122, **225**

   grave of   59, 61, 62, 64, 67, 70, 134, 146-147, 175, 281

   language skills of   236, 240

   lived at Like-A-Fishhook Village, with brother Cherry Necklace and daughters Otter Woman(3) and Cedar Woman, ca. 1845-1869   129, 172

*Index*

moved with Charbonneau to Fort Union area after 1837 smallpox 126, 129, 147, **267**, 278

preferred spelling "*Sacagawea*" adopted, 2002   118

reported alive by Gen. Henry Atkinson, 1825   157; by James P. Beckwourth, 1830s   173-**174**; by F.A. Chardon at Fort Clark, 1834   158

snake medicine of   viii, 64, 103, 180, 198, 234, 281

statues of   114, **115**, 164, 265-**266**, 270, **273**, **281**, 282

trip with Charbonneau to Idaho, 1803-04   48-49, 61, 271

trip with Lewis & Clark Expedition, 1805-1806   **5**, **45**, **50**-51, 179, 233-266, 271-272

trip with Charbonneau to St. Louis, then the Southwest, 1815-1817 107, 109, 133, 136-137, 143- 145,158-**159**, 160, 262, 274

*Sacagawea* Project Board of the Mandan, Hidatsa, & Arikara Nation iii, x, xii, **xviii**, **79**, 116, 171, 282 284, 285, 286, 296

*Sacajawea* (One Who Pulls the Boat/ Boat Launcher), a Shoshone name xvii, 36, 59, 62, 71, 112, 162, 245, 286

*Porivo*, deceased Shoshone woman, selected as "*Sacajawea*" by Grace R. Hebard   151-153, 158

graves of her sons rifled and moved by Charles A. Eastman   **150**, **152-153**

"Wyoming Story" claimed *Sacajawea* died at Fort Washakie, Wyo., 1884   149-155, 269, 285

"Fort Manuel Story" claimed *Sacajawea* died at Fort Manuel, D.T., 1812   154-157, 161, 282, 285

Saint Louis, Missouri   155, 158-**159**, 160, 161, 278

*Sakakawea*, earlier spelling of *Sacagawea*   xvii, 116-117

*Sakakawea* Village, modern honorific for site of *Awatixa* Village   6, 271, 273, 274

Salish-Kootenai College   165

Salmon River, Idaho   49, 112, 242

Salt Lake, Utah   144, **159**

Sand, Delores Parshall, Hidatsa (oldest living descendant of *Sacagawea* in 2021) x, 104, 190, **192**, **195**, **292**, 294, **295**

Sand Creek Place, Hidatsa camping area south of Wolf Point, Montana 53, 56, 58, 173, 280

Sanderson, Dr. George B. (in 1847) described Jean Baptiste

Charbonneau  173
San Diego, California  280
Sanish, N.D.  189, 202
Santa Barbara Museum of Natural History, CA  289
Santa Fe, N.M.  **133**-134, **159**
Scalp Dance, Hidatsa ceremony  **97**
Scarred Face, son of Four Bears, Mandan  52
Schroer, Blanche (research assistant to Grace R. Hebard)  said Hebard bribed Shoshone testimony about *"Sacajawea"* with free groceries  152, 154
*Seet-se-be-a*, see Midday Sun
Seven-bears  **128**
Shahuano, Maria Louisa (Spanish slant-spelling of "Charbonneau;" daughter of Jean Baptiste Charbonneau, near Bent's Fort, Colorado, 1837)  187
*Sheheke*, see White Coyote  109
She Kills, Hidatsa  108, 210, **220-221**, **224**, 287 bear medicine of,  222
Shell Creek Village, *Xoshga* Hidatsa community  13, 15, 45, **53**, **55**, 57, 126, 189
   Funeral at, 1923  46-47, 168
Sheppard, Shyla  110
Sheppard, Wanda Fox (Plenty Sage)  ii, x, xiii, **xviii**, 106-107, **110**, 178
Shoshone Butte, Dunn Co,. N.D., locale of Strong Jaw/ Wolf Woman story  41
Shoshone (Snake) Tribe  viii, ix, xi, 21-22, 26-27, 32-33, 35, 37-38, 51, 100, 111-112, 127, 139, 176, 228, 234, 242, 251-257, 296
   attacks on Strong Jaw Village, last battle with Hidatsa, 21-22, 26-27, 38
Sign language  xii, xvii, 11, 36, 100, 101, 126
Siouan language group of Hidatsa, Crow & Mandan  2
Sioux Tribes  1, 11, 59, 63-64, 123, 128
Sits On the ground  **224**
Sitting Bear Hill/ Montana  51
Sitting Bull, Hunkpapa Lakota Chief  169, 171
Sitting Crow, Hidatsa  **61**, 201
Sitting Rabbit, Mandan artist  1
Skin-worn-through  128

*Index*

Small Ankle, Hidatsa   125
Small-bull, Hidatsa   **128**
Small Child, Crow   **224**
Smallpox Epidemics   1781-1782, 1837-38 & 1866   1, 3, 11, 70, 99, 100, 129, 103, 186, 198, 200, 203, **267**, 278
Smith, Jefferson Bird, Hidatsa (MHA Tribal Court Judge), **1888-1975**   15, **16**, 41, 111, 112, 190
Smoked Lodge, Hidatsa, see Black Lodge   xvi, 48, 78, 177, 195, 197, 209, 270, 271, **293**
Snake Medicine, of *Sacagawea*'s family   viii, 64, 103, 105, 197, 237-**238**, 281
Snake Tribe,   see Shoshone Tribe
Snow, Philip   107, 204
Sobin, Margarita (Luiseno paramour of Jean Baptiste Charbonneau, 1848) 187, 290-291
Son of the Star, Hidatsa (husband of Buffalo Bird Woman)   127
Spotted Bear, Daylon   91
Spotted Horn   **58**, **61**
Standing Rock Reservation, N.D.   169
Stanton, N.D.   29
State Historical Society of North Dakota (SHSND)   vi
Stevenson, Rufus, Mandan   202-203
Stone, John   109
Stone Charging, Cleo   109
Strikes the Drum, Hidatsa/Crow   **221**
Strong Jaw, Hidatsa   20-22
Strong Jaw/ Wolf Woman story (ca. 1799)   x, 19-27, **23**, **25**, **28**, 32-39, 40-42
Sweet Grass Woman, Hidatsa (mother of Joseph Packineau)   165
Sylvester, Carl (Tribal Chairman)   85-86

**T**

Takes the Gun (*Miduxha Nootzhis*), Hidatsa (healed by Cherry Necklace) 204
Tangled Woods   **205**
Taos, N.M.   288
Tattooing, Hidatsa   **92**, **198**, 201

Thorton, Esley Fox   105
Three Affiliated Tribes (earlier designation of the Mandan, Hidatsa & Arikara Nation)   xiv, 1, 15, 92, 270, 282
Three Forks of the Missouri   xv
Three Wolves, Hidatsa, 1825   **276**
Thrust-in   **128**
Travels in the Middle, see Goes Between
Treaty of Fort Laramie, 1851   3, 198
Trobriand, Count Philippe Regis de, (soldier and artist)   **100**
Trujillo, Gregory, Luiseno   187
Twin Buttes,   15
Twists His Tail (Wraps Up His Horse's Tail for War), River Crow Head Chief, 1859   **231**
Two Crows (*Pa-ris-ka-roo-pa*), Hidatsa Chief, see Two Ravens   **89**
Two Crows, wife of, Hidatsa   ii, **89**
Two Ravens (*Pehriska-Ruhpa*), Hidatsa Chief, see Two Crows   **84, 85, 86**
Two Wolves, Hidatsa (half-brother of Bulls Eye)   **193**

## U
Ute Tribe, visited by Charbonneau & *Sacagawea*, 1816-17   144, 237

## V
Vandell, Mary Victoria, wife of Toussaint Charbonneau (2)   **292**
Van Hook, N.D.   45, 189
Van Hook American Legion Post   46
Venne, Carl (Crow Tribal Chairman)   223-226
Vernon, Mel, (Luiseno tribal official)   289

## W
Waldo, Edna LeMoore, historian   40
Walker, James, husband of Goes Between   210, 215, 217, 279
Walker, Sarah, Hidatsa/Crow, see Sarah Walker Pease
Walker, Sarah, State Historical Society of North Dakota   vi
Walks at Dusk, Hidatsa   21, 26-27
Walks with Wolves, (husband of All Moves)   210, **224**
Walla Walla Tribe   259

## Index

Ward, Joe, Hidatsa   27, 28
Washington, Booker T.   219
Water Buster Bundle, Hidatsa   146
Waters, Levi, Arikara   **16**
Wears-a-coat   **128**
Weasel Woman, Hidatsa (daughter of Bulls Eye)   **194**
Weidemann, Henry (blacksmith at Fort Berthold)   145
Weidemann, Mrs., Hidatsa (sister of Bears Arm)   141-146, 158-160
Welch, Maj. Alfred Burton, ethnologist (first publicized Bulls Eye's testimony about *Sacagawea*)   ix, 42, 45-62, **46**, **54**, **58**, 60, 72-73, 120-121, 122, 128, 165-166, 166-171, 187, 191, 282, 284
    helped survey Fort Berthold and Standing Rock reservations 141-143
Welch Family   vi, 169-170
Well Known Horse, Ana, Crow   **224**
Wells, Marcus, Jr.   91
Welsh, Dr. Michael, historian   vi, xiii, 288-296
Whipporwill (*Too Ne*), Arikara, see Riding Chief
White Cow, Hidatsa, 1825   **276**
White Coyote (*Sheheke*), Mandan Chief   5-**6**, 109, 141
White Dog, Crow   229
White-dog, Hidatsa   **128**
White Duck, Mrs., see Rattling Medicine
White Face, Hidatsa (son of Cherry Necklace)   196, **205**, **207**
Whitehouse, Joseph (crewman with Lewis & Clark)   259
White Owl Family (descendants of Cherry Necklace)   199
White Raven, Hidatsa, see George Parshall
White Shield   15, 83,
Whitman, Carl (MHA Tribal Chairman)   15, 38
Wichita Tribe, visited by Charbonneau & *Sacagawea*, 1816   144, 158
Wicked Cow, Hidatsa, 1825   **276**
Wilkinson, Helen Wolf   41, 62
Will, Oscar H./ Will Seed Company   **4**
Williston, N.D.   188
Wilson, Gilbert L., ethnologist   123-124, 125, 127
Wind River, Wyoming   118
Wolf, Malcolm   91

Wolf Chief (1), Hidatsa Head Chief, 1825  **276**
Wolf Chief (2), Hidatsa (brother of Buffalo Bird Woman)  123, **125**-126, 127, 138-140, 197, 278
Wolf-eye  **128**
Wolf-head  **128**
Wolf, Helen Pease  215, 217-222
Wolf Point, Montana  58, **69**, 121, 173, 280
Wolf's Gun, Crow  **224**
Wolf That Has No Tail, Hidatsa, 1825  **276**
Wolf-walks-with-the-wind-at-his-back  102
Wolf Woman, see Strong Jaw
Woman Now, Crow  190
Woman That Lies, Hidatsa (male), 1825  **276**
Woman Who Lives in a Bear Den, River Crow  **90**
Women's Suffrage Movement  72, 149, 151
Wooden-lodge  **128**
Wounded Knee Massacre, S.D.  149
Wurttemberg, Germany  182-**183**, 187  See Paul Wilhelm, Duke of
"Wyoming Story"  see *Sacajawea*

## X
*Xoshgas* (Renegades), Hidatsa band  13, 167, **176**, 187

## Y
Yellow, Crow  **224**
Yellow Cloud Woman  **10**
Yellow Hair, see Culbertson
Yellowstone River, Montana  51, **95**, **159**, 203, 231, 261
York, slave to William Clark  29, 37, 240
Young Bird families, Hidatsa, related to *Sacagawea* & Cherry Necklace  209, 213, 215, **224**, 268, 279, 286-287, 296
Young Bird, Joseph, family, Hidatsa  **280**
Young Bird, Marilyn  202, 226
Young Bird, Susie Walker, Hidatsa  210, 217, **221**, 222, **223**
Young Curlew, Crow  **224**
Young Curlew, Marcia  **224**
Young Wolf, Leo, Mandan  **16**

*Index*

# **Colophon**

This book is set in Georgia. Georgia is a transitional serif typeface designed in 1993 by Matthew Carter for the Microsoft Corporation. It was created for clarity on a computer monitor even at small sizes, and has a relatively large x-height. This typestyle got its name from a tabloid headline found in the state of Georgia. Georgia is a registered trademark of Microsoft.

The cover is set in Western. A block letter typeface, Western originates from wood type used in the later half of the 1800's within the United States. It is a display typestyle.

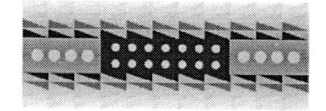

The Hidatsa Design above and found throughout, and the MHA Emblem of the Mandan, Hidatsa and Arikara Nation on the back, was developed by Dennis Fox, Jr. for this book and based upon traditional tribal design.

*End Paper Map:Hidatsa & Crow Territory during the 19th Century*
*— Barry Lawrence Ruderman Antique Maps*

*Our Story of Eagle Woman, Sacagawea*

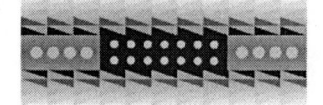

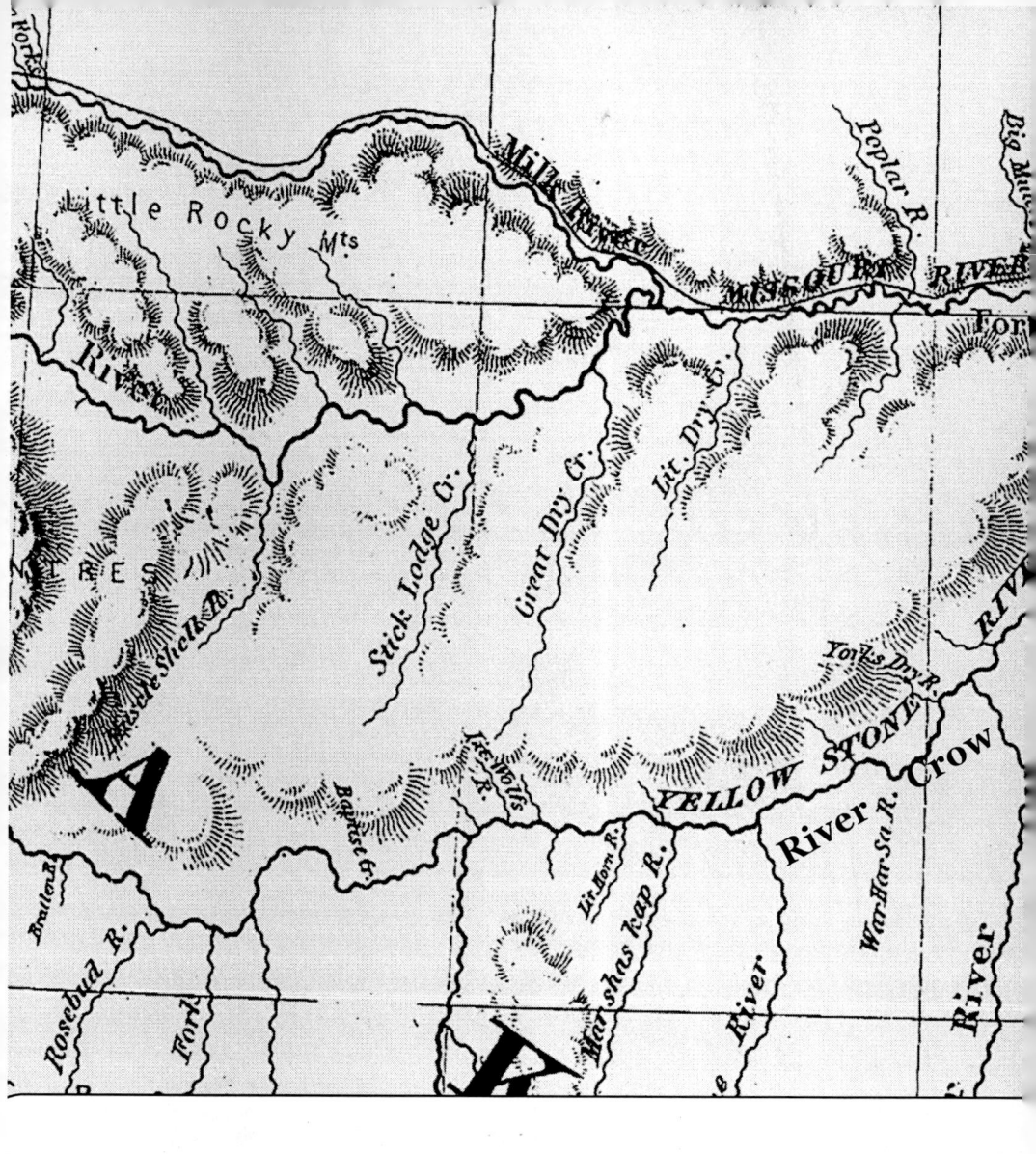

1 — 5 Knife River Earthlodge Villages, 3 Hidatsa & 2 Mandan, 1600 - 1838
2 — River Crow Earthlodge Villages, 1790s
3 — Arikara Earthlodge Villages, 1800 - 1825
4 — Fort Mandan, built by Lewis & Clark, 1804 - 1805
5 — Fort Manuel trading post, 1812 - 1813
6 — Fort Union trading post, 1829 - 1867
7 — Fort Clark trading post, 1830 - 1861
8 — Like-a-Fishhook Earthlodge Village, Hidatsa, Mandan & Arikara, 1845-18
9 — Fort Berthold trading post, 1845 - 1874
10 — Fort Buford army post, 1866 - 1895
11 — Crow Flies High Earthlodge Village, Xoshga Hidatsa, 1870 - 1884